A Man Comes from Someplace

TRANSGRESSIONS: CULTURAL STUDIES AND EDUCATION

VOLUME 126

Series Editor

Shirley R. Steinberg, *Werklund School of Education, University of Calgary, Canada*

Founding Editor

Joe L. Kincheloe (1950–2008), The Paulo and Nita Freire International Project for Critical Pedagogy

Editorial Board

Rochelle Brock, *University of North Carolina, Greensboro, USA*
Annette Coburn, *University of the West of Scotland, UK*
Kenneth Fasching-Varner, *Louisiana State University, USA*
Luis Huerta-Charles, *New Mexico State University, USA*
Christine Quail, *McMaster University, Canada*
Jackie Seidel, *University of Calgary, Canada*
Cathryn Teasley, *University of A Coruña, Spain*
Sandra Vega, *IPEC Instituto de Pedagogía Crítica, Mexico*
Mark Vicars, *Victoria University, Queensland, Australia*

This book series is dedicated to the radical love and actions of Paulo Freire, Jesus "Pato" Gomez, and Joe L. Kincheloe.

The titles published in this series are listed at *brill.com/tcse*

Scope of Series

Cultural studies provides an analytical toolbox for both making sense of educational practice and extending the insights of educational professionals into their labors. In this context *Transgressions: Cultural Studies and Education* provides a collection of books in the domain that specify this assertion. Crafted for an audience of teachers, teacher educators, scholars and students of cultural studies and others interested in cultural studies and pedagogy, the series documents both the possibilities of and the controversies surrounding the intersection of cultural studies and education. The editors and the authors of this series do not assume that the interaction of cultural studies and education devalues other types of knowledge and analytical forms. Rather the intersection of these knowledge disciplines offers a rejuvenating, optimistic, and positive perspective on education and educational institutions. Some might describe its contribution as democratic, emancipatory, and transformative. The editors and authors maintain that cultural studies helps free educators from sterile, monolithic analyses that have for too long undermined efforts to think of educational practices by providing other words, new languages, and fresh metaphors. Operating in an interdisciplinary cosmos, *Transgressions: Cultural Studies and Education* is dedicated to exploring the ways cultural studies enhances the study and practice of education. With this in mind the series focuses in a non-exclusive way on popular culture as well as other dimensions of cultural studies including social theory, social justice and positionality, cultural dimensions of technological innovation, new media and media literacy, new forms of oppression emerging in an electronic hyperreality, and postcolonial global concerns. With these concerns in mind cultural studies scholars often argue that the realm of popular culture is the most powerful educational force in contemporary culture. Indeed, in the twenty-first century this pedagogical dynamic is sweeping through the entire world. Educators, they believe, must understand these emerging realities in order to gain an important voice in the pedagogical conversation.

Without an understanding of cultural pedagogy's (education that takes place outside of formal schooling) role in the shaping of individual identity – youth identity in particular – the role educators play in the lives of their students will continue to fade. Why do so many of our students feel that life is incomprehensible and devoid of meaning? What does it mean, teachers wonder, when young people are unable to describe their moods, their affective affiliation to the society around them. Meanings provided young people by mainstream institutions often do little to help them deal with their affective complexity, their difficulty negotiating the rift between meaning and affect. School knowledge and educational expectations seem as anachronistic as a ditto machine, not that learning ways of rational thought and making sense of the world are unimportant.

But school knowledge and educational expectations often have little to offer students about making sense of the way they feel, the way their affective lives are shaped. In no way do we argue that analysis of the production of youth in an electronic mediated world demands some "touchy-feely" educational superficiality. What is needed in this context is a rigorous analysis of the interrelationship between pedagogy, popular culture, meaning making, and youth subjectivity. In an era marked by youth depression, violence, and suicide such insights become extremely important, even life saving. Pessimism about the future is the common sense of many contemporary youth with its concomitant feeling that no one can make a difference.

If affective production can be shaped to reflect these perspectives, then it can be reshaped to lay the groundwork for optimism, passionate commitment, and transformative educational and political activity. In these ways cultural studies adds a dimension to the work of education unfilled by any other sub-discipline. This is what *Transgressions: Cultural Studies and Education* seeks to produce – literature on these issues that makes a difference. It seeks to publish studies that help those who work with young people, those individuals involved in the disciplines that study children and youth, and young people themselves improve their lives in these bizarre times.

A Man Comes from Someplace

Stories, History, Memory from a Lost Time

SECOND EDITION

Foreword by Shirley R. Steinberg
New Afterword by the Author

By

Judith Pearl Summerfield

To Mark,
   I am very moved by your
article (and video) of your
dear father. Here, in return,
is the story of my father —
Lauren's grandfather — also, a
survivor.
   All the best,
   Judith Summerfield
   3/3/21

BRILL

SENSE

LEIDEN | BOSTON

Cover illustration: *Puesta de Sol en el Este*, by Norma Perel.
All photographs and documents are from Author's collection.

The Library of Congress Cataloging-in-Publication Data is available online at http://catalog.loc.gov

ISBN 978-90-04-37095-1 (paperback)
ISBN 978-90-04-37096-8 (hardback)
ISBN 978-90-04-37097-5 (e-book)

What readers are saying...

History, memory, suffering, desolation, family loss, family love—
the cries and passions of Jewish Fate—all of it winding from
Novoconstantinov to Fredericktown to Argentina; and the genetics of
why [the writer is] tall! Thank you for this invaluable and inconceivably
moving history: destined to last, both as memorial and as literature.
— Cynthia Ozick, Writer, Literary Critic

The "final solution" did not emerge out of the blue. Systemic anti-
Semitic policies, practice and violence scarred the history of Eastern
Europe for decades. Summerfield's stories are unique, a history
particular to her and her family. They are also representative of the
broader "history" of the classroom. What makes *A Man Comes from
Someplace* such a satisfying read is that the author is aware of the
multiple ways in which stories, and history, make meaning. It is a book
that I think my students would understand. Just like her father, she is
very good at telling stories.
— David Potash, Historian, President, Wilbur Wright College,
   The City Colleges of Chicago

A Man Comes from Someplace represents an original chapter in cultural
studies and social history, one that takes up the challenge of Irving
Howe's World of our Fathers' final sentence: 'Let us now praise obscure
men.'
— David Schlitt, Historian, former Director of Rauh Jewish
   History Program & Archives, Heinz History Museum
   (Affiliate of the Smithsonian), Pittsburgh, Pennsylvania

Judith has created more than an auto-biography, ethnography; she has written a living document that allows us to know her story and to relate with our own. As people of The Book, the Diaspora, we often have little information about our lives. In this beautiful story, Judith has shared her story, which belongs to us all. Our families expand into one another, and the core of our existence becomes part of the collective we. Never again are we without papers. This book, these words – these are our papers.

— Shirley Steinberg, Cultural Critic, Educator, Editor, Transgressions, from the Foreword

I love the narrative style in the book. I felt like I was sitting at a kitchen table with the writer and her father in the first part of the book, listening to the tale.. . . It is such a historically informative book in this time of turmoil and fear in our own country.

— Elissa Wilson, Social Services Training Manager, Journalist/ Writer, Traveler

For my father
who gave me
this world in stories.
And my mother and sister,
whose stories are yet to be told.

For my daughters, Lauren and Sharon, always for you.

For the next generations,
the descendants of
Chana the Long and Joseph of the Woods,
especially for Motye's great grandchildren,
Danielle, Naomi, Gabriella, Matthew, Natalie,
Max, Talia, and Pearl.
These stories are yours now to make your own.

And for all who need to tell and listen to the stories, history,
and memories of where we come from.

Contents

Foreword

Finding Our Papers

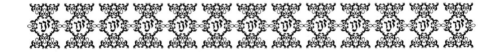

Judith is my sister. She is my heart, she is my reflection. Though we come from different stories, we have the same stories. Through this book, Judith has given me the answers to questions I've had my entire life. Questions about my father, who wouldn't speak about the old country, who was embarrassed about the old country. Questions about my Bubbie, who would ask my father a question in Polish (or was it Russian?). Dad would pause, redden and yell at her, "Speak English, speak English or I won't answer you." Judith's father answered her questions, he told her the stories. Our fathers were different, but the chicken soup that steamed through our hearts, that specific scent, the first scorching sip, that was our chicken soup, Judith's and mine. Sisters' soup. My Bubbe was Pearl. And Judith is Pearl.

My Bubbe was so tall, so thin, a white-haired lady ever with pearls and a handbag hooked on her arm. I didn't know she spoke those languages 'til long after she was gone and I wanted to understand where these tongues came from. They were the same sounds Judith's family made; the same words, the same journey, the same worlds, the same prayers. I was told I was a Litvak, Judith was from the Ukraine, but our stories began side by side, as did our countries… not yet countries, borders changing as the wind, with the wars. Our beginnings were the same, our shtetlach mirrored, the pogroms real.

Our trips were different, those of our families, different ships, different harbors, new beginnings different. I was urban, Judith was rural; we were but a day's drive from one another, our homes close to a synagogue and our chicken soup. Growing up we both reached for stories, for tales of our people, wanting to know more. Always more.

I met my sister, Judith Pearl Summerfield, in the beginning of this millennium. Our partners already brothers, they insisted we meet one another. Jewish women both married to non-WASPish, goyish menschs—we were meant to be family. My sister Judith had answers to my questions, she knew about the old country. Weaving the cloth of our past, Judith gifted me with stories from her father. We were as similar as we were dissimilar, yet we filled in the blanks of one another's observations and thoughts. Judith was the first to visit the old country, my soul rose when she told me of her visit. I followed two years later, stomping around, searching to recognize, closing the gaps.

Judith brought me to this point, to understanding that we have this story; it is particular to each of us, yet it is the same. This book, this story, reminds us that we come from someplace, and finding that someplace and our sisters and brothers brings us to completion. Judith has created more than an auto-biography/ethnography, she has written a living document which allows us to know her story and to relate with our own. As people of *The Book,* the diaspora, we often have little information about our lives, in this beautiful story, Judith has shared her story, which belongs to us all. It is not discovering the shtetl, but knowing the meaning of that shtetl and following the journeys, feeling the pain, retelling the stories, and forming the matzoh into an orb for the soup. We fold into the old country and extend our borders into the new. Our families expand into one another, and the core of our existence becomes part of the collective we. Never again are we without papers. This book, these words—these are our papers.

— Shirley R. Steinberg, University of Calgary

Shirley and Judith met as colleagues in New York, they are collaborators, friends, and sisters.

Acknowledgments

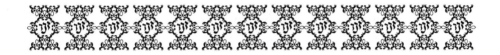

Thanks to all who have played a part in making this book:

My sister, Janet Akman, who encouraged me to take the journey.
    And to Allan, Michael, Annette. Joe and Jess.
My daughter, Lauren Azuolay, for living her grandfather's stories.
    And to Avi, Danielle, Naomi, and Gabriella.
My cousin, Silvia Perel Levin, whose lead I follow to places far and wide.
    And to Mark, Gal, Assaf, and Aviv.

For my trusted readers along the way,
Bette Ann Moskowitz, for telling me straight.
Carolyn Sacks, for wanting the stories to be told.
Rabbi Jeffrey Segelman, for urging me to cross the frozen river.
Eleanor Dreyfus, for our walking talks around the brook.
Michelle Judd Mackey, for taking the stories to heart.

To family, near and far, for their contributions, especially,
Norma Perel, for the cover painting, Puesta de Sol en el Este.
Rosa and Julio Scheines, for their insights about family stories.

Claudia Perel, for inspired archival research.
Matias Scheines, Iris Sloin, and Mario Solan for the music.
Rosa Sloin for her poetry.

Thanks to Tobin Simon, Lesley Jones, Ruth Wintner, Stuart Schulhof, Sharyn Protass, Vanesa Berenstein, Michael Akman, Gerardo Scherlis, Gabriela Scherlis, Barry Pearl, for their close readings of the book.

And to Elmer and Adie Judd, Dick and Rhoda Judd, Linda Schulhof, Carol Lazear, Ana Perel, Liliana Perel, Rosita Wachenchauzer, Pablo Jacovkis, Martin Scheines, Damian Scherlis, Rosita Gleizer, Pablo Perel, Daniel Perel, Jorge Gleizer, Mark Levin, Gal Levin, Jean Levin, Susan Levin, for their encouragement. And to all the family in the diaspora, who make the stories their own.

To translators: From the Yiddish, Lazer Misulovin, Silvia Perel Levin, Julius Akman. From the Russian, Robert Whittaker, Zhanna Kushmakova, Anna Royzner.

Thanks to these friends, colleagues, and reviewers, Janice Cimberg, Sylvia Moss, Ann Morgado, Cynthia Ozick, Nora Glickman, Dorothy Rainier, David Schlitt, David Potash, Avi Lichtenstein, Ann Andrejcak, Ellen Bartok, Rita Marlowe, June Hesler, Elizabeth Lambert, Shari Rosensweig-Lipsky, Phyllis Kelly, Karen Kolodny, Linda Hirsch, Trudy Smoke, Sondra Perl, Suzanne Reisman, Elaine Ross, Jonathan Ornstein, Ben Greenberg, Ellie Wymard, Jean Ferguson Carr, Shirley Budhos, Matthew Rosenblum, Kelsey Thayer, Valerie Faeth, Tom Watson, Elissa Wilson.

Thanks to Anna Royzner for disseminating copies of the book to teachers and students in local schools in Novokonstantinov, Ukraine.

And to those in Ukraine, who play a part in the story: Anna, Vilodin, Zina, Ivan, Nadia, "Zina of the Borders," and Alexandr Kozubovsky.

And to those who continue to influence my writing, teaching, and research on narrative: Geoffrey Summerfield, Herschel Portnoy Virginia Woolf, Joan Didion, Eric Auerbach, Abraham Heschel, William Labov, James Britton, Henry Glassie, Boris Cyrulnik, Robert Colodny, Seamus Heaney, Italo Calvino, Saul Friedlander, Sholem Aleichem, John Berger, Grace Paley, Joe Kincheloe.

To my academic home, English Department, Queens College of The City University of New York.

To my brilliant editor, Shirley Steinberg, who always brings worlds together. Thanks to Ian Steinberg for his commitment to this book and to his inspired design, and to Michel Lokhorst, Robert van Gameren, Paul Chambers, and Jolanda Karada at Brill | Sense.

Thanks to Philip Anderson, poet, musician, photographer, educator, spouse, with whom I am always in conversation.

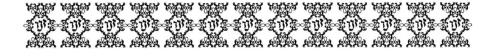

Prologue

Ukraine 2011

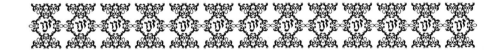

It is June 2011, and I am standing near the rocky ford in the river at the place my father came from in southwestern Ukraine. There are stone outcroppings strewn about, on land and in the water—the erosional fragments indistinguishable from the remains of the gravestones. Here on this elevation overlooking the river is the old Jewish cemetery, where my grandparents and five of their children and a grandchild are buried. The writing on the stones is indecipherable, and there are no signs or sign posts to identify this place. But my father had described the site well—as the only *elevation* in this flat fertile plain that was his home.

The local guides who are our translators and the driver from Kiev brought us here. Some of the guides are teachers. They have had no Jewish visitors, they tell us, who lived here before the First World War or the Russian Revolution and returned to the village. My father's stories link them to their past, and they want his stories for the history museum they are creating in the school.

My father was the storyteller of his family. He was the youngest of eleven children, and one of the four brothers who escaped the pogroms and civil wars of the 1920s. The politics of immigration kept the brothers separated during the rest of their lives, but now, these many years later, my father's stories are bringing the next generations of the family together—across geography and time. The stories live on for us all, these stories of a family and their survival and resilience. They have become stories to live on.

Photograph of remains of Jewish cemetery overlooking River Buh at Novokonstantinov

Introduction

So, Here's the Story

We tell stories in order to live. . . We interpret what we see. . . We live entirely, especially if we are writers, by the imposition of a narrative line upon disparate images, by the 'ideas' with which we have learned to freeze the shifting phantasmagoria which is our actual experience.
—Joan Didion, *The White Album**

It was always that moment at the frozen river that made my stomach turn. The river was the border between the Bolshevik-held Ukraine and the possibility of an escape through Romania. It was early that cold December morning in 1920, when the refugees, sleeping wherever they could find a place in the village, had been awakened by a commotion outside. And when they all pushed down to the river, they found a crowd gathered, looking to the other side where two women had been caught by the guards. Someone said, "Go back, and don't make any more commotion." The guards on this side hadn't yet come out. The crowd left, but my father, 16, and on his own, lingered a moment. A man, who was standing close by, winked at him, and said, "If you want to go across, now's the time. The guards on the other side are

* Didion, J. (2006). "The white album" in *We tell ourselves stories in order to live: Collected nonfiction*. New York, NY: Knopf.

busy with the women. The guards on this side are still asleep. Run. Go ahead. Just run. Don't look back. Run. Keep going."

My father took off without his coat or hat. Without the *tefillin* (prayer boxes) that he left in the house in the village. He slid down the bank and ran, slipped on the ice, and slipped again. The man kept urging him on. Across the frozen Dniester, he ran. And when he got to the other side, there were hills and snow drifts everywhere, piled so high he could hardly see. The wind was blowing. It was freezing. "Don't go to the left," the man had said, "go to the right." My father figured he had a short time before he froze to death. And then he heard a bell. . . .

Probably from the moment I was born, my father began to tell me his story.

He was already 39, and I was his first child. For the rest of his life, *every day and every day*, as he used to say, in one way or another, he was telling me about what had happened in those early years of his life. Somewhere along the way, I promised that I'd pass the stories on about the place he had come from and the family that was lost. Through his words, I came to know my grandparents and aunts and uncles from a world and a time that no longer existed. They were like fairy tales, and sometimes I lay awake at night wondering what might have happened to him, or my mother or me or my little sister, if he hadn't heard the bell that early morning, or if the man, who seemed to come out of nowhere, hadn't appeared and urged him to run across the frozen river.

But it wasn't a fairy tale. It all happened, and I grew up to believe when anything got rough or seemed impossible, that if my father had lived through the Russian Revolution, then I could surely live through this or that. The idea of fairy or folktales—of stories, in general, and how they become "narratives" that shape our lives—grew into an abiding passion and a literary sensibility that governed my personal and professional life as scholar and teacher. What my father lived through—and that he had, indeed, survived to tell the tales—possessed him, and began to possess me, as well. He had survived, against the odds, and the stories were impressed on my mind.

My father was born in 1903 or 1904 (depending upon which calendar he referred to) in a shtetl in western Ukraine, in what was then the Russian Empire. He was the youngest of the family, the eleventh child of his parents, Chana and Joseph. He was named Mordechai, and called Motye in Yiddish. He survived the typhoid epidemic of 1915 that killed his mother. He survived the First World War and the pogrom in 1919 that killed his father and oldest brother. He survived the Bolshevik Revolution and the subsequent Russian Civil War, a time when roughly 14,000,000 people were lost in Russia.

He set out on his own in December 1920 to find his brother in America, and a year and a week later, in December 1921, he arrived at Ellis Island. The story of the year and the week he was on the road was one that he told over and over again. It was a great escape story, of cunning and near mishap and good fortune—of taking one turn rather than another, of strangers appearing out of nowhere to point the way, and of his own daring to run across frozen rivers and continents. He was ever grateful, and incredulous, that he had somehow survived.

Some people want or need to forget, but my father needed to remember. Telling the stories was as vital to his life as the air he breathed. He wanted my sister and me and anyone who would listen to know about what had happened in the past. Every day in any conversation, no matter what the topic, he would slip in something about the past, about the family, the place, and the way things were, something about the old world would surface. And whoever crossed his path was a potential listener: family, friends, his doctors, workmen, storekeepers, neighbors, and strangers.

Ingeniously, he could capture you in his storytelling grip. "*Did I ever tell you the story about . . . ?*" or, simply, "*So here's the story. . .*"and he was off and running. There was a compulsion to tell, and a need to understand, to make sense out of what had happened to him and his family. It also became clear as we both grew older that he wanted to pass the stories on, that he wanted me to write down his words, to make sure that what he knew would be told, and that I got it right. "*This should go in the book,*" he would say. Sometimes he'd say, "*This shouldn't be told.*"

I think he was always here and there at the same time, always remembering, always needing to tell, holding on to the past and at the same time revising the memories. He had a dual vision, associating where he was and what was happening in the present moment with what had happened in the past. In a reflective moment late in life, he said, "*I'm still living it through, living it over and over again, I'm lying here, and I'm thinking, thinking about what happened then, I spent the rest of my life reliving it, that's what I'm doing. When you were living it, you couldn't stop and think about it. You can't do that.*" For him, it was always story in history, the two interconnected. It wasn't just him or his family, it was what was happening in the whole world.

In my twenties, I began to get my father's words down on the page, and during the next decades, as we talked, I kept taking notes. In the 1980's, when he and my mother moved close by, we talked even more frequently, and I began to fill in gaps. He agreed to tell his stories into a tape recorder, and we managed to get a dozen hours of interviews on tape. At one point, he drew a rough diagram of the town—a story map—so that I could see where things were, the river, the marketplace, his house, the cemetery. At the end of his life, with his memory still intact, he was still telling stories to the doctors and nurses in the hospital. After my father died in 1991, his stories continued to grow, in unforeseen ways.

First, there was Meyer, his brother. Meyer, born 1893, came to America in 1911, where he remained for the rest of his life. In 1921, working through relief efforts, he enabled my father's escape from Russia. When Meyer died in 1965, his wife, my Aunt Fan, gave my father boxes full of old letters that had been stored in the crawl space under

the front porch of their house in southwestern Pennsylvania for decades. All I knew was that somewhere in my parents' house were "Uncle Meyer's letters." I don't know if my father even opened the boxes.
Perhaps he did, but, surprisingly, he didn't say. After my mother died
in 1997, I found half a dozen old shoeboxes in my parents' apartment.
Inside were several hundred letters and postcards and other artifacts,
starting with Meyer's arrival in New York in May 1911, and continu-
ing on over the years.

It looked as if he'd saved everything: Letters from his family and
friends in the shtetl. Wedding announcements. Receipts. Newspaper
clippings. Official documents. Photographs. The letters from the shtetl
stopped mid-way through the First World War, and only began again
in 1921 with the letters my father wrote to Meyer during the year and
a week that it took him to reach America. The letters that I've had
translated from Yiddish and Russian give voice to my father's family
from a world that is gone, and amplify—or modify—the stories my
father told.

And the stories kept growing along with the children of the four
brothers who survived. Meyer and my father, Motye (who became
Martin in the new world), came to America. Two brothers, Duved
and Moishe, denied access to the United States through changes in
immigration laws in the 1920s, went instead to Buenos Aires. Over
the years, the two branches of the family have connected across time
and space in the United States, South America, Canada, Europe, and
Israel, and many of the next generations, the grandchildren and great
grandchildren of my grandparents, Chana and Joseph, want to know
the stories. My father was determined that the children would not
forget. His words, his stories of the past, are bringing the generations
together.

Finally, there is the place itself that has modified my telling: One
hundred years after Meyer left the shtetl, almost to the day, I went
back to the place we had come from. I went with my husband and

with Duved's granddaughter, Silvia, whose father was also born in the shtetl. With a driver and several guides, we went deep into southwestern Ukraine to a world, it seems, where time stood still. The stories now have a real setting in my mind, the place that figured so vividly in the stories my father told. The Jews and the shtetl are gone, but my father's stories let us touch this vanished world.

My father came from rich storytelling traditions. His was a thriving market town, where travelers' tales were common fare and where there was a strong oral tradition. His mother, Chana, who owned a store in the marketplace, was respected as a wise woman of the village, one to whom the women of the town came with their stories. I imagine my father, as the youngest, huddled close to his mother, as the women told their tales. His father, Joseph, an overseer of forestlands, traveled to cities in Eastern Europe, and I imagine brought back stories from his excursions. He also had a grandfather who told the children stories, about the family and where they had come from. Grandfather Labe lived with the family several months at a time when my father was a child, and my father remembered him as a storyteller.

While most of the stories my father told are about our immediate family and his life in the shtetl, they are rooted in the turbulent history of the times. My father was a common man, not a rabbi, not a scholar. He might have been had he been an older child. But his schooling was interrupted by events that changed history. Still, he was schooled in Yiddish, Russian, and Hebrew, even a little Polish.

Sholem Aleichem,[*] who came from a town close by, was a beloved figure by the time my father was growing up. His stories were well known. In one of the interviews, my father sings a Russian song about Tevye and his daughters, which was sung in those days in the shtetl. My father heard Tolstoy's fables and read his stories, and through his

---

[*]   Aleichem. S. (1979). *The best of Sholem Aleichem*. Howe, I. and Wisse, R. (Eds.). New York, NY: New Republic Books.
      For a recent biography, see Dauber, J. (2013). *The worlds of Sholem Aleichem: The remarkable life and afterlife of the man who created Tevye*. New York, NY: Schocken.

life, he read Gorky, Gogol, Turgenev, Pushkin, and the Yiddish writers in both Yiddish and English, including Sholem Alecheim, Isaac Bashevis Singer, Abraham Cahan, and others. He was an avid reader of the *Jewish Daily Forward*, and he listened to old Yiddish music and sang the songs he loved.

I listened to my father's stories, first and always, as his daughter, and felt the presence of the people and the past throughout my childhood. But later on, I began to pay attention to other elements in the stories– to the history he was telling of the times in which he lived. This was not just our story; this was also a story of what happened to the Jews during the terrible pogroms of that time, when my father's father and oldest brother were murdered. It was a harrowing precursor to what was to come twenty years later in the Second World War. Throughout, my father was reading what histories he could find to corroborate his own experience and shed light on his understanding of what had happened. He wanted to get the facts right.

There was also the way that he was telling stories, and I began to pay attention to what he was doing as a storyteller, to what got him going, how he led from one thing to another, and what he was saying, under the surface. In the tape recordings, you can hear how full his range was: there was joy and sorrow. You knew he was delighting in the telling, and you knew that he needed, also, to bear witness. He would remember a little story he'd read in school. Or sing a Revolutionary song that he'd heard in the marketplace. Or describe how you built a house in that part of the world.

He never presented himself as a hero in the stories. He didn't evaluate the experience or moralize (Labov, 1972, 2013).* He didn't talk about his feelings or his fears. I asked him once if he was afraid, and he was annoyed with me. Fear wasn't a question. He was describing the

---

* Labov. W. (1972). "The structural analysis of narrative," in *Language in the inner city*, Philadelphia, PA: University of Pennsylvania Press.
Labov. W. (2013). *The language of life and death: The transformation of experience in oral narrative.* Cambridge, UK: Cambridge University Press.

way things happened, the way things were, tracing lineages, connecting one thing to another, getting the story right. He was reporting on events that had happened, that he had witnessed. One of my childhood friends, who knew my father well, put it like this, "Sometimes it was almost as if it had happened to someone else, and he was in awe."*

The stories, though, kept changing over the years, grew as I grew up and my father began to fill in details—often whispering the words that weren't fit for a child to hear or that he had come to understand or know differently over the years.

His stories displayed patterns of what Vladimir Propp, the Russian scholar (1895-1970), saw as the elemental features of Russian folktales: The child (or hero) starts out on a journey. There are "interdictions" along the way; that is, someone intervenes to tell the child to go this way or that, to do this, but not that. There are of course trials and close calls, difficult tasks to complete, impossible situations, sudden changes, a rescue, and victory.** These elements all play a part in the central story of this book, my father's escape to America. In the traditional folktale, there are villains, who are ultimately punished. That was not to happen in my father's saga—or in the saga of the times. My father was caught in forces that rocked the world, forces that were much larger than himself.

In 1911, the Jewish author Shloyme-Zanvel Rappaport, who went by the pen name of An-sky, led an ethnographic expedition into Volhynia and also Podolia, where my father lived. An-sky, and others, feared that the Jewish world of the shtetl was coming to an end. For three years, he and his team of ethnographers captured the life of ordinary people in their daily lives. Through photographs and wax cylinder transcriptions, he preserved their faces, their work and their songs,

---

* (See also Summerfield, J. and Summerfield, G. (1986). "Evaluation," in *Texts and contexts: A contribution to the theory and practice of teaching composition.* New York, NY: Random House.
Summerfield. J. (1986). *Narrative compositions. An exploration of narrative in the teaching of college composition.* (Doctoral dissertation). Retrieved from ProQuest Dissertations and Theses. (Accession Order No. AAT8625656)

** Propp, V. (1968). *Morphology of the folk tale.* Austin, TX: University of Texas Press.

their synagogues and gravestones. Over the years, much of An-sky's work lay buried in museums and libraries in various places in Eastern Europe. But since the fall of the USSR in 1991, more of his materials are surfacing in this still new century, and that world which seemed so far removed is more present than ever. *

What happened to our family also happened to millions of others in the history of Eastern Europe in the last century. My father's village saw two World Wars, pogroms, revolution, civil war, famine, mass Soviet repression, and the Holocaust, as well as the rise and fall of the Union of Soviet Socialist Republics, and in 1991, the emergence of an independent democratic Ukraine. 1991 was also the year that my father died. In 2011, I was able to visit his shtetl, Novokonstantinov, to witness first hand the place where my father's life and stories originated.

To tell my father's stories has turned out to be a life-time project, and I am grateful that I can do so at this time when others are uncovering more about the world he knew. Stories about ourselves or others, though, are not fixed, they are always dialogues between what Virginia Woolf called, an "I-then, and an "I-now," our eyes of the past seen through our eyes of the present.** Our memories, interpretations, needs, and audience all influence the ways we tell stories. I am telling my father's stories through my eyes, from my point of view. In the story I'm telling, my father has a dual role. He is the parent who is the teller of the stories and also the protagonist, Motye Perel, who became Martin Pearl in America. I call him, "my father" or "Motye" in the old world or "Martin" in the new. My role is dual, as well: I am the "narratee," the daughter/listener to whom the stories are being told, and

---

*   *Photographing the Jewish nation: Pictures from S. An-sky's ethnographic expeditions.* (2009). Avrutin, E.M. et al. (Eds.). Waltham, MA: Brandeis University Press, Published by University Press of New England, Hanover and London.

**   Woolf. V. (1976) "A sketch of the past," in *Moments of being: Unpublished autobiographical writings.* Jeanne Schulkind (Ed.). (New York, NY: Harcourt Brace Jovanovich.

also the narrator, the "I," who re-presents Motye's stories and tells, as well, about the effects of the stories on her own life.

I talk about Motye's "stories," but when I connect the stories, as I do in *A Man Comes from Someplace,* I speak of them collectively as a "family story" or a "family narrative" that explores questions of where a family comes from, their history, and why that matters. The notion of a "meta-narrative" means that I am making conscious decisions about how I'm re-presenting the stories. As listener and eventual recorder of Motye's oral stories, I transcribed the oral stories into written texts. In doing so, I made textual choices about the language my father used. At times, I wanted to give the sense of immediacy of the two of us engaged in conversation, as we so often were. At other times, the stage is his, as he tells a long story, for example, about his great escape to America or the horror of his father's killing. I have deleted pauses and repetitions that I see as hiccoughs of oral speech. I have placed his words into *italics.* My objective is to represent the stories as "performances," to engage the reader as he did when he told the stories.*

My father wanted his listeners to see the world of the past as he did, of that I have no doubt, but there was much more to his telling than that. Here, I wanted to capture the range, rhythm, and textures of his storytelling "voice." So I have made what I see as *literary* choices: I wanted to capture not only what he said, but also how he said it. There are, no doubt, other ways of telling Motye's stories. But having now been to the world that my father knew, I am more than ever certain that he was always there, seeing that place, in one way or another, every day of his life. To begin here, then, is to start with the place, the world that he came from.

---

* For story as performance, see Bauman, R. (1986). *Story, performance, and event: Contextual studies of oral narrative.* New York: Cambridge University Press.

One

Time and Place

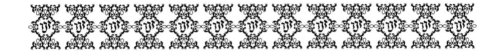

We do not live in a void. We never suffer from a fear of roaming about in the emptiness of Time. We own the past and are, hence, not afraid of what is to be.
—Abraham Heschel, *The Earth is the Lord's* *

Novokonstantinov

When you asked my father where he came from, he told you precisely. He was born and raised in a shtetl, Novokonstantinov, in the *gubernia* (province) of Podolia, in Ukraine, Russia. My father pronounced it *Neye-constanteen*, and referred to it as *Constantine*. The townspeople called themselves *Constantines*. The town was on the river, the Southern Buh (pronounced "bug"), and, until the Nazis built the European highway and bridge that bypassed the town, the ford in the river at Novokonstantinov was a vital east-west passageway for ordinary travel, commerce, and the military over the years.

Across the centuries through to the Second World War, thousands of cavalry passed through the rocky ford in the river at Novokonstan-

---

* Heschel, A. (1995). *The earth is the Lord's: The inner world of the Jew in Eastern Europe.* New York, NY: Jewish Lights Edition, published by arrangement with Farrar, Straus and Giroux.

1

tinov. The town was likely named by the Turks during their occupation of the territory in the late 17th century, but there are prehistoric remains all around. No doubt, Styroconstantinov (Old Constantine) was renamed then, too, and the new town, my father said, was seen at the time of the Turkish occupation as having the potential to become a new Constantinople. The river was a major crossroads between east and west, a trade portal connecting Europe and the Ottoman Empire.

The town[*] is about 11 miles from Khmelnick (northeast) and 8 miles from Letichev (southwest) in the heart of the Jewish Pale, that 400,000 square mile region of the Russian Empire cordoned off by Catherine the Great in 1791. The Pale demarcated the areas where Jews could or could not live. Any area "beyond the Pale" prohibited Jews from residency. This was where my father lived, in a shtetl—a small town, predominately Jewish—in the southwest border province of Podolia, near Poland, the Austro-Hungarian Empire, Romania, and Moldavia. It was several hundred miles from the Black Sea. *It was green like anything,* my father said*, with the river winding through the fields and the best fruit in the world, the seasons were like here, but the climate was colder. It was not too big of a town. It was like Brownsville* (southwestern Pennsylvani*a), maybe 5,000 or so people.*

At the turn of the 20th century, it was a thriving Jewish market town, with a big marketplace of 100 stores, several synagogues, ten or more *cheders* (Jewish schools), and a mikvah (bathhouse). There were two big churches, the Russian Orthodox and the Roman Catholic, *and there was a big mansion,* my father said*, and an orchard, at the end of the orchard was the post office, that's where we went walking, and there were some kind of benches, where the boys and girls sat talking.* The Jews were the tradespeople and merchants, selling to the local farmers who lived in town and farmed the surrounding fields. Every Sunday and ev-

---

[*] On the culture of the shtetl, see Shandler, J. (2014). *Shtetl: A vernacular history*. New Brunswick, NY: Rutgers University Press.
Roskies, D. K and Roskies, D. G. (1975). *The Shtetl book*. Jersey City, NJ: Ktav Publishing.
Petrovsky-Shtern, Y. (2014). *The golden age shtetl: A new history of Jewish life in Eastern Europe*. Princeton, NY: Princeton University Press.

Ukraine
1914 Borders

The Gubernias of 1914 Ukraine in the Russian Empire[*]

ery other Monday were market days. The farmers brought their grains, livestock, and other farm products to the market and then shopped at the stores.

Imports, canned goods, woven goods, all kinds of fabrics, were plentiful. *There was a store that sold iron,* my father said, *shoes for horses, everything was made. Across from our store, they made yard goods, oh, it was a big store, people came from all over. My brother Duved's father-in-law had manufactured stuff in his store.* There were at least two-dozen

[*] Source: http://kehilalinks.jewishgen.org/verbovets/

dealers in grain alone, five or six butchers and there were all kinds of services: cap makers and tailors, shoemakers and barbers. There were several saloons, a few teahouses and even a theatre. *In the corner of the marketplace was a guesthouse, a real big long building that you could drive in with the horses and drive out the other way.* Around the market, there were designated areas for trading horses and selling pigs and cattle. My father's mother, Chana, managed one of the general stores. She proved to be a good businesswoman and an able financial manager.

There was a mailman, he said, *but there was a Jewish woman, for years and years and years, she'd go to the post office and get everybody's mail and bring it to you, and you'd give her a penny. She couldn't read or write, but she had somebody tell her who this was for, and she'd bend it this way or that, so she'd know who to take the mail to. It was an unofficial job. Her brother was in this country, and her daughter traveled on the same carriage as me when we left Novokonstantinov.*

This Man Came from Someplace

There were horses and carts—taxis—for hire to travel from town to town. The closest train was in Derazhnya, about 20 miles away, but there was a narrow gauge connector railroad in Medzhibozh that wasn't too far. My father told me this story about a traveler who needed a ride to the next town. It was typical of the way he told stories: something would jog his memory, and you were suddenly taken for a ride:

My town, he said, *was far from the railroad station, so for transportation, there were horses and buggies that made regular trips to the bigger towns, but if you were going to a little village near by, you had to find a man to take you.*

So here, this man came from someplace but he had to go to the next village, so he hired a driver with a horse and cart and they started out and here they came to a big hill, and the driver said, 'We better walk now, because it's too hard on the horse to pull the cart up the hill.'

So they got out and walked up the hill, and when they got to the top of the hill, the driver said, 'Well, we might just as well walk down the hill, because it's hard for the horse to hold the carriage back from running away.'

So they did, and when they got to the bottom of the next hill, they were in the village, and the guy took out a ruble and a half to pay the driver.

So, the man says to him: 'Look here, Mister, I have some business here and you are here because you wanted to make a ruble and a half, that's your living, but I wonder why did we have to take the horse along?'

Is this a true story? I asked my father, and he said, *'I think, if I'm not mistaken, it was one of Sholem Aleichem's stories. He was a humorist, but in a certain way he made fun of the way things were in real life. Actually, he was born in the same part of the country that I was, and those stories were going around by mouth, there was a story going around about Tevye and his daughters. . . there was a song and everybody was singing it. In Russian, it goes like this. . . .'* And my father sang the song, and we were both laughing. That's the way it was with my father. You never knew where you'd go next, when he got going.

The River

When he was talking about the town, there was always talk of the river. The river was central to the life of the town, and there was also the creek—or *crick,* as my father pronounced it—and also the lake. The freshwater creek ran right along the street in front of their house, and that was where he played with his brother and friends, rainy days and not, and where the townspeople drew much of their drinking water. There were swamplands near the lake and the woods, where he was forbidden to go. And the river was—and still remains—a natural geological wonder.

Long, long ago, the river cut its way into the limestone bottoms of an ancient sea and moved south towards the Dniester and the Black Sea. At the current site of Novokonstantinov, the river hits solid rock and bends its way around, leaving a narrow, rocky channel. Beyond the bend, the water returns to its flattened riverbed, carving the limestone outcroppings that form the shallow rocky ford.

My father loved the river. When he was growing up, you were always at the river, getting water, bathing, washing clothes, fishing, and swimming—or playing hooky. *After my mother died, and then the war started, I didn't go to school so much and also school was interrupted, I'd go to the river to fish, if I thought it was safe.* There were designated times for women to bathe in privacy, in the early mornings during the summers. And the men could bathe or swim during the rest of the day. His mother used to take him with her when she bathed on those warm summer mornings, until the women decided that he was too old and chased him away. He remembers the time a group of young boys got up early to spy on the women bathing—and when they were spotted, they ran away fast.

I had imagined the land to be hilly, but it isn't. *'It was flat,'* my father explained, *'there is only one hill—an elevation—in the town, right above the river bend, and that's where the Jewish cemetery is. Jewish cemeteries always had to be outside the boundary of the town.'* Factories dotted the area when my father was growing up at the turn of the last century—manufacturing tobacco, sugar, bricks, paper, and, of course, grain. There was a flourmill and a vodka distillery near the cemetery.

A Good Place to Be

In the early part of the last century, Novokonstantinov was a good place to live, this world that my father left when he was sixteen. It was a restricted place to be sure, but for many years, Jews had been allowed to live there and raise their families. According to the local history that the townspeople are currently writing, the synagogue in the town was built in 1788, along with St. Anna Cathedral. The building was destroyed in the Second World War.

By 1900, there were about 5000 inhabitants in the village, among them 1299 Orthodox, 600 Catholics and 3000 Jews. There were Jewish and Polish schools there. Ten two storied buildings were built in the village that had the length of 50 meters. There were 500 Jewish houses. In 1905-1906 at the end of Novokonstantinov on the road to Letichev a school was built that was ruined in 1944 during German occupation.*

Under the stores of the marketplace, there was an underground passageway that had been built at the period of Turkish rule (1672-1699). During the bad times the underground tunnels served as hiding places. *Pogroms* is the historic term used for those outbreaks of violence against the Jews—robbery, pillaging, rape, beatings, killings—that plagued Jews from the 10th century on throughout Europe, and particularly in the Pale, and became full-out massacres at various times. Pogroms could happen any time, spurred by pervasive anti-Semitism that was instigated (and condoned) by the church or local culture or a particular group or nation. As one of Sholem Aleichem's characters, says, "Anyway, can you find a place nowadays which hasn't had a pogrom?"**

The scenes my father draws, of his life in the town, are filled with hazards on the road, outcrops of danger around the corner, a place where poverty was in abundance, and the young people had few opportunities to make a living. But there was a Jewish community, where people knew and took care of each other. The shtetl was also a bridge between the past and the present, where traditions held strong but the big changes that were happening or about to happen throughout the world reverberated in the shtetlach. In the town, even dress for the young people was becoming fashionable and modern. The women were not all covering their heads, and men were cutting their beards, some growing moustaches. This was no utopia—life was precarious—

* Personal correspondence. (2011). Novokonstantinov town history. Town committee, translated from the Ukrainian, by Anna Royzner.

** Aleichem, S. (1999). "The Village of Habne," *The old country*. (C. Leviant, Trans.). New York, NY: Sholem Aleichem Family Publications, 304.

but there was also for my father a sense of belonging to a world where you had a place.

On Saturday nights, he said, *right after sundown, the young Jewish kids would get all dressed up and go strolling, up and down the main street of town, starting at the garden wall by the church, walking to the other end of the long street, the boys walking arm in arm, and the girls walking arm and arm, up and down the street, passing each other up and back, and stopping to greet each other.*

'Hello.'

'How are you?'

'What's new?'

We were flirting. We were having fun, enjoying ourselves.

I asked my father if he ever had a girlfriend, and he said, *I was maybe 11 or 12, the time I'm talking about now, and there was an aristocratic family, very modern, the show people of the town. I was very shy. This was my first encounter. There was a school teacher in Russian, and me and another boy, we used to go there to the house, and she'd tutor us in Russian, and she had a little sister, the same age as I was. I was very backward, but she would talk to me and talk to me. . . and we played post office, where you send notes. Here, she sent me, in Russian, that 'I care for you,' and asked how I feel in return. Of course, I was blushing like anything. I started talking to her.*

We had a neighbor over there, who grew flowers, and I'd steal into the garden, and pick some flowers, and every other day, I'd bring her flowers, and then, my father at that time during the War, it was 1914, had bought a few acres of timberland, about five or six miles from town, and he'd come home, once or twice a week, and he'd let me go downtown to buy some feed for the horse, and I'd go by her house and take her for a ride. There was no talk, just blushing, that's all.

One time, my father bought a new horse, it was an Army reject, a real tall white horse, and some horses when they get to be a certain age, they don't budge anymore, they just stop. So we go riding and the horse stops and wouldn't go any farther. And I had to carry her.

All this here was before, and I didn't have too much of it. It was beautiful. The nights were beautiful. The stars and the moon. And on Saturday nights, the whole town of young people, 15 or 16 of us, the Jewish kids would take our walk.

This was the way it was for that short time in his life, before the First World War and all that came afterwards.

Two

Family

"Behind every name, there is a story."
—Dasa Drndic, *Trieste* [*]

Chana the Long and Joseph of the Woods

*T*he story goes like this, my father says. *My cousin Mendel Peril told me this, when I was here in this country. Mendel was at my mother and father's wedding in Vinnytsia in 1882 and he remembered how the bride and groom were standing under the chupah, and the two of them were exactly the same height. But after they got married, my mother grew taller than my father. She grew a lot taller and everyone called her Chana the Long, or Chana the Tall One. And Joseph was called the Husband of Chana the Long. And also because he worked as a manager in the forests, he was called Yosel of the Woods, and he had lifts built into his boots, to make himself look taller.*

My father's parents, my grandparents, were Chana Dina Uler (c1866-1915) and Joseph or Yosel Perel (c1861-1919). Chana's par-

---

* Drndic, D. (2014). *Trieste*. (E. Elias-Bursac, Trans.). New York, NY: Houghton Mifflin Harcourt.

ents were Malka and Boruch Lepa. Yosel's parents were Sur and Labe. Labe was born around 1830 and died in 1912. Labe's father Paci came to the region from Poland around 1860. Joseph was the youngest, the only child born in Ukraine. Labe came with Polish landowners to a farm village near Zozulynits, not too far from the town of Pikov near Vinnytsia, about 25 miles from Novokonstantinov. Chana's people also lived close by in the same kind of farm village.*

The *dorf* (Yiddish for *village*) belonged to the Polish overlords. The serfs lived in the villages and then went out to the fields to farm. The landowner employed one Jewish family, who was permitted to live in the village and manage concessions: a general store, a tavern, and perhaps an inn. The Jew was a "go-between" for the landowner and the dealers of the farm products. Then a law was passed that only the oldest son could live in the village and manage his father's business. Yosel was the youngest son, so he had to leave when he grew up. Then after that they didn't allow Jews to live in the villages at all; they had to move to the towns.

The changes in laws reflected the changes in the times, and who owned what territory. That part of the world was a border country that changed hands many times over the centuries: Poles, Lithuanians, Turks, Russians, Austro-Hungarians, Germans, and, of course, the Ukrainian nationalists. There were roaming bands of robbers and bandits. There were times of relative calm, but always the Jews could be counted on to be hated and terrorized by someone. As my father said, *there were good times and bad times.*

Yosel's Family

Chana and Yosel both came from large families. Since their families lived in neighboring farm villages, they all knew each other. Their fa-

---

* Dynner. G. (2014). *Yankel's tavern: Jews, liquor, and life in the kingdom of Poland.* Oxford, UK: Oxford University Press.

thers were in the same business for their *dorf.* They were storekeepers. The marriage, as most, was arranged. Chana was 16, and Yosel was 21.

Like my father, Yosel was the youngest in the family. Of his father Yosel's family, *there were all kinds of mingled up stories,* my father said. Yosel's father married twice: he had a son Willy with his first wife, Rachel, and then she died. Then he married Sur, a widow who had one daughter, whose name was Beila. In all, there were seven children in the family. Sur's daughter Beila from her first marriage, and Labe's son Willy from his first marriage, and then Labe and Sur had five children together, with Yosel, the youngest.

So Beila and Willy were stepsister and brother. They grew up together, fell in love, and got married. And that's how they were all mixed up, my father said. *There were two halves put together. But you know what happened?* He would insist. It was a large extended family, and it was hard to keep track of my father's own brothers and sisters, yet alone the aunts and uncles and cousins, as well. But my father was determined that I knew who was who, how they were related, and how the parts all came together.

So Willy was my father (Yosel's) half-brother, and he married Beila, my father's half-sister. But Willy was killed when he was young. He had the same kind of job my father (Yosel) had, and one day Willy was walking in the woods, and someone killed him, and then Beila came to this country. Her two sons, Mendel and Philip, [my father's first cousins] *came first to America, before my brother Meyer came, and then they brought their mother Beila over too. She, too, died a tragic death. You know what happened—you could write books about it—she died the same day my father died in Europe.*

She came to this country. Mendel, her eldest son, got married in Europe. He had got married to a girl from our town, who didn't get along with her mother-in-law. (They left his mother Beila behind.) When the younger son Philip got married to Liza in the States, they decided to bring Beila over here to Baltimore. This daughter-in-law was the apple of her eye. Eventually, though, she didn't get along with her mother-in-law either. So they rented a room for Beila in Baltimore. The day before Shavuot, she was getting ready for the holiday, and she got on top of a table to dust something to get the house ready, and she fell down and got killed. This was the same day, but not the same year that my father was killed.

There was also another son of Labe and Sur, whose name was Motye, for whom my father, Motye, was named. He died young and left a daughter. When my father was traveling back to Novokonstantinov from his sister Beila's in 1920, before he came to America, he stopped overnight in the town where she lived, and she wanted to meet him, but she wasn't home when he called and they never met.

My father remembered that after his grandmother died, his grandfather Labe gave up his home in Zozulynits and would spend two or three months at a time with first one of his grown children and then the other. His father had the two brothers, Paci and Motye, and two sisters, Bessie and Zilpa. The children would chip in for keeping their father, Labe. My father remembers that his grandfather used to tell the children stories, all kinds of stories, perhaps about the family, and how they got to where they were. *He looked like my father,* he said, *only older, and he'd spend time with us, sitting there by the furnace, and telling us stories.*

My grandfather Yosel's sister, Bessie, lived in Letichev. She had four daughters and no sons. The oldest daughter was Manya, who was a seamstress. My father said that *they had just come out with machines that made women's stockings. So the family got together and bought a machine, and she used to make stockings and sell them. Of the four daughters, the youngest was my age. They were after my brother Duved to marry one of the daughters, and then they were after me. Somewhere I got a letter from her asking me to write her back and to show my 'decency.' (That I had good intentions.) But I never did write back. I used to walk on the road to Letichev to visit my aunt.* Later, my father's half-brother Willy moved to Letichev, too.

My grandfather's sister Zilpa lived in Khelmnick. *She was a widow and had three sons and a daughter. In that town was a gymnasium, and she used to keep boarders. She wasn't doing very well. So every year, she'd visit rich relatives to see if she could get help from them. Zilpa had a daughter living in Philadelphia.*

I now understand that because Yosel was the youngest child of Labe and Sur, he had to move from the farm village to make a living. Not too long after that another law came out that no Jew could live in that village at all. That's why the family was so spread out. There were aunts and uncles throughout the country. You went where you could find work, to the towns, to America.

Chana's Family

Chana had three sisters and two brothers. They had a Willy, too. Uncle Willy also came to America, and left his wife and two boys behind. They were about my father's age. There was some worry that he was not going to send for them, but he did. Uncle Willy moved to Toledo, Ohio, and one son moved to Detroit, and another to Chicago, and he also had a daughter in Toledo. *Uncle Willy Uler was the one who sent Meyer a ticket. In those days, it used to be that you'd buy a ticket on payment. $50 was the ticket, and the payments were 50 cents a week. Meyer paid him back when he got a job.* Meyer lived with Uncle Willy for a short while when he first came to New York, and when my father came to Pennsylvania, Uncle Willy came to visit him several times.

In the summers, Chana would stay with her parents (Boruch Lepa and Malka) and also her sisters, Iradice and Mollie, in the farm villages near Zozulynits, and she sent Beila, her second daughter, Meilach's twin, to be raised by her parents in the village. There was a third sister, but my father didn't mention her name. She lived near Kiev.

Chana and Yosel were married in 1882, and they settled in the town right after the wedding because Novokonstantinov was close to where Yosel was working. He secured a steady job with a steady income for over thirty years, as an overseer or manager of timberlands. At first, Yosel worked for local concerns, and then for the Germans, until the First World War broke out. He supervised the cutting and shipping of the logs, which were sent mostly to Germany. And Chana managed a store in the marketplace.

In the early years of the marriage, the forest he timbered was close to the village, but as the land was cleared, he moved farther away from his home, farther south. To have moved the family along with him when he changed locations *'would have made them gypsies,'* he said, and so Chana remained with the children in the town, and Yosel returned in the later years only once or twice a year—at Rosh Hashanah and Pesach.

It was noted that the youngest children, my father and his brother, Moishe, were each born nine months after Pesach, exactly nine months after their father's annual visit. Yosel worked on commission, but had a monthly salary, as well. He got a portion of his income from selling branches of trees that had been felled. The company provided Yosel with a house and a cook and a manservant. The same couple stayed with him for many years, until the job ended and he came back to live in Novokonstantinov. By that time, Chana had died. During the war, he bought a few acres of timber and sold wood for fuel to make a living. He eventually took over Chana's store at the marketplace.

I remember that in the summers when we were little, my mother would take us to stay with my father in the woods for several weeks at a time. I remember once that me and my brother Moishe got lost in the woods. We must have been five or six. A man stopped to talk to us and wanted to take us home, but we wouldn't go because we weren't supposed to go with strangers. We were lost for about three or four hours, and we cried and cried, and they were all looking all over for us everywhere. Oh, it was a big story that we told all the time, how we got lost in the woods.

Yosel of the Woods was a small man with a full beard. He was much shorter than his wife, and the children knew that he had extra inches built into his heels to appear taller. He knew five languages: He was schooled both in Hebrew and Russian, but he was also literate in Polish and German, and, of course, he could speak, read and write Yiddish. *Of my father Yosel, I have real good memories. I would go to shul with him. I remember one Simchas Torah, and there was a big celebration, he was so happy, he kept hugging us boys. My father had a twinkle in his eye. He was a man who could read a Russian newspaper and write in Russian. He had a Russian newspaper delivered to the house every week. Always, there was a neighbor sitting on the sun porch or in the living room, who'd come to the house to read the weekly Russian paper.*

My father did a lot of traveling. He was a worldly man. He would get a telegraph from the Germans. 'Meet me in Warsaw.' And he used to have to go to auctions to sell individual acres. He liked to play dominoes, and he liked his schnapps. He would bring us playing cards from Germany. I remember once they were plastic. He liked his tea as hot as could be, right from the samovar. It was a thrill for me when he came home with his horse and buggy.

One time we did something like this. Over there, Friday night, you're not allowed to ride or do anything, or Saturday, the whole day. But Saturday night, it's a celebration, you can do everything. So sometimes my father used to go to a neighbor on Saturday nights or the neighbor would come to our house and they'd play dominoes.

One time he went to a neighbor's, and we went and took out the horse. It was a real nice wintery day. It just started snowing. Actually it takes a little while before the big snow presses down and freezes. Before then, it's very nice to ride.

And we got together some boys and girls, and we took the horse out with the sleigh. We had a nice time, but, of course, we figured we didn't have much time, so we had to make it hurry up, make it real fast. We had to cover some territory and get back before my father got back.

The horse was running real fast for a few miles, and of course the horse was sweating a lot. And we had to put him back in the barn before my father came back.

So my father got back right after that, and he said, 'But before I go to sleep, I want to feed the horse.' So he went out to the barn. He used to like animals very much, my father, and especially this horse. It was a real good horse. They had a nickname for him, 'Mutlick,' because he could swallow up the road real fast.

And here I was holding the kerosene lamp for my father. And he went and threw down some hay for the night. We were about to go, but then he had to go and pet the horse, and he could feel that the horse was all sweaty. He laughed and said, 'I figured you guys would pull something like that.' He laughed, but he didn't get mad.

I asked, "Did he ever get angry with you?" *'Oh, sometimes if we didn't behave,'* he said, *'he'd get mad, but he was a good guy, he wasn't mad at us that night.'*

The House

Their house was the last in a row of seven houses right near the horse-trading street, where Jews and gentiles lived side by side. *The guy next door had a 'chicany,' this was a threshing machine, which was pulled inside the barn by blind horses, they'd run and run and turn the wheels, but if they see they get dizzy, that's why they're blinded. Next to him was an old man and his wife, living very poor, my mother would give them a couple of glasses of milk every day. They were gentiles, but we got along real good. One was Polish and the other Ukrainian. Right next to the house were open fields and then the swamps and then the woods began. You had to know where to walk. Turn off the main road, a Jewish boy, and the gentile boys would throw stones at you and call you names and something else could happen, too.* Often, that would happen. He always remembered that his father's half-brother Willy was shot and killed in the woods.

He remembered it when he thought of that time that he and Moishe got lost in the woods and everybody was looking for them.

They all had gardens in front and in back of their house, my father said, and their house was the start of the *eruv*, the enclosure of poles with ropes or cables attached between them that enabled Jews to transport objects that are not allowed to be carried on the Sabbath. Their house was a double house. In the house next door were cousins, with a boy my father's age who, along with his brother, Moishe, was his constant playmate. I remember that my father and his cousin reconnected years later in the 1960's. His cousin was living in Moscow, and they wrote to each other for a while.

Their house was built of logs on a stone foundation, as were most of the houses in the area. *I saw them build houses there,* my father said. *On the sides, they have it notched out for the logs. The logs were then covered with yellow clay and straw. Usually women did that, the yellow clay is mixed with water, to make it hold together. The clay holds the logs in place. The house takes a long time to build over there, a couple of years, then you leave it sit there for a year. The walls are real thick, to keep you warm. It was a real nice house. There was a dugout, a cellar, underneath, where you could try to hide during the bad times.*

There was a big fence all around the house, with a gate opening up to a long garden with a fruit orchard of plums, cherries, apples, and acacia and lilac trees, and sunflowers. In front of the house was a large sun-porch—or entrance hall—with windows all around, and a slatted roof that could be pulleyed up in the fall to make the Succoth. There on the sun-porch, on rainy days, you could watch the street outside, and dream about playing in the gutter or fishing in the river.

Inside, the house was comfortable and airy, the thick clay walls whitewashed, the oak floors cleaned twice a week, and the big kitchen hearth stove with a sleeping nook on top. There were two halves to the house, with four big rooms, two on either side. On the right side was the sun-porch that entered into the dining room with a small eating table and that room led to the kitchen. On the left was the living room with a big oak dining table and a big cedar chest for clothes, and that room led to Yosel and Chana's bedroom. There were doors between the two halves. The dining room opened to the living room, and led to the bedroom, which also led to the kitchen.

In each of the two sides, in the front rooms, there were *riba* (Yiddish), which were wood-burning furnaces enclosed in stone, that kept the front rooms warm. The windows in the front were set low to the ground. By the standards of the times, the family had all they needed, even more.

"Did they have bathrooms?" I asked my father. *There were no bathrooms in the house. A few houses in town had outhouses, but most people used the gardens in back of the houses—there was a designated place in the garden, or if you were in town, you used the alleys. Sometimes you'd be walking past an alley and see a woman squatting. The women in the house used pans, they emptied them in the back garden. And there was no running water. You'd use slop buckets in the kitchen. You'd get water from the rain barrels, the fresh water creek, the artisanal wells, or the river. You'd change your clothes once a week. There was a bathhouse, a mikvah. And once a month, a woman came to the house for the whole day to do the laundry. She'd take the clothing to the crick to wash.* (Chana died in 1915 from typhoid fever, which is known to be caused by contaminated drinking water.)

Chana and Yosel had the only beds in the house, two wooden beds with straw mattresses, and when the children were little, and his father wasn't home, the younger children would crawl into one of the beds to sleep. The other three rooms, the living room, dining room, and kitchen, all became sleeping rooms. You'd sleep on the wooden benches, the couches filled with straw, and even on the straight-backed chairs. You'd pull two chairs together and make a bed, and you'd also sleep on the floor, too, wherever you found a space. You'd also make room for guests, and for Grandfather Labe, who stayed with the family several months at a time.

The house felt safe for sleeping in those days. The draperies were drawn, the straw and pillows and comforters pulled out for the long winter nights, and all was secure. My father's favorite sleeping space was the wooden couch in the dining room that sat against the warm wall of the *riba*.

In the back of the house were two unfinished rooms, the roof already in place. Yosel had planned to enlarge the house, in case one of the older boys wanted to bring a wife and live with them. A ladder led to the unfinished upper story, where there were sacks filled with dried potatoes and other root vegetables. That's also where the Passover dishes were stored. Those rooms, though, were never finished.

Behind the unfinished rooms was the stable for the horse and cow (only five or six Jewish families in the town had a cow), and a garden beyond the stable, and around the side of the house, and even in front of the house, every inch of land was used for growing corn, enough for the whole winter, for potatoes, beans, carrots, cucumbers, and tomatoes. Food was plentiful. His father had said, "All we need is bread," and there was food enough to contribute to feeding the poor of the town. The kitchen was always alive with cooking and baking. The oven was always ready, and the samovar, too. There were plenty of cups of tea and lumps of sugar.

And there was Sofia, who was like a second mother to my father. She was a widow, who helped to raise all the children. She slept on top of the stove in the kitchen, and she was there through it all, for thirty years, and stayed after Chana died. She kept a special eye on my father, the youngest, who was always running in from play for a snack. My father remembered her. *She was very good,* he said, *I remember that Duved was called up again for the army, and that he had to go to the county seat, and she cried like anything. He didn't go. That may have been when he blinded himself in one eye, so as not to go.*

Every day, there was good food, there was milk from their cow, which Sofia milked twice a day, and there was extra to give away to the poor or sell at the market. There was a peasant boy who took the cow out to pasture every day. There were potatoes, meat, fruit and vegetables. They baked bread twice a week, on Sunday for the week, and then on Friday for the Sabbath. On Friday morning, there were latkes. Every Sabbath would bring with it chicken soup and boiled chicken, the daily potatoes, and that was the day the younger children received an extra penny to buy sweets at one of the local merchants. Motye counted himself rich. His pockets were always full of hard candy (he called it *sucky candy*), and the Sabbath multiplied the weekly supply.

My father says that his mother, Chana, was *a serious, hard-working woman*. She was *highly respected in the town*. "How does a woman become so respected," I asked him, and he said, *'By her deeds. By what she does. By what she did for others. People could talk to her. Women would come to her with their tsuris, their troubles. Someone was always there in the house, having a cup of tea. And she would listen and help if she could.'*

She managed her store, as well as the household. With her husband away, she was in charge of the family's finances, and offered guidance to other women of the shtetl on how to handle their money. She vouched for the women who needed a loan, and she was a trusted confidant. There were many poor people in the town, and she always shared what she had. There was a place by the oven where she kept change, and every day there was someone at the door. She carried out *tzedakah*—giving to others who have less than you—because doing so was an essence of Jewish life. She gave away bread twice a week, half a loaf, a whole loaf, whatever was needed. A few old men, who came regularly, she gave them a big chunk of bread in the bags they carried. They didn't eat much. Every Friday, she awakened at 4 o'clock to prepare for the meal. The challah were in the oven, there were at least a dozen loaves, and Shabbos meals for the regulars who lined up at the door. There was a *landsman* in New York who told my father, *'I remember the meals you got from Chana Yosel, and so many challahs every Friday, so many challahs that she gave away.'*

She allowed no photograph to be taken of herself; she had her children to remember, she said. She couldn't read or write, but I hear her voice in the letters she had written for her by her husband and children to the son who left for America in 1911. She cried over him, she wanted to hear from him, she worried, she warned him. *Don't walk in the middle of the street, walk on the sidewalk.* And missed him, *Come home, come home for Passover.* Six children died during her lifetime. What happened to the other five, she never knew.

"Were you rich?" I asked my father, and he said, *"Yes, we were rich for the standards over there, but being rich over there was poor."* In my father's stories, it is his family who were the riches of his life. And his mother, Chana the Long, was the center of his world who instilled in him a love of the sweetness and beauty of daily life—a loving kindness, what Abraham Heschel called a *life-feeling.* Being alive was a blessing—the air he breathed, the food on our table, the sky and trees, most of all, his wife and children, his family. We were his wealth.

I missed having grandparents. I never knew Chana or Joseph, and my mother's parents died when I was very young. But through the years, I've felt connected to my grandmother, Chana the Long. I am tall like her, and I imagine she would recognize me as belonging to her. I talk to her in my head, write to her in notebooks and letters, in poems, and here on these pages, and tell her about all that she missed. I want her to know that there were four sons who survived the terrible times. Meyer, Duved, Moishe, and my father, Motye. They married and had children and lived good lives. And there were grandchildren and now great grandchildren and great-great grandchildren.

I want most to tell her about my father, the eleventh child, her youngest, who I know inherited her beautiful soul. "All things are mortal," says Isaac Babel, in one of his stories, "Only a mother is accorded eternal life. And when the mother is not among the living, she leaves a memory . . . that [sic] nourishes compassion within us, just as the ocean, the boundless ocean, nourishes the rivers that cut through the universe."*

Chana's Children:
Brucha, Paci, Yeta, Meilach, Beila,
Duved, Meyer, Samuel, William, Moishe, Motye

Chana and Yosel had eleven children. My father was the eleventh child. In the white leather English translation of *The Holy Scriptures*** that I received in 1957, on my confirmation from Sunday School, from the Ladies Auxiliary of Temple O'Have Israel in Brownsville, Pennsylvania, both my mother and father recorded the names and birthdates of their parents and siblings. On the following page, in my father's handwriting, is his list. I knew my mother's parents only briefly, they both died when I was young, but I knew my aunts and uncles and cousins. My father's family was mostly gone, but for my father it was essential that both my sister and I come to know them all. So we learned Meyer's story and Meilach's, Yeta's and Paci's, and all of them, all his brothers and sisters.

Of Chana's eleven children, there were eight boys, and three girls. The first girl, Brucha, died at birth. As did the fifth son, Samuel. The sixth, Willy, died at three of scarlet fever. But it was a miracle in those times that eight children were growing strong, six boys and two girls. There were two clusters of children. The older children were Paci, Yeta, the twins, Meilach and Beila, and Duved and Meyer. There was a space in between, because the two little boys, Samuel and Willy, had both died. So there were nine years between Meyer and Moishe, and eleven years between Meyer and my father.

---

* Babel, I. (2002). "The Rabbi." *The complete works of Isaac Babel.* (P. Constantine Trans.). New York, NY: Norton, 234.

** *The Holy Scriptures: A New Translation.* (1956). Philadelphia: The Jewish Publication Society of America.

Martin Pearl ‏פ‏רל‏ ‏ווורשען‏

1-16-1904 ‏כ‏ה‏ ‏טבת‏ ‏טלן‏

NovoKonstantinov Prov. Podolia

Ukrain Russia

Joseph Perel 1861-1919

Hana Tina Uler Perel 1865-1915

Brucha

Perach 1884-1919

Yeta 1886-1912

Meilach 1889-1908

Beila Takser 1889-

David 1891-

Meyer 1893-

Samuel

Willian

Moishe 1901-

Mordechai 1903-

MARtin

10-16-57 FREDERickTowN, PA.

Genealogy: My father's hand-written list

Joseph Perel (1861-1919)   m.   **Chana Dina Uler** (1865-1915)
(murdered)   (typhoid fever)

Eleven Children:

Brucha b. 1882?

Pesach
1884-1919 (murdered)
Married Hutka in 1908.
One son, Lev, born in 1916 (fate unknown).

Yeta
1886-1912 (died in childbirth)
Married Aaron Trachtenburg in 1911.
One daughter, Malka, 1912-1915 (typhoid fever)

Melach and **Beila** b. 1889
Meilach d. 1908 (suicide)
Beilach d. 1942 (murdered)
Married David Takser.
(Three daughters murdered))

Duved
1891-1971 (buried in Argentina)
Married Dina Serebrier.
Three children, Ana, José, Herman.

Meyer
1893-1965 (buried in Pennsylvania)
Married Fanny Eisenberg.
One son, Berne.

Samuel b. 1894?

William b. 1896?

Moishe
1901-1983 (buried in Argentina)
Married Rosa Silber.
Three children, José, Ana, Rebecca.

Mordechai (Motye, Martin)
1903-1991 (buried in New York)
Married Bessie Judkovitz.
Two daughters, Judith and Janet.

A family story in history

It was confusing: my father records two birthdates in the Bible, 1903 and 1904. The confusion came from the translation from the Jewish calendar to the Gregorian. The Russian military draft may also have entered into the equation. The later the year was recorded for a Jewish boy, the better, for the birthdate determined when he would be called into the draft. Both Paci and Duved maimed themselves to avoid going to the Czar's army for 25 years. Paci had all his teeth pulled. And Duved blinded his left eye. At all costs, you avoided conscription, by making yourself lame, cutting off a thumb, or an ear or making yourself partially blind or unable to chew properly.

Paci was already twenty when my father was born, and shortly afterwards he moved out to a neighboring town to oversee the felling and distribution of lumber, like his father. Yeta was eighteen, and as yet unmarried, and Meilach and Beila were sixteen.

When Beila was born, she was sent to live with Chana's family in the farm village. It was understood that it was difficult to raise twins, *there was not enough milk for two,* my father said, *even with a wet nurse.* But I always wondered if there were other reasons. Perhaps Chana's own mother, Malka, needed the company of a young child, or needed the help, so Beila was sent away, and only came to live in the house in Novokonstantinov when she was in her teens.

Also, in the house were Duved, the eighth child, born in 1891. He was bar mitzvah the year my father was born. I know that it was Duved who watched over my father when he was young. He scolded him when he didn't do his homework or misbehaved. My father always called him *my Duved.* He became well learned, a teacher in the town, kept the store after his father died, and married his sweetheart Dina. They immigrated to Argentina, with two children in 1926. Meyer was the ninth child. He was eleven when my father was born. He left for America in 1911, and in 1921, Meyer made it possible for my father to find his way to him in America. They were devoted to each other throughout their lives.

Moishe was a year and eleven months older than my father. He was his constant companion, his best friend and protector, his closest brother. They played together, and wrestled and pushed each other out of trees. They were both remarkably physical and sturdy. But Moishe was always bigger, and when they were little, he dragged the little brother along wherever he went. The two were inseparable as boys, and bonded throughout their lives, although they lived their adult lives a continent apart. My father gained entry to the United States in 1921. Moishe emigrated to Buenos Aires two years later, and with the national lottery money he won, sent for his wife and son a year or two later.

So Motye was the eleventh and last child, the little one that Chana and Yeta and Sofia and then, Beila, all doted over. He knew that he was spoiled. "Motele," they called him, and if he didn't get his way, he would bang his leather boots on the hard wooden bench in the living room, and Chana and Yosel, when he was home, would laugh and hug him. "The littlest one, the baby," and they would keep him safe, give him an extra penny, and send him on his way to play in the street, along the running stream that ran through the gutter when it rained, where he took his home-made boat with Moishe, and imagined they were sailing to far and distant places.

The street was where he lived when he could, when he lived freely those first years, and before they tried to tie him down to *cheder* and home tutoring in Russian. He didn't like school. His sister Yeta helped him with his letters, which he mixed up. Duved warned him that he would be a *dumkop* if he didn't learn, he'd be *nothing more than a horse and cart driver. I worked so hard, but it didn't come easy to me.* Maybe he had dyslexia, he thought years later, because he was always mixing up his letters, even in English. Yeta tutored him. *She was a doll,* my father said, *she treated me like kids are treated here. There, you wouldn't worry too much about kids. You just put them out to play. But Yeta would say, 'go wash yourself, comb your hair.' She would encourage me about school. Bei-*

la was very quiet. *Of course, she couldn't write herself. My mother encouraged me to go to school, telling me I would regret it if I didn't go, giving me a penny to go. I wanted to read. I was taking Russian lessons, but there was no one to help me find children's books. I got "Mother" by Maxim Gorky.*[*] *I was too young, I couldn't understand it.* (In the final days of his life, my father wanted his copy of Gorky's *Mother* beside him.)

A Place in the World

When he was growing up, he had a place in the world. There was a world inside the house, and the world outside called to him: the stream that formed in the gutter on the horse-trading street near their house, the river that encircled the town, where he learned to swim, the trees where he climbed as high as he could, to look out over the fields. This is where he wanted to live, and this is where you would find him and Moishe, racing their dog to the river, throwing off their clothes on a summer's day, and diving into the water. *Once, years later, Moishe and I found the body of a young Jewish girl caught in a trap in the river. She had been missing for days, and the whole town was looking for her.*

But here in these early years, the water was clear and cool and inviting, and they were free. He became a strong swimmer. And later, after his mother died, he could easily escape from school, and spend his days down at the river, fishing, swimming, jumping from rock to rock, or walking along the road to Letichev to visit his aunt, when it was safe, and in the winter, there was ice skating.

There was his brother, Moishe, always connected to him, they were always together. There were the dogs: he remembered, *there was a dog, we called her Halvah, because that was the color, grey, and oh, we had her a long time, but over there they used to have dogcatchers, the dogs didn't have tags on them, and the dogcatchers would catch the dogs and put them in a cage, and then you'd go and buy them, but this one dogcatcher, he'd catch them and kill them. He'd get something out of it, something to make soap out of, and he caught her. When I left for America, we had a dog that was hers, only black, and she had some pups, too, that looked just like her. There was always a cat there, too.*

What was my life like when I was a child? We always had bread. We had plain rye bread. I'd run into the house and break off a piece of bread and then run back outside and play. Sometimes I'd take an apple. We had a cow. In the morning, we'd have a glass of milk and a piece of bread. My mother would make potatoes. Around 10 or 11, we'd have potatoes. At lunch, we'd have meat often.

They left the kids to play by themselves. There was a gutter across the street from us, and when it rained, it got to be like a little crick, with the water running real fast, and so we'd go out there and we'd make a dam out of mud to stop the water, and then we'd make little holes, so the water would spout through, and then we'd run through barefooted. We had no toys. . . but there would be a box from shoe polish, we'd clean it out real good. and we'd take the two lids, and put a long wire between and make a telephone out of it and holler so loud, 'Can you hear me?' 'Yes, we can hear you. . . .'

And we'd get spools from thread, stuff like that.

Once we found a caster. . . . I never saw anything like it in my life. . . it was from a bed. I was little, about five years old. So we tied it to a broomstick and ran all over with it. Nobody had a bicycle, but one of the neighbor's kids had a little tricycle. It was the only one I ever saw.

But life was different there than here. . . it was kind of rough. . . but we had fun. . we had fun, that is, before the First World War. In the summer, we had a lot of fun. My father had two sisters. One of them lived about 9 miles from us one way (Letichev). . . the other lived 11 miles the other way (Khelmnick). And we'd go visit. . . I'd go visit, sometimes on foot. . . I'd go, not to the one 11 miles away, because it was a different country, you'd get a little bit scared, there was a lot of woods, and hills, but to the other one, I used to walk, it would take me a couple of hours, two or three hours. . .

and I'd stay overnight. Bessie, she was a widow woman, she had four daughters, four girls. . . . and then after a while, my father's half brother (Willy) moved into that town.

My mother used to take us, me and Moishe, in the summer, that was a big deal. She had a big family living in different little towns, maybe 25 miles away, some lived in towns, some lived in villages, where she was born, so she'll take us, maybe two or three weeks, and we'd go visit one and stay a couple of days, and then another, and then come back here. I remember my mother's mother, I remember her just sitting there. She died when I was about two. I remember when my grandfather died. We were all sad that he died. She had sisters and the one brother, he was younger, he came to this country and sent Uncle Meyer the ticket.

Our life over there, he said, *was happier and more ordinary when I was a young boy. And then it all changed.*

Motye, 1916, age 13

Three

End of a World

The spectator can know nothing of the truth.
—William James, *"On a Certain Blindness in Human Beings"* *

Knowing your Place

I remember it as if it were yesterday: I'd just come out on the street one morning, with Moishe and the boy next door, who was a cousin. I was chewing on a piece of rye bread. I was wearing a woolen cap and chewing on the bread, and a policeman rides by on his horse. We had been taught that whenever a policeman rides by, you have to take off your hat, but I was all mixed up because I was also taught that a Jew cannot remove a hat while you're eating. The other two swallowed the bread and took off their hats, but I bit off too big a piece to swallow. The policeman on the horse came up to me and screamed, 'Take it off, you good for nothing Jew. Take it off before I give you what you deserve. I should strip the skin off your behind, you miserable little Jew.'

What my father learned during his foundational years was that there was danger in the air outside the house. There was a history

---

* James, W. (1958). "On a certain blindness in Human Beings." In *Talks to teachers*. New York, NY: Norton.

33

that pressed in on you every moment of your life. As a Jew, you didn't walk out onto the roads alone, without remembering the warnings and reminders. You heard the stories of the wars against the Jews, the stories in the Bible, of course, and the stories of the *pogroms,* here and now, the spontaneous outbursts against the Jews, the little ones and big ones. The stories were real, and you learned the lessons early.

There was a litany of local and world events that he could recite: the recurring attempts of the local Ukrainians to establish a Ukrainian state; the Russian Empire reasserting its power in one political guise or another: czars or Bolsheviks or Soviets defeating the local insurgents and foreign insurgents, the Poles, Turks, or the Germans or the international forces that tried to quell the Revolution. *It was all mixed up, and during the Revolution, things would change overnight. One day the Poles would be in charge, the next, the Bolsheviks.* I learned the history lessons, too, from my father. Khmelnitsky was a household name, as were the pogroms in Proskurov of the seventeenth century.

My father was born into a time of enormous social unrest in Russia. In 1905, the Russians were defeated in the Russo-Japanese War, there were revolts against the government (Bloody Sunday, 1905), increased calls for the overthrow of the monarchy, peasant uprisings and workers' strikes, and repeated attacks against Jews, students, and intellectuals. When he was a boy, my father said, *there was a lot of talk in the marketplace about how the Russian fleet had been defeated so fast. Nobody could believe it. Before the war, they used to say that the Russians, all they had to do was throw their caps at the Japanese, and they'd defeat them, because there were so many Russians. Many Jews were happy that the Czar was defeated, but they didn't say it too loud.*

They used to catch Jewish boys and send them to the army for 25 years. Nobody wanted to go to the army, first you couldn't eat kosher, how did you go to the army and give up your Jewishness? Some of them cut off their thumbs to avoid going and they'd shake hands with the hand with the missing thumb. It's funny what you remember. The price of flour was high, and the Jews were accused of causing the bad economy and causing the revolution. Most wanted to come to America, some went to Palestine. There were no jobs, there was nothing to do.

For the young Jews, it was increasingly clear that no matter which side they belonged on, they were always caught between two worlds: Jew and non-Jew. Jews had come to Ukraine with the Poles, but the lessons of the past taught them that they were the ones who would be sacrificed. The Jews, no matter what kind of poverty they suffered, or what kind of work they did, were associated with the moneyed classes, as feeding off the backs of the real workers—the peasants and, later, the proletariat.

My father remembered that there was always talk about the way things should be, about the world being just, and where everyone, even Jews, would be treated fairly. No one would feed off another, like the fly in the parable that he often recited to me.

A farmer went out to plow the fields. He had two oxen, and here was a fly sitting on the neck of one ox, sucking on him, and bothering him no end, but the ox couldn't do anything about it, he kept turning his head and wiggling his ears, but that didn't chase the fly away, and so it went on the whole day long, that fly sat on the ox's neck and fed off him, and towards the evening, when they came back to the village, the fly met her friend, another fly, and the friend said, 'Where were you the whole day long?' And the fly said, 'We were plowing.' In Russian, my father said, *'me pakhali.' 'We were working. We were laboring.'*

But the fly wasn't working at all, I used to say, he was just sucking on the neck of the poor ox.

There was another world, they were told—across the ocean—where it was possible to live another kind of life. It was a land of opportunity. Some said the streets were lined with gold. That's where the young people wanted to go.

Paci and Meilach, 1908

Pesach (Paci) the oldest son was tall like his mother. He was a firm, gentle man, well-schooled in Hebrew, and learned in the scriptures. He had the learning to become a rabbi, as did Meilach and Duved. But like most young men of the community, Paci spent much of his young manhood looking for work, moving from one job to another, returning from time to time to live with his parents. He found a job like his father's, in timber, but with a different company. He married Hutka in 1908 when he was already 25. Their wedding proved to be bittersweet.

Meilach, in 1908 was 19, six years younger than Paci. Motye remembered him as tall, like Paci, with a brisk moustache. He, too, was a gentle man, like his father, like Paci. During that year after the Russo-Japanese War when his father lost his job, Meilach helped support the family. *He brought the family food, a chicken, some meat, flour.* But jobs were scarce, and prospects for the young were limited. Like many, he wanted to leave, he was clamoring to go to America. *He wanted to go in the worst way, but my mother didn't want him to, and my father didn't want him to go.*

This is where the details get murky. There were rumors later that Meilach had fallen in love with Paci's fiancée. That she was flirting with him. Or that he was embarrassed because he didn't have the money to pay the musicians at his brother's wedding, which was what a brother was expected to do. But who knows? Suicide among the young in those times was not uncommon. What we know is that he died by his own hand in the unfinished room two weeks before his brother's wedding, and that Motele, then four, remembers Meilach lying on the ground where they laid him at the bottom of the ladder. *He was so quiet,* my father said, *he wasn't moving.* Everybody was gathered around.

There was a law that an autopsy had to be performed on presumed suicides. Yosel was called back from the woods to be there. *They never told my mother about the autopsy.* And after that, nobody wanted to finish the second story of the house, because that was where Meilach had died.

Soon after Meilach's death, my father was climbing the ladder up to the unfinished rooms, and something flew into his eye and damaged the sight in that one eye. Things went dark, *and my eye was jumping, jumping,* and then he could see for a little while, and then not. He always saw *blurry* out of that eye. His peripheral vision was damaged. "Did you ever tell anyone," I asked him, "Did they ever take you to a doctor?" and he said, *'No, things like that just happened, you just lived with it. They didn't listen to kids, anyhow.'*

Chana and Yosel buried one son and married off another within a month. The wedding was one of my father's earliest memories: everyone in the house was rushing about, ignoring him, and he climbed onto the wooden bench in the front room and banged his leather boots *real loud.* Someone came by and calmly removed his shoes. They all went to Letichev, the bride's town, for the wedding, and as many as could fit, they stayed with Aunt Bessie.

He remembered the party afterwards, and being held by his father's mother, Baba Sur, who was wearing a fancy dress with sequins, and he wanted to pull them off. He remembered his Aunt Bessie dancing. He remembered all the wedding guests marching over to the riverbank and throwing in fistfuls of coins to wish the couple good luck. And to show that they had enough money to throw away.

The bride and groom married and moved to a village close by, and Paci moved from job to job, and they returned home from time to time to live with his parents. Paci and Hutka were childless for the first eight years of their marriage and then had a son, Lev, who was three when his father was killed. A second pregnancy ended in a miscarriage. I wonder how much Paci carried the death of his brother, Meilach, on his shoulders the rest of his life.

Meyer leaves for America, 1911

My father also remembered the day in May 1911 that Meyer left for America. In 1911, Meyer was 17 years old and, for a long time, trying to persuade his mother to let him leave. Chana finally gave in, apparently fearful that if she didn't, she might lose him, too, as she had lost Meilach.

Both Duved and Meyer lived in the house when the little ones were growing up. In 1911, Moishe was already 9 and Motye was 7. My father remembered Meyer sitting at the dining room table, singing. *He was a jolly guy and ready to move out into the bigger world. And there were plenty of girls. Meyer was a kind of ladies' man. He had girlfriends, but he had no spending money. So he and his friend, Hymie Fox, decided they'd go to the United States, make some money, and then they'd come back home. He wrote a letter to our mother's brother, Willy (Uler), who was already in New York, for a ticket, and he sent it.*

That Saturday night in May, everybody and everybody in the town came to the house to say goodbye. There were people in the streets, so big an event it was. Everybody was there, all the neighbors, the family, everybody. And in the morning, the whole family got into carriages, and we went to Letichev, where Aunt Bessie lived.

On the way, all the carriages stopped at a crossroads to water the horses, and I looked up and saw an icon with a cross on it, and was trying to find my cap to cover my head. You had to cover your head if you saw a Christian symbol like that. All these years later, I remember that.

In Letichev, they left me there with my aunt. I was too little. And they all carried on by carriage to the next town [Medzhibozh], where they met the narrow gauge railroad, which they took to Derazhinia, where you got the big train. That's where my father met them, he had come from his job, and the whole town took the carriages to Medzhibozh and then came back. The three of them, my father, my mother and Meyer carried on to Derazhinia. And when Meyer's train pulled away from the station, my mother went running after it on the tracks, until the train was out of sight.

It was so hard, Meyer said, all the good-bye-ing. He had that picture in his mind for the rest of his life, of my mother running after the train.

I remember how she cried and cried for days afterwards, and how they used to look out for Meyer's letters, for a postcard from him.

Yeta, Beila, and Chana, 1912-1915

Yeta was the apple of her mother's eye, the daughter she had by her side throughout their lives together. The first daughter, Brucha, had died at birth. Paci came next in 1884, and then Yeta, two years later, in 1886. The next were Meilach and Beila. Beila was raised by her Uler grandparents. The Perel girls were educated, the Uler girls were not. It was also the difference between the town and the country. In Novokonstantinov, there was a thriving Jewish community.

In the farm village, the Jews were few and far between. In the town were synagogues and cheders, and it was expected, as well, in the merchant classes that a secular education would happen at home. When Beila finally came home, at 15, and Yeta was 17, the two girls did not get on. Beila sat in the corner, silent. And Yeta most likely objected to this sister-intruder. Yeta was town-bred, and schooled. Beila was a farm yokel, and illiterate. She did not call Chana, *Mother*. Both played significant roles at different times in my father's life—as second mothers.

Yeta was eighteen when my father was born, and certainly eligible for a *shidduch* (arranged marriage), which she objected to. She was learned, having been tutored at home in Hebrew, Russian, and Yiddish. She herself became a tutor, probably in Novokonstantinov. There is no mention that she left home to tutor, so I gather that she taught in local homes. She was a lover of books, that was clear, and she minded my father, as a second mother, and was able, as Chana was not, to help him with his homework.

She resisted the matchmakers, and finally, already 20, she reluctantly agreed to marry a cousin from a distant village. *You see, my mother had another sister living far away. She was a nice person. She had a son. Yisroel was his name. And he used to come to visit. I remember him. He was going to kill himself if Yeta didn't marry him. Finally she gave in. And I guess he wasn't doing anything, but mostly Jewish boys didn't have anything to do. His parents had to set him up in something. My mother had a big dowry saved for her. A couple of thousand rubles. It was a fortune in those days. They gave him the money. And here one day, he confessed that he'd fallen in love with someone else and that he was breaking off the engagement. It wasn't that Yeta loved him, but she figured she had to get married at that point. And now she was ashamed she was jilted. The town he came from was close to Kiev, but a long way from us. I remember my mother went to see him, by train, and she brought back the money. Over there you didn't have a safe or anything, and we put the money in a pillow, and every time we needed some money, she would send me to go and find the pillow.*

Yeta resisted the matchmakers for another five years, and then relented. It was agreed in 1911, just after Meyer left for America that she would marry Asher Trachtenberg. He was a good man, my father said, from a good family, but like so many others, he needed a job. First, he tried to get work close by Novokonstantinov, but it was impossible, so both he and Yeta went to the city of Uman, where they figured the prospects were better. They took the dowry money and together they opened a store. Chana even went to help her, taking the children (Moishe and my father) along. But they had no success in the store, and they lost a good bit of the money. A few months later, Yeta was back in Novokonstantinov, living with her mother once more, while Asher got work at a distant flourmill.

She was now pregnant, and it was a difficult pregnancy. My father remembered her *humiliation*. She was embarrassed, my father said, that her husband could not make a living, and that she was pregnant. She took to her bed, and my father recalls the weeping, his mother's soothing words, and what was to come. The birth was terrible. Yeta was in labor for days, and finally the baby came, *a beautiful little girl*, my father said. They named her Malka, after Chana's mother. And Yeta began to bleed, but the mid-wife couldn't help, and since there wasn't a doctor in the town, the barber was called in. My father blamed the barber, who punctured the womb, and peritonitis set in, and, *oh, was she in agony*, my father said. This was in 1912. He was eight or nine, and I imagine him listening, watching when no one noticed him off in the corner in the room.

The baby survived, but Yeta died, and Chana took care of Yeta's little girl. My father remembered her well. Malka. There was a big rubber tree plant in the house that she would pull herself up on when she was learning to walk. She was a beautiful, joyful little girl, my father said. Chana never got over the death of her daughter, Yeta, who died at 27. *I remember when Yeta died. Everyone was sad. Meyer said that no one wrote to him, you didn't write bad news, so he didn't know until he approached a landsman, my old teacher Moisman, who came to this country, and he said, what have you heard of my sister, and he told him.*

After Yeta's death, Beila and her mother cared for Yeta's daughter, and sometime later there was an arrangement for her to marry her sister's husband and to raise the little girl. But in 1915, there was a terrible typhoid epidemic. Malka, who was three, and Moishe contracted the disease. Chana nursed them both. Moishe survived, but both grandmother and granddaughter died. Chana was 49. And my father, at 12, was motherless. Beila then stayed on to keep house for her father and the two boys, Moishe, and my father.

So Meilach died in 1908, when my father was four. Meyer left for America in 1911 when my father was seven. Yeta died in 1912 when my father was eight. Chana died in 1915 when my father was twelve. Yosel and Paci died in 1919 when my father was 15.

There was no photograph taken of the family until after Chana died. Meyer had begged that they send him a photograph, and then

Family portrait, 1916

Yeta was gone and now his mother. In 1916, this photograph was taken to send to Meyer.

In the back row, left to right are Beila, Duved, and Moishe. In the front row, left to right, are my father Motye, Yosel, Paci and his wife Hutka (standing). Of the eleven children, there were six remaining. Five of them lived in or near Novokonstantinov, Paci, Beila, Duved, Moishe, and Motye, my father. Meyer lived in Masontown, Pennsylvania, U.S.A.

With both his mother and Yeta gone, and the world in turmoil, my father's studies were interrupted. Most likely he did not have a formal bar mitzvah at 13. He evaded the question when I asked. Beila became like a mother to him, but she couldn't help with his studies, so he was pretty much left on his own. And Beila found a secret love, a man who had deserted from the Russian army and was living in hiding next door in the adjoining house. He had assumed the name of a soldier who had died in the war, but the 1917 Revolution brought with it a general amnesty and a pardon for deserters. So he was able to come out of hiding, and they married that same year. His name was David Takser, and Beila and he moved to the town of Dunaivtsi near Kamanetz-Podolsky. My father lived with them in 1920.

As long as Beila took care of the house, Yosel did not remarry. But after she left, he was urged not to be alone. My father said that *a man needed caring for, he didn't know how to cook for himself, or keep house. He needed a wife.*

My grandfather's second wife was a widow with a daughter my father's age. Several months after they married, my father said, *they made a hold-up to us one time. In the middle of the night, robbers broke into the house. They smashed the window at the back of the house in the bedroom right next to the bed where my stepmother was sleeping. My father was in the bed next to her. I was on the couch near the 'riba,' and Moishe was sleeping, we were the only ones home, and here six men broke in. They were packing everything they could, from the cedar chest, everything, demanding money, okay if you don't tell us, I'll give you five minutes. They brought Moishe over to where my father was. I stayed on the couch and didn't get up. They hit Moishe on the head with a rifle butt to show that they meant business. They hit him real hard and knocked him down. They were about to shoot him in the head. What happened, I don't know, but suddenly they heard something and got up and left, they must have heard a sound from outside the window, and ran away.* My father said that his stepmother never spoke another word. She died three or four days later. The young daughter, who was my father's age, was sent to live with his stepmother's sister in a neighboring town. This was one of the stories that my father told me late in his life.

Right before his death in 1919, Yosel married a third time, but he died before the marriage was consummated. Since the mikvah in Novokonstantinov was now gone, his wife-to-be had to travel to a nearby town for the ceremonial mikvah. Before she came back, Yosel was killed.

Chaos

Our family troubles were set within one of the most tumultuous times in the history of the Western world. In 1914, World War I began. Russia, one of the Allied nations fighting against Germany, became a battleground. Early on, Podolia, as well as other parts of Ukraine, was occupied by Austrian troops.

The ford at the River Buh at Novokonstantinov provided passage for the opposing factions during the war. My father remembered thousands of troops coming through the town, on horseback and on foot. He remembered Austrian soldiers garrisoned in the house. Initially, everyday life in the shtetl remained relatively quiet for the time being.

In 1917, Russia erupted into Revolution. In March, Tsar Nicholas II was overthrown, and Alexander Kerensky chosen as the head of the Provisional Government. With the encouragement of the Allies, Kerensky intensified the offensive against the Germans, and the fighting in the south continued. But the Russian army was exhausted and hungry, and the conditions were ripe for the Bolsheviks to seize power, as they did in Petrograd in November 1917. The Soviets wanted to end the fighting with Germany.

In early 1918, the Treaty of Brest-Litovsk was signed, which ended hostilities between Germany and the new Soviet government. Russia ceded a number of territories, and recognized the independence of Ukraine. World War I ended November 11, 1918, but the Russian Civil War, as well as the war with Poland, spanned the next five years. An estimated 14,000,000 people died, more than the total number of casualties on both sides in World War I. From countryside to city, Russia was bleeding. Ukraine's independence was short-lived, and it was not until 70 years later, in 1991, with the break-up of the Soviet Union that it became an independent nation.

In the early days of the Revolution, there was a prominent Jewish presence among the revolutionaries. In many towns in Ukraine, when the Bolsheviks gained control, the Jews became part of the town's governance. My father remembered the revolutionary songs being sung in the marketplace in the town, and the promise of better days for all.

But the next years of the Revolution and Civil War were not good for the Jews. The pogroms against the Jews in Ukraine intensified. Here was the greatest concentration of Jews in all of Eastern Europe, and the Jew was the common enemy. In the aftermath of World War I, during the turmoil of the Revolution, entire families and whole Jewish villages were destroyed.

Ukraine was in chaos. There was prolonged fighting among the key factions: the "Whites," the counter-revolutionary forces, were fighting for the old regime, against the revolutionary "Reds," the Bolsheviks. At the same time, the Ukrainian nationalists were fighting for an independent Ukraine. After the war, the Poles tried to regain a foothold in Ukraine. The Poles were supported by an army of international brigades.

Again, the Jews were caught in the middle. The Whites accused the Jews of being Bolsheviks, as did the Poles. And virulent anti-Semitism spread world-wide, particularly through pamphlets such as "The Protocols of the Elders of Zion," first published in Russia in 1903, but drawn from a long history of similar diatribes against the Jews. In the early 20th century, Jews were seen by some as a driving force behind the Russian Revolution. Killing Jews, therefore, was synonymous with killing Communists.[*]

---

[*] See Webman, E. (Ed.) (2011). *The global impact of the protocols of the elders of zion*. A century-old myth. London and New York, NY: Routledge.

In 1919, the Red Cross sent a delegation to Ukraine to investigate the growing reports of what the head of the commission, Elias Heifetz, called the *gory carnival* that was happening in Ukraine. The delegation, named the All-Ukrainian Relief Committee for the Victims of Pogroms, was not only to supply "money, food, and clothing to the victims, render medical aid to the wounded and mutilated, and take care of the orphaned children, [but] also investigate—to determine the true character of the events and ascertain the circumstances in which they occurred." The Committee's report, *The Slaughter of the Jews in the Ukraine in 1919,* provides a history of pogroms in Ukraine in the context of the larger political history, and publishes page after page of eyewitness accounts of the killing of the Jews. *

My father was an eyewitness to the pogroms of Novokonstantinov in 1919. He was orphaned that day in June, when his father and also his oldest brother were killed in their house in the shtetl. For the rest of his life, he relived what happened that day, replaying the memories, revisiting the scene. He was there as *participant,* in the midst of the day's event as they was unfolding. But an event is not a story. *Story* is not only *what happened,* but also how we make sense of it all. We impose a "narrative line upon disparate images," says Didion. We learn to "freeze the shifting phantasmagoria, which is our actual experience" by ascribing meanings and interpretations, lessons and morals, to the narrative. It is how we get to some kind of truth, or understanding. It is how we remember.

My father needed to remember and report on what he had witnessed that day—the shifting disparate images. What did happen in the house that day? What was the sequence of events? Who came into the house and killed his father and brother? He didn't know for certain. And *what if?* What would have happened to him—or to Moishe— if they hadn't escaped? What propelled him that day to run out the

---

* Heifetz, E. (1921). *The slaughter of the Jews in Ukraine in 1919.* New York: Thomas Seltzer. BiblioLife Reproduction.

back door? Should he have stayed and tried to defend his father? What could he have done differently?

He needed to keep the story alive, and he also needed to get the story right, to be sure of the *facts*, as they were knowable. So he became a researcher—of that moment, and of that history, as the history, through the years, was being written. He kept reading whatever he could find in Russian, Yiddish, or English about what had happened during his lifetime. He talked and talked to his brother, Moishe, who was there that day, too. I found among his papers, Heifetz's *Slaughter of the Jews,* in Yiddish. I also found in his papers a newspaper clipping of an eyewitness account of the 1919 pogrom in Novokonstantinov, published in the Yiddish paper, the *Forward,* in July of that year. I assume that his brother Meyer gave him a copy—and perhaps that is how Meyer found out about the deaths of his father and brother on June 3, 1919.

Sivan 5/5679 – June 3, 1919

The day my grandfather and Paci were killed was the day before Shavuoth in 1919. Life was ordered by the Jewish calendar, and Jew-killing was, historically, coincident with Jewish holidays and festivals. By the Gregorian calendar, it was Tuesday, June 3, 1919, and my father remembered that it was a beautiful day, Sivan 5. The political situation in Russia kept changing. Officially, Ukraine was now under Bolshevik rule, but the town itself had been abandoned, left without any official in charge. The Bolshevik officials had fled.

The town itself had been occupied during the war by Austrian troops. In 1918, after the peace treaty, my father said that the Austrians dropped their guns and ammunition right where they were and went home. The munitions were left for anyone who grabbed them first. After the Austrians left, and during the beginning of the Revolution, the Cossacks, under the rule of Simon Petliura, seized control of Ukraine as an independent republic. It is estimated that 250,000

Jews were slaughtered by his Ukrainian Army. On one day, February 15, 1919, there were 1700 Jews massacred in Proskurov (now Khmelnitsky), and another 600 in Felshtin. Petliura was the commander of the forces and also Ukrainian prime minister. In 1926, Petliura was assassinated in Paris in retribution for his atrocities. The assassin was the Russian anarchist and Yiddish poet, Sholom Schwarzbard. A French court found him not guilty.[*]

Eventually the Bolsheviks returned, but in Podolia, they had difficulty holding on. Guerilla warfare was the order of the day, with bands of peasants joining in the fight against the Red Army. These guerillas robbed and pillaged, and gained control over the towns near Novokonstantinov. Stephan Shepel was known to be the leader—*ataman*—of the peasant guerillas who attacked the towns, including Novokonstantinov in the spring of 1919. After several days of fighting, the Bolsheviks retreated, and the town was occupied by the guerillas. My father said that the whole town fled on foot to Letichev.[**]

So it was back and forth—between the Bolsheviks and the guerillas. The Bolsheviks occupied the territory, but they abandoned the towns they could not hold. The guerillas would gain a foothold, be pushed back, but they persisted, plundering and brutalizing the villagers, usually when they were low on supplies. You were never safe. One spring day, the bandits came in and killed 60 people. Another day, more were killed.

After two or three weeks of living in the next town, Duved and his family, Moishe, and my father, all without food for days, learned that the bandits had left the town. My grandfather Yosel had stayed in Novokonstantinov alone, refusing to move. When they all returned home, things were quiet. But after a month, on June 3, the day before Shavuoth, soldiers on horseback appeared in the town again. Paci and

[*] Friedman, S. S. (1976). *Pogromchik: The Assassination of Simon Petliura*. New York, NY. Hart Publishing Co.

[**] For a comprehensive history of the Russian Revolution, see Figes, O. (1996). *A people's tragedy: The Russian Revolution: 1891-1924*. London: Jonathan Cape.

Joseph Perel (left) and Paci Perel

his wife and young son had come to the house to stay for the holidays. Several horsemen stopped at the house, demanding food, and looting.

They held us at gunpoint, my father said. *After they got what they wanted — food, clothing, bedding, things they could carry, they left. Several times during the day, the soldiers appeared at the house, doing the same thing.*

This was the First Soviet Division. They passed through the town by the thousands. This went on throughout the day, as the Bolsheviks filed through Podolia, on their way west. Around three o'clock that afternoon, it seemed they had all gone. Someone suggested that we could have some lunch. As the family was about to sit down at the table, we heard shots for the first time that day. We looked out the window and saw several soldiers tying their horses at the gate. I said not to open the door this time, because of the shooting. But my father said that nothing would happen this time either.

As my father went to the front door, I ran out the back door. Outside, I investigated the shooting. They told me they were about to kill a neighbor, but he escaped. I started to turn back to the house to warn them, but as I came near the house, Moishe was jumping out a window, he grabbed me and said, 'Let's run, they're killers.' We ran into a neighbor's house, and we heard them coming into the house, so we separated. Moishe ran through the back door, and I hid up in their attic. They entered that house and I heard shooting and screaming. I stayed in the attic until I heard local people come in the house to investigate. After that I came down. There was blood all over the house. They killed a pregnant woman. Then I returned to our house and met Moishe there. In the house, we found our father shot in the back of the head. He had run out the back to the unfinished room, and they shot him in the back of the head, going up the ladder. We found Paci there under the high-legged sofa in the front room. He was also shot in the back of the head.

Paci's wife Hutka had jumped out the front window. And Moishe followed. The baby was sleeping in the bedroom, with the door closed. There were twelve people killed that day, men, women, and children. The entire regiment of Soviet soldiers had passed through the town. About 15 murderers stayed behind. Who knows who they were. The same mercenaries would join different sides, depending on where they could get a meal. There was no investigation, no report. Why, what, no one knows.

Another bunch appeared later that day. Moishe and I went up to the attic and didn't come down until the next day. That next night, under darkness so as not to attract attention, they buried my father and Paci in the cemetery up on the hill. After that, for the rest of the year, we never slept in a bed, we slept in secret bunkers, in attics, anywhere we thought was safe. That's the way it was for a long time.

Among my father's papers is the following eyewitness account of the pogroms in Novokonstantinov, which was published in the *For-*

ward sometime in July. The report,[*] below, translated from the Yiddish lists eight victims from Novokonstantinov, two of whom are my Grandfather Yosel and Uncle Paci:

Forward, July___, 1919:

"The account of the Pogrom in Novokonstantinov"

This is taken from a private letter about victims of a pogrom. The letter from Mr.(name omitted) of Henry Street was received from his brother-in-law, who reports on the pogrom.

It is two days since I was in Lemburg. The two days were like two years. You can't live in Lemburg with less than 40 kronin per day. I don't know where I'll get them. Getting food is a daily problem. One time I bought the London Times and had to pay 6 kronin. It's pretty good for me here, far better than for other Jews who have been in the Ukraine. I will not readily forget what I have experienced. The horrible scenes that people saw, the terrible things. Writings don't express what has happened in the Ukraine. In our shtetl, Novokonstantinov, 70 Jews were killed. The Jews left are in big trouble. All the clothes were burnt. To carry on a business is impossible. The danger for our people is very great. We sleep with fright and are afraid of shadows. We sleep in the basement. I am at a loss to explain what has transpired. . . .Greetings to my *landsleit* who came to America. A small town has been ruined. When I stop to think about my close friends who were left in the town, a cold feeling runs through my body. It is terrible and Lord knows when the conditions will improve. We don't know what will happen later. We don't know what is happening in the other small towns. Like blind people, we are walking around in the dark. We don't know where we are in the world. Ask our *landsleit* if they could see what they can do to help the people who are left in Novokonstantinov. Because in our town, we are starving from hunger. Women whose men are in America must know and help. To close I will send you the names of the victims who fell in the pogrom:

Yankel Kozak, 70 years old	Yankel Weinelvin, 52
Yosel Perel, 60	Avraham Rabinovitch, 45
Paice Perel, 28	Yosef Tretian, 30
Chaim Bernerman, 62	Toibe Asnem, 50

Lots of people were killed, but I don't remember their names. It bothers my mind and the tears fall from my eyes.

---

[*] Eye-witness account of the pogrom in Novokonstantinov, undated newspaper clipping from the *Jewish Daily Forward*. Presumably early July 1919, page unknown. Translated by Julius Akman and Silvia Perel Levin.

During the next several months, the town was caught in a bitter struggle between the Bolsheviks and the guerillas. Sometimes the Bolsheviks would come to the town and stay for a while, then the guerillas. One Saturday afternoon, the guerillas came in and killed one Jewish boy. Another time, they demanded gasoline. The following day, they killed 60 people. It was another beautiful summer day, my father said, and then word was sent by a farmer nearby, that the guerillas had stopped at his farm to have dinner, and he heard them talking, saying that *they were in the mood for killing.* Somehow the farmer got the message to the townspeople. My father tells what happened:

Some of us were on lookout, and others slept in bunkers. It was dark, almost night, and all of a sudden, we saw them coming. They broke into the house, calling names. We stayed in the bunker for three or four hours, and then heard voices. When we came out, we saw the whole village burning, the shops, the marketplace. Sixty people were stood up in a line, so that the guerillas could see how far one bullet would travel—how many they could kill with just one bullet. We slept in the bunker, there was a baby crying, and someone wanted to smother her, but she stopped. We all left town again, the whole town again went to Letichev. From then on, we never slept in a bed, we slept in secret basements, but not in the house.

In August 1919, the Civil War was still raging. After several weeks, the Ukrainian locals returned, having reorganized in Poland, and the guerillas joined them. They told the villagers from Novokonstantinov that they would provide an escort so that they could go home, and promised everything would be all right. At this point, the Allies were helping the Ukrainians, with an understanding that they had to be good to the local population. During the Russian Civil War, 14 Allied countries, including the United States, Britain, France, Poland, Romania, and Serbia were supporting the anti-Bolshevik factions.

There were now five in the family in Novokonstantinov: Duved and his wife Dina, and their new baby, Ana (born in February 1919), Moishe, who was 17, and my father, who was 15. They all returned to the house and began to organize themselves around survival. There was no food or money. All you could do was barter. In the yard, they found a sled, and a nearby Polish blacksmith gave them potatoes for the steel rods from the sled.

My father laughed about the soup they made. *None of us were cooks.* Somehow they made a soup out of potatoes and dough that was inedible. He remembered it half a century later. They sold the chairs and tables and eventually bought food.

But, again, the Ukrainians were driven out by the Bolsheviks, and this time, an entire Soviet regiment was stationed near town. There was no trouble for a time. Paci's widow, Hutka, and their son moved into the house. They lived through the winter, and early spring, and then the war with Poland began—a strategic part of the Allied intervention. After several days fighting, the town was occupied by Polish troops.

Beila and Motye (1920)

My father wanted very much to go to his sister Beila's, some 80 miles away (127 kilometers), but the roads were impassable. As he told it:

Since my father's death in June 1919, I had been looking for a way to go to my sister Beila's. It was not a direct route to Dunaivtsi, which was in the guberniya (administrative province) of Podilsky, about 80 miles southwest of our town, Novokonstantinov. And during the chaos of the Russian Civil War, there had been virtually no transportation, until now in the spring of 1920, when the Polish had pushed the Bolsheviks out of our territory in southwestern Ukraine. Some commodities, which had been very scarce, now began to appear. One day in town, I noticed a carriage piled high with barrels of kerosene (we had nothing to light our houses all through the long winter), and I asked the driver where he was going. He said he was on his way to Medzhibozh, some thirty miles west, and right then and there, I arranged for him to take me there. I left with him that day.

When they got to Medzhibozh, my father found a guesthouse to stay overnight, but he only had a permit to travel to that town. So, he spent the whole next morning, waiting to be issued a permit from the Polish authorities to go on. When he got the permit, he began to walk to the next town, another thirty miles away.

I got half way, to a farm village, and by now it was dark. It was an all-Christian village, and I asked if I could stay overnight. I walked to another house, and they said, sure, and the farmer's wife put some straw out in the living room, and I went to sleep there, and I couldn't fall asleep, I heard the farmer talking to his wife, 'How poor he looks, he's such a nice guy.' She went and baked some potatoes, and said, 'Are you sleeping?' and she asked if I wanted to eat. In the morning, they borrowed a piece of bread from a neighbor to give to me.

These are the moments he remembered the rest of his life—the kindness of a stranger—in this event, the Ukrainian peasants, who took him in, took pity on him, and helped him survive. The next morning he walked another fifteen miles to the next town, where he found a "China shop" for a cup of tea and *bulkas* (small rolls). It was a big town, Proskurov, and he began to wander about, looking for a ride.

In a little while, he found a carriage driver who agreed to take him to Dunaivtsi. He told the driver that his brother-in-law would pay his way when they arrived in the town. As it turned out, there was a man riding in the carriage who knew Beila's husband, David, and offered to pay his fare, and then collect it from David when they got to Dunaivtsi. They headed south, and he remembers:

It was on the last stretch of the road, with this carriage driver, who had been in America for a while, that we passed by a troop of Polish soldiers, who had just finished clearing a number of trees, and were now chopping them and piling them into wagons. They called to the carriage driver to stop, but he kept right on going. The Polish captain then fired two shots into the air, and the wagoner stopped. The captain strode over to the wagon and raised his rifle, and mumbled, 'God damned son of a bitch.' The wagoner then responded, in English, 'Excuse me, Sir. I didn't know that you wanted me to stop.' They then began to speak to each other, in English, and he let us go on.

The Polish captain, it turned out, was an American, part of the volunteer Polish army that had been organized in America and Canada, as reinforcements for the Polish war against the Bolsheviks (with support from the United States).

Later on, the wagoner explained to us, 'Whenever you want to stop someone from doing something, you simply say, 'excuse me,' and he will stop.'

This was the first time I heard English.

He had plans to stay with Beila for a short time and try to leave for Poland from there.

I was 15. I stayed with my sister and brother-in-law that spring and summer. She took care of me, deloused my body, got me new clothes, fed me. It was a wonderful summer. I joined a soccer game, got a job in a tobacco factory, saved money to buy a suit. I had the best time in years. I went swimming, bathing, fishing. I registered there. There was civil rule, so you could travel without a military permit. That summer we were occupied by Poland, and from Poland you could go anyplace, you could even come to this country without a passport or visa. Around 1921-22, that's when the first quotas started. I wanted to go. People were going, and you could go almost for nothing. It was not too far from the Polish border, people were taking empty wagons, to bring stuff from there. So you could get a ride. My brother-in-law David talked me out of it. 'You should wait six or seven weeks.' It was too bad, because it would have been a different story anyhow, maybe Moishe would have been here too, if I could have gone sooner. So I stayed with Beila, and at the end of the summer, I decided to go back home and get my belongings, and then return to my sister's for good. I took a carriage, and halfway there, we were stopped by the Polish military. It turned out that the Polish were retreating, and you needed a special permit to travel. They took me off the carriage, and kept me in the army barracks, and were nice to me. They asked me if I wanted to go back or forward, and I said forward—but that took me right into the front.

Now I was under arrest by the Polish, and they were taking me to military headquarters with two escorts. Two other soldiers attacked me on the wagon, calling me Jew, Bolshevik. I was taken to the commander's house, but he was not there, so the soldiers continued to beat me, hitting me repeatedly in the ear, with a log, asking if I was a Bolshevik.

The commander returned, and I told him my story. He began to whip me with a dozen leather straps, making me lean over the bed, whipping me a dozen times. Then he told me to run. I'd never been in that town before, but I knew a friend of Meyer's who lived in the town. They had taken away my identification paper, and without it, if you were caught, you'd be killed.

I found Meyer's friends and told them the story. The woman went to see the commander to get the I.D. card back, and the next morning I went to the commander's house, and was offered tea and cookies and the I.D. card. The commander told me to go, but asked me why I had said those things about him.

But there was no question of going on, so I started back to Beila's, without a permit, again. I was close to the next town, and I was stopped again, and taken off the carriage again. A Polish soldier and I walked into town, and I was taken to headquarters where I slept on the floor.

There were many cases the next day. One lady brought me bread while I was waiting for my 'next' to get to see the commander. I was the last case he called in. I went in. The commander, a nice man, heard my case. He had the paper from the Polish commander in the first town. He wrote an I.D. card with permission to go to my sister's town.

So they let me go, but it was nighttime, and where to go? I found a synagogue, and asked a man there if I could stay overnight, but he said that the military doesn't permit that. The door was locked.

He suggested that I stay in the orchard, so I lay down under the trees, but that was where the soldiers and girls were coming to be together, and one couple almost stepped on me, so I tried the door of the synagogue, and it was open.

It was about 20 miles back to Dunaivtsi. I started out on foot, hungry. It was about 11 o'clock in the morning, and I was about half way to a Jewish town. I got bread at one house. The roads were dangerous. There were killings on the road. In July 1920, two American doctors from the Joint Distribution Committee had been robbed and killed on the road near Yarmolinitz [which was close to where he was walking]. *This was a couple of weeks ago.*

I started again to walk, I was barefoot, and after a few miles, I met a young woman carrying a pack, and we walked together. And she kept repeating how the Jews killed Jesus, with tears in her eyes.

We heard shooting. Behind us were soldiers in a carriage, trying to kill a dog on the road. They invited us to ride with them. I got back to Beila's, and they were so glad to see me. I couldn't walk for a week. But I rested up. The Bolsheviks were now back, but there was little fighting. There were rumors that people were going to the Bessarabian or Romanian borders and then going to the United States.

I decided to go home to say goodbye. I got all the documents I needed to go back, but now the Bolshevik commander refused to stamp them. He said I didn't need to go home. But I decided to go anyway, and traveled back through the same town where Meyer's friends had helped me and stayed with them again. There were a couple of narrow escapes on the road. One time, a man suddenly appeared out of the blue when I was at a crossroads, and he warned me to take one road and not the other. I heard later that there was a killing on the road that I didn't take. I had it in my mind now to find my way to America.

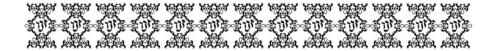

Four

Going to America

"On the eve of World War I, about five million Jews, 94 percent of Russian Jewry was still living in the Pale."
—Samuel Kassow[*]

Motye: 1920

The world in 1920 was not good for the Jews of Ukraine, particularly in the western provinces, where my father and his two brothers and sister still lived. The country was caught in a brutal civil war, with the old czarist factions, the Whites, pitted against the Red army. Poland was fighting to regain a hold in the east, and the Ukrainian nationalists were fighting to establish their own state. The international interventions in support of anti-Bolshevik forces intensified the conflicts. You didn't know from day to day in the borderlands of Podolia who was in charge. There were many days that the towns were left with no civil authority at all. Bandits and robbers roamed freely in many parts.

---

[*]   Kassow, S. http://www.yivoencyclopedia.org/article.aspx/Shtetl

*Ukraine and borders**

Unrest reigned throughout the early 1920's. Pogroms were now rampant, with the numbers of Jews killed in 1919-1920 reaching 250,000—or a million. Numbers are unclear. The only hope was to get out. When my father was living with his sister Beila in Dunaivtsi, he had been hearing that many Jews were trying to escape the massacres in Russia by stealing across the borders to Romania or Moldavia or Poland, where you could leave without a passport. He wanted to go in the worst way when he was in Dunaivtsi, but Beila's husband and mother-in-law urged him to stay. Now it seemed as if there was no way out. In Podolia, as my father found out, if you went anywhere without carrying your papers, your life was in danger. You could be picked up, and without question, killed.

In early 1919, his brother Moishe had made his way some 250 treacherous miles to Odessa to find a way out. Given that the French and English occupied Odessa at the time, it was still possible to leave

---

*   Source: http://upload.wikimedia.org/wikipedia/commons/8/8a/HistRegUkr.jpg

through the Black Sea and Turkey. Whatever happened in Odessa for Moishe, how long he stayed there, where he stayed, what he did, that part of the story is unclear, but the results, we know: Moishe made his way back—250 miles back—to Novokonstantinov, as my father had done from Dunaivtsi.

Soon after, the French and English left Odessa, and later, changes in immigration laws made it impossible to get into the United States. Moishe fled to Buenos Aires in 1923, his ticket paid for by a Jewish relief organization. He went to Medanos, a Jewish agricultural community, where he did manual labor, my father said, working on the farm, then installing hardwood floors. Two years later, he won money enough in the national lottery to send for his wife and son, who were still in Novokonstantinov.

He would blame his brother Meyer for not helping him when he was waiting in Odessa and writing to Meyer in Pennsylvania. But did Meyer get the letters? It's doubtful. There are a few letters to Meyer from Moishe in 1922, 1923, but it was impossible then to get the necessary papers to enter the U.S., particularly for whole families.

The world was turned upside down. When Meyer left in 1911, it was different. It was expected, in fact, that Meyer would go to the U.S., make enough money, and then return to Novokonstantinov. From 1911 until 1914, his father kept asking him when he was coming home. In one of the letters from his father, dated January 1914, Yosel told Meyer to "save your money, so that you can come home for Passover." But things had already changed. Yosel tells him:

Meanwhile, may you not know any suffering from us. God Almighty will hopefully help. My only request is that you save up money, however much you can, and come home. I want to know how much money you've saved until now, because Tzvi Fuchs tells me that Chaim earns twenty dollars a week, but I have no idea about your earnings . . . . Mother is sitting near me and shedding a tear. She sends you her regards. She's insisting that I write more, but I don't know what else to say to you.

His brother Duved told him that the situation in Constantine was getting worse and worse, and that he should send him a ticket.

> I've already begun to think of Palestine or Brazil, but you write that you want to send me a ship ticket. I ask you, beloved brother, do me the favor and send it to me as soon as you receive this letter because I want to apply for a passport and I can't until I receive the ship ticket. If I already had the ticket, I would be in America. I beg you to fulfill my request.

It was still thinkable at that time that the son who had emigrated to America could—and would—return, and that Meyer would be able to send his brother a ship ticket at any time. During those years, he sent Duved tickets at three separate times, but Duved could not make up his mind to leave. Then the war came, and it was impossible. Now in the fall of 1920, Duved was married to Dina and had a daughter, a year old. It was not until the end of 1925 that Duved and his family, his wife and two children, left for Buenos Aires with the help of his brothers.

In the meantime, in 1916, Meyer married Fanny Eisenberg, who was American-born, and their son Berne was born in 1917. He was named after Chana's father, Boruch Lepa. Meyer and his family were living in the mountains of southwestern Pennsylvania, in small towns, Masontown, Republic, Farrell, and then Uniontown, where he was still struggling to make a living. The letters from the shtetl had stopped coming right after the First World War began. In Meyer's boxes of letters, I found the letters that he wrote to the shtetl, returned. One is marked June 1919: It is a desperate plea to his father to write. His father had already been killed.*

> Masontown, PA, May 6, 1919
> Dear Father!
> To tell the truth, I do not know if you will receive this letter, because it has already been so long since I have received anything from you but I am writing still, only I know that you will not receive it. It may be, though, that God will grant that you will indeed receive it. Oh, how happy I would be to receive something from you

---

* Meyer's letter in Russian, translated by Robert Whittaker.

and to know that you are healthy, and I hope that soon it will be possible to hear from one another. For this reason I ask that when it is possible to write that you would write very often and about everything and about everyone. I am living very well. I have a very handsome son. My wife sends her greetings to you, also to Paci with his wife and son, also to Beila and her husband Duved, and perhaps also to others… Also to Duved, Moishe, and Moyte, and I ask everyone to write.

Your son
Meyer Pearl
Masontown, PA.

Meyer's Message

But news was seeping out to the Jewish communities in the States that the massacres were happening daily in all parts of Russia. There were eyewitness accounts describing the horrific killings of the Jews in 1919 throughout Ukraine. Whole towns were pillaged and destroyed. There were refugees from the shtetlach, who were escaping to the cities, Kiev and Yekaterinoslav, and telling their stories. As a reader of the *Forward*, Meyer no doubt read the eyewitness account of the pogrom in Novokonstantinov in June 1919, where the names of his father and oldest brother were listed. The Heifetz Red Cross Report, *The Slaughter of the Jews, 1919*, was published in 1920, detailing the atrocities across Ukraine. The reports were harrowing. He was keeping in close contact with his friends in New York who were members of the organizations of *landsmanshaftn*, the townspeople of the shtetlach who organized burial (and social) "societies" in the new country. It was through them, in the fall 1920, that he learned of the relief efforts being organized to help the people of Novokonstantinov. Here is the announcement that he received in October 1920:

> At last! On Shabbos, November 6, emissaries will be leaving for Nova Konstantine with the relief aid that we acquired for them here. It is for this purpose that we arranged a mass meeting to take place on Sunday, October 31, 2 o'clock at 80 Clinton St. Room 4.
>
> Nobody from Nova Konstantine should miss this meeting to bid farewell to the emissaries and wish them success. We'll also give them a photo of all of Nova Konstantine's men, women and children who will be present at the meeting. At

this meeting you will also have an opportunity to send home letters and regards. We also arranged for two good cantors to recite the El male rachamim for those who fell in the Nova Konstantine pogrom.

It will be one of the most unforgettable meetings you have ever attended. Whoever misses this meeting will be committing a crime for which he will never be able to forgive himself.

Therefore, people of Nova Konstantine, everyone as one, put aside your work and business and together with your wife and children take part, and come to accompany our first emissaries to Nova Konstantine. For the sake of God don't miss out on the photo. Don't cause any grief to your family, for they already have enough. You'll also have the opportunity to receive regards from two people who just returned from Nova Konstantine.

The Nova Konstantine Relief Committee

P.S. At this meeting all of the people from Nova Konstantine from around New York, as well as Philadelphia, Baltimore, Boston and Chicago will be present. The following people will address the meeting:

Shmuel Kristel
Gavriel Goldin
Pesach Axelbank
Lazer Flacks
Shalom Kalish

Below the announcement is this postscript to Meyer from his friends, Lazer Flacks and Pesach Axelbank:

Friend Mr. Meir Pearl, you won't be able to come to the meeting, however you can utilize the opportunity as all other people from Nova Konstantine. The two emissaries are Aron Liebson (Vovke's son) and Moshe Asnis (Itzik Mane's son). If you trust them you can send money with them for your family. (Ten percent of all the money goes to the relief for expenses).

We are sending you a form where you can fill out the top section. Write as much as you want on both sides. The bottom section would be for the response. $2.00 for a letter. If you want to take out your own [family] through them, sign an affidavit and send money for the expenses to last until whatever city you wish, Warsaw, Paris etc.

Your friends,
Lazer
Pesach Axelbank
Nova Konstantine Relief Association

Honorable friend Meir Pearl,
At last we have the opportunity to send aid and help home. Two emissaries will
be traveling for Nova Konstantine in ten days. If you would like to send regards
and find out about your family back home, don't miss out and write. This is your
only opportunity! Write your regards on two pieces of paper and send it right
away, together with two dollars. Write only your name and from whom you wish
to receive regards in return.
The Committee

In November 1920, it was clear that Motye could not go back to
his sister's house in Dunaivtsi. He had planned to come back to Novokonstantinov, gather his belongings and then return to Beila. The journey home had been hazardous, and there was no telling what would
happen now that he was back in the shtetl. There seemed to be no way
out. In the meantime, the relief workers from New York were making
their way to the town, to reach family members of *landsmen* who had
been cut off from the rest of the world.

There had been no mail getting in or out for over five years. No one
at home knew if Meyer even knew that his father and oldest brother
had been killed nearly eighteen months before. The family who remained, Duved and Moishe and their wives, were living in the house
with Paci's widow Hutka and their son, Lev. Now my father returned.
They were trying to survive, bartering the furnishings of the house for
food, and picking up odd jobs whenever they could.

My father got a job in the tobacco factory in the town. He made
enough before Rosh Hashanah to buy a pair of boots. One day in late
November, when he was working in the tobacco fields, someone came
running through the town, my father said,

*"There's news, there's mail from the United States in the synagogue,
they're distributing it right now," so like a bullet I was there, I was the
only one there from the family. So what happened, there's in New York, a
Society, we still have it, they got everyone who had family in the village to
write a note, for about $10, and there was a man going to Poland, and he
got somebody to bring it to our town, but when I came to synagogue, they
had a tablet, and a message, written in Meyer's own handwriting, a little*

note, and they had an index. Number 1 belongs to this one, number 2 for this one, and finally it was for me. Joseph of the Wold. They cut it out and gave it to me:

'I know everything that's going on over there, and what happened, find a way out of Russia and I'll do everything I can to help you.'

That was Meyer's message.

And then, my father began the story that he told over and over, day in and day out, throughout the rest of his long life. I imagine that he replayed the scenes from his journey again and again, watching the story unfold as if it were happening to someone else. And when he captured a listener, he'd often hold them spellbound for hours. I watched him do it. I heard many versions of the story over the years, with some details appearing in one version and not the other. Somehow or another, something about the story—or something about the past—would slip into any conversation you'd have with him.

Here are his words, taken from our many conversations together over the years and from the one hundred or so letters that he wrote to Meyer during the long trip from Novokonstantinov, south through Romania, across Europe to Liverpool, to Ellis Island, and then, finally, to Farrell, Pennsylvania. He left the shtetl, never to return, on December 5, 1920, and arrived at Ellis Island on December 12, 1921, a year and a week later. As Meyer had written, "I know everything that happened and that's going on, find a way out of Russia and I'll do whatever I can to help you." With Meyer's words as beacon, he was ready.

Crossing the River

Now I got a fever. And began preparing to leave. There were stories about people stealing across the Romanian borders. I found two carriages that would be going south in a month, with 12 people in all. There was one family in one carriage, and five in the other, with room enough for me. In the meantime, the Polish came back, they stayed for four or five weeks, and then concluded peace with Russia. The Poles retreated peacefully, and we were again occupied by the Bolsheviks.

The house and furniture belonged to me and my brother Moishe, that's the way it had been settled with the rabbi. So I had to get myself ready. I took my father's boots and I fixed them, I took the uppers and had them fixed. I had a shoemaker lower the heels, and I sold my share of the house to Duved, who agreed to pay for my trip to the border, and we went to the rabbi and signed it over to him. I sold the kitchen table to a farmer for a live duck and 40 pounds of rye. So, the next day, I took the rye to the flour mill on my back to make flour out of it. I took the duck to the shochet [ritual slaughterer] *and had it killed, and then I took the duck and the rye to a woman who cooked me the duck and baked me seven or eight loaves of bread, and we packed it in a sack. I had my boots, my father's coat, it was fur lined. I had my father's fur cap, the duck in a sack and seven loaves of bread, and tefillin, you can't travel without that. I had a little bit of money, maybe 500 Russian rubles.*

We left December 5, 1920 in the middle of the night, with instructions to travel by night and rest during the day. There was trouble on the road right away. There was a transport leaving from Khmelnick, 11 miles away from where my aunt lived. Maybe, 20-25 carriages, so our two carriages were to go together with them, but somehow, someone changed our plans, and we were going by ourselves, but we came to one little town, and here that transport had just arrived there, and they were held up, and we were lucky we went by ourselves, that transport had been robbed, and everything taken away from them, a little baby was smothered, in fact, it was a relative of ours, I never met him, but he was a cousin of mine, and he and his wife had a baby, and the baby was smothered.

The change of plans meant that I never got to say goodbye to my brother Moishe. He had plans to meet the carriage at Khmelnick, and he waited there for me, but we headed south instead from another road. I wouldn't see him again for twelve years, when I went to Buenos Aires.

So, now, we came south to Sharhorod and were stopped by Bolsheviks, but they made a mistake and let us go and then tried to find us. We all ran into different houses. Then we reassembled and continued on to Yaruha. On the way, we came across a soldier on horseback, a Bolshevik, who was half frozen. He offered us protection, and tied his horse to the wagon and rode with us. Three days later, we came to the little town, Yaruha, where the Dniester River is. We stopped at a farmhouse before we got into town, and then walked into town in pairs. There was a girl there, a first cousin of mine, my aunt's daughter from Khmelnick, who was also on that transport. She had a boyfriend in the United States who was sending for her. She was picked up entering that town and was sent home by the Bolsheviks. She never got to the United States, I don't know what happened to her.

People in my carriage had money and had money waiting for them in Romania. I stayed with them. We were called refugees and were maybe 5000 people. Yaruha had, maybe, 500 people. I found out that the whole town was full of people trying to cross the border. I thought I was the only one, and the whole world was there.

We all found lodging in one house. It was a two-room house and a family of six, and there were twelve of us in our carriages. The Moisman family were six and another five and me. I slept under a table in the house, and someone else was on top of the table. There was no other place to stay. Contrabands took you across the Dniester at night if you had the money.

The river had just frozen over completely. Three of our crowd had money and were smuggled across the river one night. Then one morning, very early, there was a big commotion. The youngest of our crowd came running in with a story that two women just ran across the frozen river. I was encouraged by the people in the house to try. So I ran to investigate. It was December, a very cold day. I wasn't heavily dressed, I left the fur hat in the house. And also the pillow and my tefillin. I came close to the bank of the river, there was a synagogue. Outside several men with prayer shawls on their arms were watching across the river. They told me that the Bolsheviks who were on watch went into the building to warm up and fell asleep and the two women ran across and were intercepted on the other side and taken away. I told them I wanted to run too. Most of them advised me to wait till the next day, they said if you go earlier, you have a better chance. People said let's disperse in case the Bolsheviks come out. The Romanians will ship people back.

I started walking away. Then one man winks at me, saying, let everyone go. "Look here, there's nobody watching. The Bolsheviks are not here, they probably fell asleep. The women were taken away on the other side, so no one is there. Now is a good time." I listened to him and started out. There was a steep bank down. He kept guiding me, saying keep on going, run. I slipped on the ice, got up and ran, slipped again and he said, 'Don't look back, keep going. Just go.' I got to the other side and I was there. But now where?

I knew of a town, Zgurita in Bessarabia, 20 miles away, where I wanted to go. The man said don't go to the left, that's where the village is and you'll be caught, keep to the right. Snow was blowing; there were hills. It was freezing cold. I keep walking; the road can't be seen, there are drifts.

I heard a bell ringing and thought it was a carriage with a horse and sleigh, and figured it could be an official. I had left my winter hat, pillow, and tefillin behind. I figured I would freeze if I didn't have my hat, so I might as well go in the direction of the sound of the bell, and saw it was a boy driving sheep and one of them had a bell on. He spoke to me in Russian and asked me if I was the lost one. I knew I was lost but I didn't know why he was looking for me. So he asked me to go with him to a farmhouse where I would find my comrades. He took me to a house with 12 Jewish people, 4 girls, and 8 men. They paid a high price to be taken across and were waiting in the house until night to go on to Zgurita. While coming across the river, one of the group got lost. They sent the boy out to find him, pretending he was to look for sheep. He found me, instead.

The boy asked the group, is this the lost person? They said yes, but the farmer found out that I was not. I gave him a little money so he would feed me during the day and help me go on. He cooked us some dinner. They made me mamaliga (a Bessarabian dish) and gave me some straw to sleep on. A woman visitor came from the next farm, and she saw us and objected to us being there. So the farmer decided to lock us in the house and he went away so not to get any more visitors. Right after that, the police came. It was late in the afternoon already. They knocked at the window. I stood up and asked what they wanted, in Russian.

Soon they came back with the owner, all beaten up, he was crying. Two police took us to their headquarters and searched us. They piled up the baggage in a shanty. It was late. One of the men said he'd put us up in different houses, and the next day he would take us to headquarters. He had an eye on one of the girls. He said she could stay with him, but the girls wouldn't be separated, so he said he would make room for all four. Two other guys and I were sent to the home of an old Russian man; he was so nice to us. He had nothing to eat himself, but borrowed some potatoes. He told us if we could escape, he would accept responsibility. In the middle of the night, someone knocked on the door and told us to come.

It was a big business to help people. Someone was waiting in Zgurita to receive this group. When they didn't come, they sent someone out to look for them. They got three sleighs and horses. They found out where we were and got the baggage stored in the shanty. We were told to get in fast and we took off to Zgurita. The whole way there, the girls were hysterical, crying and crying that they were all ruined. That was a Thursday night, near dawn. Near the town, the men dumped us out of the sleighs, baggage and all. They didn't want to be seen bringing people in, so we all walked into town. I helped a man and carried his baggage on my back as daylight broke.

As it turned out, the smugglers set everybody free, without knowing that I wasn't a part of the group.

Zgurita

We all got into town early morning. There was a bakery open and someone there opened a door and saw us and said something in Romanian. We got scared and ran in different directions. I saw a man walking with a prayer shawl to synagogue so I followed him. I was so cold and there was an open stove. I got close and burned a hole in my coat.

That first morning was a Thursday morning, and some people were still asleep in the synagogue, anywhere you could find a place, on the steps, on the floor, everywhere. The sleigh drivers were looking for me. Everyone was getting paid by the head. They realized someone was missing. Also I was carrying a feather cushion for someone and I still had that. They found me in the synagogue. I gave the bundle back and paid the sleigh driver something. They let me stay in the synagogue. A man invited me for dinner that Friday night. They gave me a sack to put straw in to sleep on in the synagogue. It was cold at night. I asked how to make a living and how to get in touch with the United States.

There were about 100 families in the town, and several thousand refugees. I slept about two nights in the first synagogue on the floor. The fire was not kept up and it was very cold.

Zgurita was built on a hill, with one long street, and there were only three wells in the town at the top of the hill. The wells were very deep, and the water was far down, and you pulled up your bucket with a big, long chain. Since there were so many people, there were long lines to wait, and water was scarce. I knocked on doors asking to carry water. I was paid a lei for two buckets of water. I found two customers to work for regularly. One needed six buckets of water a day, the other needed four. Every morning I did this, collected three lei from one, four from the other. On that I lived. You could buy a couple pounds of bread, herring and occasionally hot water for tea.

A few days later I wrote to Meyer. I had to wait until someone was going to the next town, Kishinev, to take it for me. I had memorized Meyer's address—Meyer Pearl, Masontovin, PA. (Masontown, Pennsylvania). I knew how to write it. I was told it was 6-8 weeks before you would get a reply, that you gave your address in Kishinev, that's the capital of

Bessarabia, where there was a HIAS office,* maybe 100 miles away. When I wrote the letter, I gave my address in Kishinev. I got the address from someone from the Joint Distribution Committee.

I made contact with a family named Baumberg, they were also refugees from another town, and were distant relatives. He was my grandfather's sister's grandson. All my life a tall man, probably 6'6", came to visit us, and I remembered him. This was the same man. They invited me to eat with them every Friday night. So once a week I had a meal. Life continued like this for several weeks. Then I got a toothache. My face was swollen. I went to a dentist, he wouldn't do anything. The tooth quit hurting, but the swelling remained. Then they took me to a clinic, and they gave me a black salve.

I wanted to get to Kishinev; I wanted to get away farther. Zgurita is the town where I suffered for 4 or 5 weeks. That's not so long, but of course, it's long enough to die from hunger. I carried water and slept in my clothes. My pillow I had left to pay for my rent in the town on the border where I stayed before crossing into Romania. The Moismans, the family that was traveling with me, brought me my tefillin when they met up with me in Kishinev.

I started writing letters to my brother in America. You'd look around for people going to the next town to take the letters. That was in January of 1921. There was a lot of mud. I never took my boots off, never took my clothes off. I worked for 3 or 4 weeks. One morning I started on my job and felt dizzy. I just carried six buckets of water. They only gave me two lei, they were short. I couldn't go on for more water. I went to the synagogue, bought a loaf of white bread, but couldn't eat it. I had a fever. I lay there for a few days without any food. Somebody brought me water. There was no doctor. About the third day, a young man came in, inquiring about people from the next town to ours, Khmelnick. He asked where I was from.

---

*   A number of Jewish refugee aid societies were engaged in the effort to help my father and other Jews flee-
     ing the Civil War and pogroms in Russia: HIAS (Hebrew Immigrant Aid Society), the Joint Distribution
     Committee, and the Novokonstantinov Relief Effort. See Soyer. D. (2001). *Jewish immigrant associations and
     American identity in New York, 1880-1939.* Detroit, MI., Wayne State University Press.

He asked what I was doing, if I had any money. He gave me five lei. I sent a boy out to get me some sucky candies, which I lived on for a few days.

On the fifth day, one girl who also lived at the place where the Baumbergs were staying came running into the synagogue, screaming at the top of her voice that a letter was received from Kishinev saying that there were two delegates from America and they had money for me. Immediately, I inherited friends and some oranges and a person bought me a chicken and made me some soup. I soon got better.

It turned out Uncle Meyer was writing letters but they weren't getting through, and the relief organization (Novokonstantinov Relief Fund) had sent some delegates to Romania to try to get their relatives out of Russia. So my brother Meyer gave them $50 and said if you come across any of my family, give him this money and if you need money, telegraph for more. Uncle Meyer didn't know I was on my way. These men were in Kishinev and some of our group was there and they got word that I was in Zgurita. Pretty soon, someone advanced some money for me to Zgurita.

Three days later these delegates from America came to find me in the synagogue. I was sewing up my coat sleeve that was torn. They measured me for a suit, had it made up, got me other things I needed and rented me a room with board. He gave me some more money, $50.00, and said if I needed more, whatever I needed, he'd write to Meyer and get it. This man was a landsman from our hometown. He had thousands of dollars that people were sending to their relatives.

Now, I figured that maybe my financial troubles were over, Meyer promised to take care of everything, the question was how to get to the United States.

Two things held me back. First, my cousin, Yosel, was interfering with the mail, and also I had no legal status, no passport, nothing. All I had was a birth certificate. So Yosel, was my cousin from my aunt in Khmelnick, and he was in Zgurita with me. It turned out, he somehow got my tefillin that I left in Yaruha. Then he somehow went to Kishinev. I had been expecting direct mail from Meyer in Kishinev. The Joint Distribu-

tion Committee would put up lists outside in Kishinev of who had mail. If days passed and mail was not picked up, lists of mail not claimed would be published in the Jewish newspaper, which we could get in Zgurita. So that was what I was reading, looking for my name. Then all of sudden, we had to register—all of the Russians had to register. We had to report to the police. I told them my story, they gathered up a group of 120 people and sent us by train to Beltz, and housed us there in synagogues with one policeman watching the doors. Some people paid off officials to get papers illegally. We were not supposed to leave the shul, but we came and went as we pleased. They took us in groups to a board of inquiry and after we were all interrogated, we were sent back to Zgurita with a transit permit to stay in Romania They gave me permission to stay in the country for 60 days and gave me permission to go to Kishinev. Then they sent us back to Zgurita.

When I got back, I saw my name in the paper. So a few days later, I left for Kishinev. I went and got the letters from Meyer. Meyer said that this is the third or fourth letter he's writing me. I met a fellow I knew in Kishinev and he told me that Yosel had been taking my mail. I found Yosel and he even had a check that he hadn't cashed yet. I then received a few checks from Meyer, one for 500 lei, one for 1500 lei. I had given my address at the Joint Distribution Committee. Now there was no way to continue on, unless I had papers.

Kishinev

My father traveled by train to Kishinev, where he lived for the next four months of his year and a week's voyage to America. By now, he had been gone nearly five months, having left the shtetl in the middle of the night of December 5, 1920, and made his way to the Ukrainian border town of Yaruha, where he escaped across the frozen Dniester to Zgurita in Bessarabia/Romania (the borders kept shifting). There he had nearly died of what he later knew to be hunger-fever. He was found by the rescue workers from the Novokonstantinov society, and given money that had been sent by his brother, Meyer, in southwestern Pennsylvania. He had money to pay for food and lodging and a new suit of clothes.

For months, he had lived in the clothes on his back, and he had not taken off his boots. So now it was spring, May 1921, in Kishinev, Romania, in what my father called "a beautiful Russian city, with nice parks, movies and restaurants." It must have felt as if he had awakened to a dream. He had turned 17 in January, and now he was on holiday in a city of refugees. Everyone was on the move, everyone was trying to get somewhere, to get papers, legal or not, to get out. There were *landsmen* everywhere: the two girls working in the restaurant were from Novokonstantinov, as was the seamstress who made him several sets of white cotton pleated underwear. The Moismans, the family who left on one of the carriages of the same transport, were there. They helped him find a place in Kishinev near them. They were all from Nye-Constantine. They were "Constantines," as they all said. Some of them made it to America, others turned back.

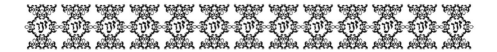

Five

A Brother's Keeper

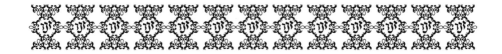

A Story of a Family: Meyer 1911

Meyer persevered, finding ways through the bureaucracies here and abroad to get my father out. He negotiated with officials, the mayor of the town, local judges, his congressman, the senator, the relief agencies in the United States, the bank, the ship company, to make it possible for my father to enter the country. This was a time when the gates to immigrants from Eastern Europe were closing, fast. It must have seemed interminable for both brothers.

I don't remember talking about it in the family as if Uncle Meyer had done anything out of the ordinary in helping my father. It was what you did as a brother, as a *mensch*. I've come to realize, too, that it was what you did as a Constantine. And I've come to understand through the letters that my father wrote to Meyer during the year that it took him to get to America, that this is a story of a family. Everyone—and all that happened to them—played a part in the story. *If it wasn't for Meyer,* my father said again and again, *I wouldn't be here.*

Letter (in Yiddish) to Meyer, from family in Novokonstantinov, 1911

In May 1911, Meyer (Perel, Peril, Pearl, it seems that the spelling was not settled until he was married) left for America to meet his friend Hymie Fox (Chaim Fuchs), who had arrived in New York in March. Meyer was 17. It was a different world, before the First World War, before the Bolshevik Revolution and Russian Civil War. Although jobs were scarce and the young people were restless to leave, travel back and forth between Eastern Europe and the United States was relatively unrestricted. You could come and go, if you had the money. Meyer was itching to go.

My father said that his mother blamed herself for her son Meilach's suicide in 1908. When Meilach wanted to leave for America, she held him back. She finally agreed that Meyer could go, but with the promise that he come back, and that he'd have money in his pockets to help the family, and also boost his lifestyle in Novokonstantinov. Chana had an older brother, Velvel (Willy) in New York, where he could stay. Yosel also had cousins in Pennsylvania, Mendel and Philip Peril, who invited him to stay with them. Uncle Willy sent Meyer a ticket for $50, with the agreement that Meyer pay him back.

Letters from the Shtetl, 1911

Meyer left a family in a world relatively intact in 1911. The voices of those he left behind come to life in the hundreds of letters* from the shtetl that Meyer saved and that somehow survived over a century. His mother, in her mid 40's, and his father, not yet 50, were both alive and well. His two sisters, Yeta and Beila, were at home. Yeta, at 25, was about to marry Asher Trachtenberg.

A week after the wedding, on June 8, 1911, Yeta wrote to her younger brother. She was 26 and Meyer was 17. Her concern for him and the intimacy between them are apparent. Both Yeta's and Asher's

---

* All letters in this chapter and the next were translated from the Yiddish by Lazer Misulovin. http://www.yiddishtranslating.com/about.html

letters to Meyer give us a glimpse into their lives, and how they tried to manage in a world of diminishing opportunity.

> June 8, 1911
> Beloved brother Meyer,
> We received your postcard yesterday. We are very worried that you are ill. Tell us what is the nature of your illness.
>
> I gather that you are longing to be back. But, of course, it is natural to long for home. God will help and we will see each other soon, and everything will be good.
>
> Now I will tell you: eight days ago was my Chupah [wedding ceremony]. There is no need to mention that I missed your presence. Write to me about what you are dong. What is your work? How do you feel? Don't hold anything back. There's no news to tell. Write to us often.
>
> A few guests are still with us. Chana and Uncle Paises.
> Be well and happy.
> Your sister,
> Yeta
> Mother and the children send their regards. [The two "children" were Moishe, who was nine years old, and Motye, who was seven.]

Yeta and Asher's life together began in Novokonstantinov, with Asher trying to find work nearby. He found a job in the flourmills, worked for a few months, but then was out of work again. In July, they were still in the shtetl, most likely living in the house with Chana and the two children. Duved was in and out, depending upon where he was working. In July, Asher wrote that they just had their photos taken, and promised to send copies to Meyer. "About myself," he says, "I am searching for business opportunities. May God help that it happen quickly."

In a note at the end of this letter, Yeta wrote that there was no news, but urged Meyer to keep writing. "You write to me that we have lots of news to write. If anything was happening we would tell you. It is boring here." She mentioned that "Motele [my father] left with Mother for the country."

In August, she wrote that Asher was not home, he left to look for work. She was home with her mother, her sister Beila, Moishe and Motele. She was wondering if their oldest brother Paci, who was working in the forests, had written. In September, she wrote a long postcard, offering sisterly counsel to her brother, who, in many ways, was suffering the same challenges as she and Asher were, to find work and make a living.

September 1, 1911
Novo Konstantine
Beloved brother Meyer, may you live and be well.
I received your postcard today. With tears, I read that you are not in a good situation and that you are out of work.

Beloved brother, it is not so bad as you make it to be. Bad times pass and good times come. During the bad times, do not despair, or have depressing thoughts. God will help everything to pass, and we will be together, with God's help, and able to tell of everything, with great joy.

Now, my beloved brother, I want to ask you to promise me two things:

First, I beg you, do not allow yourself to suffer. Do not think you are alone. You have devoted friends. Everyone in our family is ready to act on your behalf and do whatever in the world is possible to help you. Although we are far from each other, with our souls, we are very close to you.

Second, beloved brother, I beg you to tell me the real truth of how things are with you, and if you are on good terms with Uncle. Write to me about everything truthfully. Perhaps you are in need of food to survive the bad times. Don't be embarrassed, and write to me about everything else soon. Answer this postcard. We are very concerned, especially Mother. Her pain is not to be described.

Stay healthy and be well.
Your sister, Yeta
Regards from the children
Asher sends his regards

In the middle of September, they still have not heard from him. His mother is exhausted from worry. (Yeta, presumably, is writing for her mother.)

September 18, 1911
Friday, Erev Rosh Hashanah, the New Year of 5672
Konstantine
To my dear son, Maskil Kesht [Title of honor, meaning scholar or enlightened man], Meyer, May His light shine.
Thank God for my health. May God Almighty help that we see each other very soon.

Dear Meyer! Why are you causing me so much grief? More than two weeks have passed since I received a letter from you. Why can't you at least provide me with some comfort and write to me often? You know quite well how time goes by and when I don't receive a letter from you, I am in great pain. Especially since you wrote that you are out of work and that you don't know what to do, I am even more worried.

I beg you, if you want to give me some relief, write to me often. I am very concerned. Since you left for America, when I don't receive a letter from you, so much of my strength is exhausted.

There is no other news.

Be well,

From me, your mother,

Chana

I wish you a good year.

In this same Rosh Hashanah letter, his brother Duved wrote a few lines, telling Meyer that they are all concerned that they haven't heard from him for two weeks. "Our grief is not to be described." He adds, "Father, who has been away for many months, has just now arrived" and the family is gathering for the holidays. Yeta, too, adds a few lines, "Write soon, beloved Meyer, about what is happening, write everything. We would be happy if you could celebrate the holidays together with us. Now at least write to us good letters. Be well and may God grant us a good holiday and happy year."

Asher, in the meantime, had no luck finding other work, and so Yeta and he decided they would be better off in the city. Sometime in October, they set out for Uman, some 100 miles southeast. Chana came along to help in the new shop, then Duved came, and Beila, too. In early November, she wrote from Uman, with the roles now reversed. She is apologizing to Meyer for not writing:

November 7, 1911

Uman

Beloved brother Meyer, may you live with much happiness.

I am so sorry, beloved brother that I haven't written to you for a long time. But you must not reproach me. When one comes to a new place, and spends time alone, one forgets about everyone in the world. I know that you'll forgive me.

I won't write a lot but I'll write to you about everything briefly. Mother has already left from here. I was longing for home. I wrote home and asked for someone to come to me. They soon sent Beila and Duved.

Duved stayed for four days and left today. Beila will remain here for sometime until I become more accustomed to being here. I already have made some acquaintances. People visit us and we visit them. Last night we were at the theatre. They performed an interesting piece. I gather things are getting better for you. They brought us a letter. I was very happy to see that you moved into an apartment. I assume you won't be hopping around.

Be well and write to me often.

Your sister who wishes you all the best,

Yeta Trachtenberg

Asher sends his regards, as well as Beila.

On this same date, his oldest brother Pesach (Paci) writes from the shtetl, in a tone far different from anything we've heard before from the family. Paci doesn't mince words about the postcard that Meyer sent to a neighbor, the mother of Meyer's friend, Hymie Fox.

November 7, 1911

Novo Konstantine

Dear brother Meyer, May His light shine.

I stayed home another day, so I had the chance to read a postcard that you sent to Tsvi Fuchs, where you complain that your parents don't write to you. I was very disappointed. One does not cut off correspondence with parents so easily, even if a month passes by that they don't write to you, there is still no reason to be so angry as to decide not to write. One has to consider all possibilities. Perhaps it is not possible to write. Perhaps they wrote, but the letter was lost.

Mother says that she writes every week. So I don't know why you haven't received her letters. As bad as things are here already, your postcard has made matters even worse. Mother has enough pain, now you added more. What are you doing?

Be happy and well.

Your brother, Pesach.

We sent a letter yesterday, but today I read the postcard. Don't be a child.

Mother sends her regards.

In December, in a letter from the family, Paci brought up the issue again, and urges Meyer not to hold hard feelings towards any of his sisters or brothers. Perhaps Meyer has written that he was annoyed with the way Paci had talked to him, but Paci reminds him that, as the oldest brother, he has every right to speak his mind:

> I'm sorry if I said something to offend you, but you must understand that if someone speaks his mind, he should not be considered an enemy. I am an older brother, and I grew up believing that I have the right to speak my mind to my younger brother.
>
> Why is it important to talk about the past, of what happened and how it happened, since it's already too late? There's no need to talk about it. I do not want us to become distant from each other. Rather, we must stay connected, and treat each other well, even though you are gone to America. How can we help ourselves? We can only hope for the future. When God will help us and bring us together, we will discuss everything, happily.
>
> Be happy and healthy.
>
> From me, your brother, Paci.
>
> Please write often and forget trivial matters. Write about your current situation. How are things with you? Are you still longing for home? How much do you earn? Are you working too hard? When do you plan on coming home?
> [Paci then sends regards to his friend Yankl and sends him this note. When I saw your handwriting, I reminded myself of our old friendship and how we gradually forget.]

There are only a few letters from Duved during these early years when Meyer is in America. Who knows how many of the letters were lost, including Meyer's? Duved, three years older, was torn between staying and leaving. In his early letters, he speaks of moving from place to place to find work, doing varied jobs, trying to make a living. He is so busy that he has no time to write, he says. He travels to the forest to be with Pesach, perhaps to work with him. He tells Meyer that he has just come in from planting beets. He does not hold back from telling Meyer that life in Konstantine is becoming unbearable.

> I cannot describe to you how much I am disgusted with Konstantine and how desolate it is. Don't long for Konstantine. Be happy and thank God for your lot. You have good reason to be thankful that you are not here. Only work for a better lot and be happy. God willing, one day we will see each other.

He lends his voice to the chorus who tell Meyer to write. On September 19, Duved reports that a letter has arrived, and the family is joyful:

September 19, 1911
Nova Konstantine
Beloved brother Meir, may you live and be well.
I was home last night for Kaparos [a ritual before Yom Kippur, where one transfers one's sins to a live chicken, which is then killed and given to the poor for the pre-fast meal].

When I saw Mother, all she could talk about was that she hadn't received a letter from you. I am also concerned. But today, the day before Yom Kippur, we went to the post office, and there was a letter from you. You cannot imagine our joy. We ran to tell Mother the good news, and she was happy.

Yeta is not at home. She is in Uman, and rents a shop there. Don't be upset that Mother is not writing because there is no one to write on her behalf. God willing, after Yom Kippur, when Yeta is here, she will write a letter to you from her. Last week, Asher wrote a letter for Mother. Beloved brother, don't be angry with me. I have been very busy lately. I already started to plant the beets. I'll write soon.

Be well,
Your brother, Duved.
I am wishing you all the best. May God help us see each other soon.

Duved wanted to leave, too, to come to America, and longed for them all to be together. The closeness between Meyer and Duved is apparent, and I know from my father that during the ensuing years, Meyer sent tickets to Duved. My father said, *He had three times tickets. Meyer sent them. But Duved changed his mind himself, he let himself talk himself out of it, he didn't want to leave Dina, so Meyer cancelled the ticket, and lost some money. He sent him another ticket, the third time again, and Meyer said he was just going to leave it for him, so he could come whenever he decided, but then the war broke out, and then he couldn't leave.*

In the letters, the one member of the family who is barely visible is Beila, but in one postscript to Meyer in the following year, November 1912, we have a glimpse of her character. Beila, who has Yeta write for her, tells Meyer that she has his photo by her bedside: "I look at the photo all the time. I look at your hands and they are dried out. The veins are showing. Write to me if that's true."

The letters from the shtetl are a window into the dynamics of my father's family. Of course, neither he nor his brother Moishe, referred to as "the children" were writing, but they were there, witnessing Meyer's leaving, and, now, during this first year that he was gone, knowing the pangs of loss. "*Oh how my mother cried,*" my father remembered,

Meyer and his friend, Hymie Fox, in New York, 1911

when he talked about the day that Meyer left, and the days afterward. *"She knew that she would never see him again and she didn't."*

And for Meyer, the ties to the family and to the people of the shtetl held strong. The box of letters contained letters from his friends, who tell of the comings and goings of village life, the love affairs and heart-break, the news and events, the stasis. They tell him that things are bad in the shtetl. They want to know about America. They urge him to write, and apologize for not writing. They ask him to give so and so a message. They give him assignments. They want photos. They are a chorus of voices, Asher G., Chaike F., David T., Itzik L., Chaike P.

> May 29. I visited your home for the Choson Mal [special meal for the groom the night before the wedding]. I walked by and she came towards me and squeezed my hand. Afterwards, she went alone to the city and I didn't want to follow because I thought that she should come over to me, otherwise there's no point. But Meyer, I must have it my way. There's no reason to run after her, to wander about for two hours until she utters a word, and only when I beg. Menasha, son of Like, made up with Sara Sheid, who was angry over Lozer Ber.

> June 9. Meyer, please send me the photo that you took with Chaim. Perhaps you also took a photo of yourself. Please don't refuse my request. You don't write to me although I write to you.
>
> If you are interested to know some news, I can tell you that two couples be-came engaged, Motl with Esther and Yitzchak Wakim with Frida. Do you remem-ber them, Meyer, or have you already forgotten everyone in Konstantine? You American! At least, be interested in those who are now engaged in Konstantine.
>
> It's late, there's nothing more to write. I just came from Avram Krasner. He played very well. The whole of Konstantine was outside, and I was reminded of you and how you are so far away.

> July 5. I got your address from Asher and I'm sending a postcard. The news here is that Konstantine has become desolate. There's no sight of a living being. Four or five weeks have passed since I've been home. There's no reason for you to regret the fact that you have left for America. Don't long for home. It will get better.

> July 6. I received your letter. Thank you very much. Please write to me every week. Meir, about Brucha. I don't want to make up with her. I almost felt like making up with her, but I didn't. Hershl is not in good health. He left for Khmelnick today to see the doctor. The doctor here tortures him. Don't let Chaim see this postcard.

July 15. I am angry with you that you forgot me. You don't write me any letters. But I gather that you have no time. Please write me. Write about everything.

August 25. If you see Chaim, tell him that he should be ashamed of himself. It has been five months since the rascal left and he doesn't write me a postcard. He should be ashamed of himself.

Mid-September, 1911, and the family was together for the holidays, Yosel and Chana, Paci and Hutka, Yeta and Asher, Beila, Duved, Moishe, and Motye. This was the first holiday that Meyer was gone, and all were wishing him a good year. *"Be well and may God help us that we have a good and happy year,"* said Yeta on September 18. But it was not to be a good year, nor the next or the next. Yeta died in childbirth in the following months, leaving behind a little girl, Malka, for her mother to raise. My father said that Chana never recovered. Two of her grown children had died. Meilach in 1908. Yeta, four years later. My grandmother would not live to know that her oldest son and her husband were killed in 1919.

In 1915, typhoid fever was epidemic in the shtetl. Moishe became ill. His mother nursed him, and then she became sick, and the baby, too. Moishe survived, but Chana and the baby did not.

My father said that Meyer found out about his sister's death, and then his mother's death through *landsmen*. The family would not write bad news, but the news of his sister's death got to him, my father said, through someone from Pennsylvania hearing the news from someone who talked with one of the Moisman family in New York. My father didn't say how Meyer found out about the deaths of his mother and Yeta's daughter, Malka. Perhaps he heard the news from Hymie Fox, who was living near him in Pennsylvania. Perhaps Fox heard the news from *landsmen* in New York, or perhaps he received a letter from the shtetl. But the First World War had begun, and mail was erratic.

Somehow, Meyer found out, and now he insisted that the family take a photograph, and they listened to him. I know this photo by heart: Everyone is looking into the camera, even my grandfather Yosel, whose hands are folded. My father's hands are on the wooden bench. Paci's are on his lap, and his wife Hutka's right hand is on his shoulder. Beila's hair is pulled back. She is not yet married. Duved has a moustache, but Moishe is clean-shaven, his hair cropped. Hutka's hair does not look like a wig. Is it? Paci has a neatly trimmed beard. None wears a skullcap, except my bearded grandfather. This is the only photograph we have of my grandfather or Paci or Beila or Hutka. We have none of Yeta or Meilach or my grandmother, Chana.

In 1912, Meyer moved from New York to southwestern Pennsylvania, where his cousins, Mendel and Philip Peril, were living. He married an American-born girl, Fanny, and their one child, a son, Berne, was born in 1917. By now, it was clear that he was not returning, and the letters from the shtetl were few and far between. Among his papers are five letters to his father, Mr. Yosel Peril, that were returned, and stamped, undeliverable: "Returned to sender for the reason that service is suspended. There are no means for transmission of the article to destination"

There are returned letters from 1915, 1918, 1919, and 1920. He began to send money through the relief organizations for any of his family who might be alive, but it was not until the spring of 1921 that he learned from the emissaries that his youngest brother, Motye, was alive and on his way. Here is the returned envelope of a letter, dated August 20, 1920, with a "returned to sender" stamp from a New York post office, with these words: "There are no means available for transmission of the article to destination."

He began to send money through the relief organizations for any of his family who might be alive, but it is not until the spring of 1921 that he learned from the emissaries that his youngest brother, Motye, was alive and on his way. On the following page is a returned letter, dated August 20, 1920, with the returned envelope from a New York post office.

Meyer's returned envelope

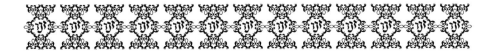

Six

A Man without Papers

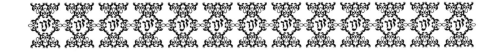

"And what is a man without papers? Rather less, let me tell you, than papers without a man!"

—Joseph Roth, *The Wandering Jews*[*]

Letters from Motye (1921)

For my father in Romania, the whole world seemed to be on the move, everyone trying to get somewhere, to Canada, South America, Palestine, but mostly to the United States. As I re-read my notes, listen again to the taped interviews with my father, and now read the letters that he and others from the shtetl were writing to Meyer, I understand more fully the desperation of those in flight. This was what it was in the early 1920's in these border areas that surrounded the crumbling Russian Empire. Everyone who could get across the borders was trying to get to the closest port, trying to reach somewhere and someone who would help them. And many who were on the move from Novokonstantinov—my

---

* Roth, J. (2001). *The wandering Jews.* (M.Hofmann, Trans.) New York, NY: Norton.

father and a dozen others, family and friends—were asking my Uncle Meyer for his help.*

What Meyer knew from Aron Liebson, one of the emissaries sent from the Novokonstantinov Society in New York, was that Meyer's youngest brother Motye was now with him in Kishinev in the spring of 1921, and that he was working to help him get the papers he needed to get out. The first letter from Motye to Meyer is marked March 10, 1921, sent from Kishinev. It was three months since he had left home. He wrote that he received the money that Meyer sent through the emissaries, but had not yet received a letter from his brother, and he didn't know what if anything Meyer knew of the family who remained in Russia, since the mail had not been getting through. What my father told me was that he, along with other refugees who had no papers, were taken back across the border to a "concentration camp" in Beltz (in Bessarabia, northwest of Kishinev) and that they were treated very badly, and then released. Some were given a permit to go on to Kishinev, with permission to stay in Romania for 60 days.

March 10, 1921
Beltz
Dear Brother Meyer Perel,
Thank God I am now healthy and I hope to hear the same from you.

　　Dear Brother, I left home because it was impossible to survive. When I was taken to Bessarabia I did not have any money, and I suffered a lot. Moishe and Aron came two weeks ago, and they gave me the money that you sent through them. Aron may go to Paris soon, to collect additional funds. I know that it will

---

* Motye's Journey: Motye left Novokonstantinov in evening on December 2, 1920, traveled in a horse and carriage carrying six people to Sharhorod, then to Yaruha (border town) on the Dneister, where he ran across the frozen river. The refugees were taken to Zguritsa, Romania, then to Beltz, Bessarabia (a camp), where he "suffered." He came back to Zguritsa, then to Kishinev and to Bucharest. Through Briggs and Company, he was taken to Antwerp, through Transylvania, Prague, Leipzig, and Antwerp, then to Dover. He took train to London, then Liverpool, and sailed December 2, 1921. A week later, December 9, he arrived on Ellis Island (Friday night). On Monday, he was taken to B&O RR station, New York. Train stopped in Philadelphia on way to Connellsville (train did not stop in Uniontown). He was to wait four hours for train coming from Pittsburgh to Uniontown, but the man he was with said to take a streetcar. He thought they were going to restaurant, so he went along, but found himself in Uniontown three hours early. He had address, 80 Pittsburgh Street, a tailor shop, where Italian tailor knew he was coming and called Philip Peril. Meyer lived in Farrell, and he met him the next day.

take a long time before I can come to you. I would like to be with you soon, but it all depends on God.

You should know that our Moishe got married to Rosa. Duved, Dina, and their daughter Chanusya, are alive and healthy. Beila gave birth, but I do not know if it is a girl or a boy. Hutka and her son Lev are alive and healthy.

Meyer, I wrote a lot of letters to you, but I did not hear back from you. I am here already for almost four weeks, and every week I write to you, but I have not received an answer. As soon as you get my letter, please answer me.

Your brother,

Motye Perel

Say hello to your wife and beautiful son.

By March 19, my father had arrived in Kishinev, and he wrote that he retrieved four letters from Meyer from the Joint Distribution Committee, along with a check for 1500 lei, which he was trying to cash at the bank. He assured his brother that he would check at the bank every day to see if the funds had been cleared. Once he heard that his brother was en route, Meyer began sending checks made out to Motye, but cashing the checks in Romania proved to be nearly impossible. In this letter, my father wrote that Meyer mentioned another $100 he had sent, but that he had not yet received that check, nor was he able to cash the check for 1500 lei.

The Novokonstantinov Society in New York had urged its members to send cash with the two emissaries, Aron and Moishe. Aron was now traveling to Paris to retrieve funds that had been cabled there. This was one of the persistent challenges the refugees and their sponsors faced: sending and receiving money through the various channels. And then there was the complicated matter of getting papers. Minute by minute, it seems, the rules for entry into the United States were changing, or the refugees were not getting the right information or the right guidance:

Meyer, now they are saying that they are only allowing children to enter America, children to their fathers. You should send a telegram that I am a child.

In his March 28 letter, my father sent more news of the family in the shtetl.

Moshe is already married. There are people here who were at his wedding. He lives at Chaim Shimon's. He started a candle factory, and he traveled with his brother-in-law for wax. He was caught, and they found the money, and confiscated it. They imprisoned them for ten days. They pleaded, and they returned the money and were released. Now they are working little by little and earning.

Duved and Dina, with their child, are also healthy, but their life is not the best.

I didn't hear from Beila for a long time. I was there after Father's passing. Then her life was good. She has a very dear husband. He's Slobke Pearl's daughter's son.

Duved and Adke with their child are healthy. She is home.

I received a letter from Aaron. He'll be here tomorrow.

I don't have anything further to write.

Be well and may God grant that we meet soon.

Regards to your wife and child.

M. Pearl

Tobe Zeiger has already left.

Yosel sends his regards.

In April, my father wrote that now he was not well, and that he still had not received any letters from Meyer, and that he should not send him any money, but rather send it through Aron. He said that he was at the Moisman's and they had already obtained passports, which cost 4500 lei for one person. There was a chance that Aaron would take him along with him to Paris, but he didn't know for certain. He had no money. And he had been waiting since January for a birth certificate and passport.

He also told him that his cousin Yosel needed money, "as much as possible." Yosel was the cousin who apparently had been taking the letters that Meyer was sending to Kishinev for my father. My father told me that *Yosel maybe thought he might forge my identity in order to cash one of the checks, I don't really know.* And then, he told me, *there's the story of the tefillin. I saw a man using my tefillin in Zgurita, and asked him where he had gotten them. I recognized the sack. He said that Yosel had sold them to him. Yosel kept on writing to Meyer, but Meyer didn't help him because he thought he had a big family and he didn't know how many he would have to help. So Yosel went to Philip Perel, who was a*

cousin too. Finally Philip said he'd send a ticket if Meyer would pay half.
Meyer agreed and sent him a ticket and some money.

I kept asking my father what happened to Yosel, but he never really answered. I never heard that he had come to the United States. And I never found out how my father actually got his tefillin back. He told me what he wanted me to know. At one point in the letters, there is mention of Philip Peril and Meyer sharing the cost of the ticket for Yosel, and at another point, Yosel told Meyer that he was going to Canada, and then since he couldn't get a visa, he was returning to Novokonstantinov. At the end of June, my father told Meyer that Yosel was staying behind in Kishinev. "He cannot do anymore now, and I don't know what will end up with him now. He's again without a penny." How many others had to return? In the papers that Meyer saved, there are at least another fifty letters from Yosel and others cousins and friends, who were begging him to help, and as the gates were closing to the States, it was getting worse in the *shtetlach*.

Yosel told Meyer on March 9,

> There are new pogroms at home. Many people are being killed by the murderers. The voices of our brothers can be heard here. They are screaming, 'Why don't you save us?' But we cannot help them, because we ourselves are in great trouble. Do the best that you can, so that we can be saved, because those who are still there cannot be helped at all. Do something now so that we can be saved.

At the end of April, my father wrote a long letter, in which he tried to explain, again, that Meyer should "not send money, but wait until Aron travels to a port and telegraphs you to send him money." He was now worried because Meyer said that he had sent him a ship ticket, but he hadn't received it yet. By the beginning of May, he had received two letters from Meyer, and a check for 5000 lei, and also the forms for a visa, as well as a ship ticket and a photograph of his brother. So now he had two checks, the first for 1500 lei and the second for 5000 lei, and in the letter he details how he has gone to several banks to cash them both, and, finally, at the third bank, for a 5% fee, he has been able to cash the second check. He still cannot cash the first check, but he says that he thinks he'll "have enough money until America, if there aren't any incidents."

He also tells him that "here in the newspapers they write that as of the first of May, they won't allow entry into America, except through those people whose friends in America have been citizens from before 1910."

How many letters along the way were lost? Did Meyer answer all the letters he got from Yosel, and from the others? The chorus of voices of the past tells of the refugees' plight:

> I've written, but you've not.
> I have nothing to write, there is nothing new, except I am waiting, waiting.
> Don't send money that way, send it this way.
> Send a ship ticket.
> Don't send a ship ticket,
> I'm now not eligible.
> Say that I am your child. How will I ever get out?

Motye, at 17, was as old as Meyer was when he left for America. He lived through one rupture after another, and his letters shed light on the child/man that he is in 1921. Now, Meyer, at 28, was father to his own son at home, and acting as a father to his brother. Meyer asked Motye to write to him every day, no matter what. Motye promised he would:

> I promise to write to you every day. Now, I don't know what to write. But I must. There's no news now, and it is not the time to write old news. I will write to you every day, although I don't know what to write. But because you asked that I write to you every day, I will obey you and do as you ask.

Here are glimpses of Motye's life in Kishinev in the early spring and summer before he left for Bucharest, to wait for his *next* in order to get his visa:

> May 12, 1921
> I received a letter from you today. I'm very glad that you have already received my letter because lately I've been receiving letters from you in which you tell me that you haven't received letters from me. Now since I arrived in Kishinev, I'm writing

to you more often, and I believe that you are receiving them, because now it seems that the letters are not getting lost. I've already received fourteen letters from you.

Meyer, you write to me asking if I'll be able to recognize you. I'd recognize you. I remember you well. You left me when I was still a little boy. You assume that I'm a grown mensch by now. We'll I'm already grown, but I'm not yet a mensch. When I come to you, then I shall become a mensch. I still remember when Mother and I accompanied you to the train station. Then Mother traveled with you to Yaniv, and I stayed in Khmelnick.

You ask about my Kishinev life. I'm staying at a tailor's house. I pay 150 lei a month for sleeping and they also prepare food for me. There's no good bed. Even during the day, there's nowhere to sit down. I wake early in the morning, and I must leave the *house right away*. I go to Yosel. He stays at a shul. He's struggling. There's nowhere to earn even one lei.

May 21
I ask you, Brother, don't be concerned about me. I see in your letters that you are very worried. Don't worry, dear Brother, I have already survived worse. So everything is all right with me. God will bring me to you in peace. I am living for the moment that my number for my visa is announced, because it's worse to sit here and be depressed. There's no work to be found because the city is full of refugees, and everyone is looking for work. I have to wait for another 2500 names until mine will be called. It's going quickly now, though, I hope it won't take long.

May 29
Things have become pretty bad now. Also, they are not issuing any visas. They're only issuing visas to children under twenty who are going to their parents, wives who are going to their husbands, or fathers over sixty who are going to their children. Also, that anyone going has to be a citizen of a country. Now I ask for your advice about what to do. If it's possible, perhaps you can find some means over there for this matter. Maybe you can influence Washington to issue a visa for my passport. If not, maybe we can send applications that I'm traveling to my father who has citizen papers. We may use other papers. There's no requirement that we use the same name, we can use other ones.

I don't know what to do or where I should go. I don't have any home, and I don't know now who to turn to, besides you.

A new fire has now been ignited here. [He's referring to more pogroms in the shtetl.] Who knows how our brothers are doing.

June 5.
Over here they tell me that they could issue me a visa because I'm left alone with no parents. Dear Brother, I beg you, do not change your mind about me.

There were two sets of papers that my father needed. He needed a Russian passport and he needed an American visa. He was a man without a home. He needed to prove that he had come from somewhere, that he was a citizen of someplace, to get a visa to travel. It took a while for him to figure that out. What he had was a Russian birth certificate but no Russian passport. The American delegates, Aron and Moishe, were able to help him get a passport at the Russian Consulate in Kishinev, and also to get a "number" in the line to apply for a visa at the American Consulate in Bucharest. That's what my father meant when he said that there were 2500 names before him in line to apply for the visa. Then he'd be *next in line.* That's what he meant when he said, "I was waiting for my next." It was now six months since he had left home.

Bucharest

By the end of June, he decided to go to Bucharest to wait. At first he stayed at a hotel, he said, and then he took room and board at a private home. Aron and Moishe returned to the United States, and he put himself under the care of HIAS (Hebrew Immigrant Aid Society). They were the ones who advised him to approach the American Consulate to ask that they send an inquiry to Washington about the status of his position on the preference list. He was at the bottom of the list for family members. The preference was wives, then children, sisters, and finally brothers. There were thousands of people before him waiting in line for their next.

The wait was interminable, and the complications unpredictable. The letters from Motye to Meyer now tell of my father's anguish:

> July 25
> Oh, Brother, my strength fails me. I'm not sure we'll ever see each other again. With what have we so greatly sinned? I do not know. For three weeks here in Bucharest, they have stopped issuing visas to America, and when they did issue visas, they didn't want to give any visas to a brother.
> Aron is sending a few young Constantine boys to Canada.

August 1

You asked me about the visa.

Dear Brother, the same laws that exist in our country are in effect here, as well. They allow 8,000 Romanians a year, and 52,000 Russians. The number is divided into months, every month a certain quota. But there's another law that the first in line should be women who are traveling to their husbands, children traveling to parents, and parents traveling to children. These three categories are issued first, and afterwards, if the quota is not full, they will allow a brother to travel to a brother. They say that it will take another two months until they start to issue visas for brothers. I was at the American committee today, and I inquired over there. He told me that I should wait it out for a period of time.

Write to me what I should do, where I should travel. It is no good staying here.

August 10

I won't be able to come to America until I receive a permit from Washington. I telegraphed you yesterday about the matter and also asked that you send me 200 dollars. I would return to Bessarabia, but I cannot return. Let Pesach Schwan know that his children are also in Bucharest. They also have a long wait. Send everything to the HIAS. The Joint Distribution is already closed.

August 15

I haven't received a letter from you in weeks. Please do not change your mind about me.

What it meant to be at the bottom of the preference list, my father found out when he went to the American Consulate to seek advice. If you were high up on the list—a wife waiting to be reunited with her husband, or a child, with a father—the Consulate would send a cablegram to the sponsor in the States, and ask for a cablegram in reply. The sponsor was to make the request for the visa, and verify the relationship of the two parties. If you did not fall into the top category, they would send a letter, instead, which could take six or more weeks to reach the right office in the United States, and another six or eight weeks or more to receive a response. In my father's case, the American Consulate sent the inquiry by mail, because he was last on the family preference list. In August, he wrote to Meyer, telling him that he submitted the letter to the Council, and they sent a letter to Washington to inquire about a permit.

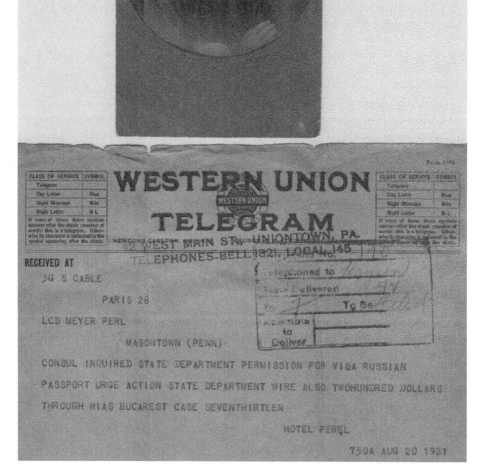

Motye in Bucharest, 1921, telegram from Motye to Meyer

August 13

It's already been two weeks that I'm waiting for an answer. They say that it will take a very long time. I would rather travel to Canada. Over here, all of the Constantine brothers are traveling to Canada to their brothers. Meir Fox is already in Antwerp. He is also traveling to Canada. I would travel there too now, but I telegraphed you for money, so I'll wait. And also, maybe the answer will come from Washington. Now the Council is not accepting any letters of inquiry.

August 18

It's a very bad time. It's already two months since they stopped issuing any visas. Now they are officially issuing visas, but there's a long wait for one. Is it possible to be patient? Lots of people are now going to Canada. Yakov Chariton received a telegram from America saying that he should not go to Canada, but he's going anyway. I would also travel to Canada, but I telegraphed you for $200, so I can't leave because the money would be lost. When it arrives, and if the situation doesn't improve, I will go to Canada. I have not received a reply from Washington, they say, it will be another four or five months.

August 31

I would leave for Canada now, but I will wait until I hear from you. Today, Moishe Asnis arrived from Antwerp. He says I should go to Canada because there's talk that Canada will also close its borders, and that an answer from Washington will take another four months. It's been over three weeks since I telegraphed you for $200. If I receive it, but do not have anything from Washington, I will go to Canada.

September 16

If it's like this, it's meant to be this way.

I haven't heard from you, I haven't heard from Washington. I owe Aron $300.

I would return to Bessarabia, but one can't travel back, and also, it's very bad in Bessarabia for our people. They are gathering all the Ukrainians in Bessarabia into a camp. Two boys have been sitting in a camp in Beltz for four weeks.

September 22

I don't know what to think. I still have not heard anything from you. I'm walking around these days literally a meshuge. I wrote and telegraphed you. I don't have a penny. It is six weeks, and I've not heard a thing. You used to write to me three times a week. I've borrowed money from Aron, now he's leaving for America. It's already cold and I don't have a coat. I have not heard from the Council. Pesach Schwan's children received their visas today. Moishe Asnis did them a favor and placed them in the queue, saying they were children, and their visas were issued. They're leaving in three days.

September 23

I received a postcard from you today. Thank you for your effort on my behalf.
I wrote to you many times that I told the council that I was born in Konstantinov.
My name is Motel Pearl. Make sure there's no mistake when they ask you.
I am writing to you often, fulfilling your request that I keep writing to you often.
May the New Year that is now approaching be with mazel and peace for you.

September 27

Aron is leaving to go to America tomorrow night. Moshe is also returning with
him, as well as Pesach's children. The rest of the Constantines are staying behind.
I received word that Duved is rebuilding our store. They burned it.
May God help that we see each other very soon.

September 29

Aron and Moshe left for America yesterday. I don't have any money left.
Yesterday, we sent you a secured letter.
Be healthy and happy with your wife and child.

October 8

I received a letter from you yesterday. Thank you very much for the effort you are
making on my behalf. I already thought you had forgot about me. You didn't write
to me for such a long time, I didn't know what to think. I still haven't received
anything from Washington. No money has arrived from you yet.
Regards to your wife and child from the depths of my heart.

October 21

I have no news. I haven't had another letter from you.

October 25

I received $98 yesterday at HIAS. That's how much arrived, I was told. Nothing
yet from the council from Washington about me.
I heard a rumor that Yosel was home for Sukkot.
Be healthy and happy together with your wife and child.

America, at Last

In the boxes of letters that Meyer saved, there were more than eighty
from his brother Motye, en route to America. The first was March 10,
1921; the last was October 25. It was Motye's last letter from the old
world. Meyer's letters to my father during these months were not getting through to Romania, so my father didn't know that his brother
Meyer had taken matters into his own hands.

I never heard this angle of the story, how anguished my father was at that time, how impossible the situation was. He never talked about his emotions, about what he felt. That wasn't the way he told the story. I didn't know that there was a chance that he would go back—as his brother Moishe did a few years before, or as his cousin Yosel presumably did, or that he might have gone to Canada, as others from the shtetl were doing. Here is my father telling what happened, in his own words, sixty years later:

In the meantime, there was no way to continue, you had to have a passport, some kind of passport. So there was a Russian Consulate in Kishinev, Romania, and with the birth certificate with me, with that, I got a Russian passport, and then they applied to the American Consulate in Bucharest for a visa for me, so after a few months, three or four months, I had a real big number, and when it came close to my number, I picked up and went to Bucharest, and I finally went to the American Consulate there, and the man says he had to inquire from the United States, Labor Department, whether I'm permitted to come here, so he took a letter from me, it cost $1.00, and they wrote a letter of inquiry to my brother, and he had to give witnesses, and so on.

But, and it never happened before like that, that when my brother got the letter, instead of sending a letter back, which would have taken months, my brother went and got people to be witnesses and then got the Labor Department to send a cable back. You see, he lived in a small town, so he went to the banker, he went to the mayor, to the chief of police of the town, a judge, and to the congressman, and they all wrote letters saying that it was urgent, that I was just a young boy and my people were killed and he would very much appreciate it if they would send a cablegram and sure enough they sent a cablegram. In ten weeks, we got the permission to grant the visa.

Now I had to wait in line to get the visa. But the problem was that I was in Romania, and the American Consulate was concerned with Romanian affairs five days a week. Only on Saturday, from 9-12 (noon), did they take care of Russian visas. I had #9210. Every week they called 100 numbers, but they could only attend to 30 or so, and 70 were left for the next week. The next week, they called another 100. The line started to form Friday night, and it was a couple of thousand long.

But there was also the business about the age on my passport. I was advised to have my passport changed to say I was 15 years old, rather than 17. But it was a bad job, with a different ink. Meanwhile, my number came up. I asked HIAS about my age being changed and showed them the different ink. I was told not to present that affidavit. I had a different affidavit still showing my age as 17. I had to be careful. I went to the Consul; there was a sign that Russian business would be taken until noon. It was after that and I wouldn't be able to come back for another week. I told them I had other business and I live far away. The man scratched out on the passport in red ink the 15 and put in 17. I gave him some money.

I still had to wait for my next. Finally my number was called. I got there 4 A.M. Saturday. The line was already six blocks long, and there were several hundred ahead of me, but I still got in line. About 9, the Consulate gate opened, and a few people walked up. The street was black with people. Then a friend of mine, Rubenstein, and his brother Berl came. He had his brother Berl stand in line for me, and he and I went to the front of the line to investigate what could be done. He indicated to a policeman that he had some money and then pushed me to run to the front of the line. I ran in. I gave my papers, and in 5 to 10 minutes, I had my visa. It was November 18th.

I started to pack. I had the ship ticket that Meyer sent in May, so I went to see the agent for Briggs and Company. I didn't know that Meyer was sending money through the company. Everything was paid for, and they reimbursed me the $10 for the visa. Meyer had sent me money, but he was afraid someone would steal the money and then I wouldn't have enough for the visa, so he made sure to pay for that, too. When I got the visa, the company formed a group of 65 people. They told me to report on Thursday. They had a man travel with us to Antwerp. I didn't have to *worry about border crossings; they did and they fed us. We traveled through Transylvania, Prague, Leipzig, where we stayed overnight, and then Antwerp, Belgium. A representative of the White Star Line picked me up.*

In Belgium we had to go through physicals because we had come from an infested area. We stayed a week. We went through a steam bath to be disinfected, and the suitcases were put through a steam bath too. There was a box of brown shoe polish in the suitcase, and it ran all over my clothes. Everything was red when it came out. The new white underwear that I had made for me in Kishinev was all red. We were taken to a small town on the channel. The Germans were repairing the city. It was a rough boat ride to Dover. I got seasick. We got on a train to London. There on the train, I ate a sandwich, it tasted pretty good. I opened it up to see what was in it. It looked like it might have been ham. I asked someone what it was, and he verified my suspicions. I opened up the window and threw up. In London, we stacked our baggage at the railroad station and went to a hotel where we stayed overnight.

We then got to Liverpool. The next day several boats were leaving. All the hotels were full. Someone asked if there was anyone Jewish there. A man had an extra bed and wanted someone Jewish who he could talk to. This man at one time lived in Novo Konstantine, but he moved away. He was traveling with his wife. She died in childbirth, and the child died several months later. He had to face her family now in the United States.

The next day, Friday, December 2, 1921, I sent a telegram to Meyer and boarded the White Star liner, the Baltic, for the United States. We got into Ellis Island the next Friday night. We had to wait until Monday until we could get off. At Ellis Island, we had a physical examination. Then they put us in a room and put numbers on us. Then they took us to the B&O Station. Of the 65 people, there was only one man still with me on the train to Pittsburgh. We stopped in Philadelphia. We went to a restaurant and we had coffee and pie. I had money with me. The biggest impression it made on me was that there was a bowl of sugar and you could take all you

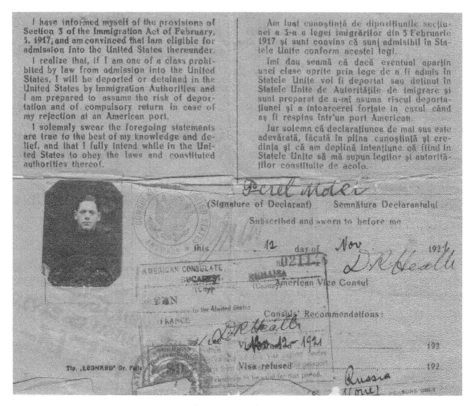

Motye's passport photo, 1921

want. In Europe, they gave you one spoon of sugar. Here you could take all you want. What if you took three spoons!

This is how I got to Uniontown, which is south of Pittsburgh. The B&O from NY didn't go to Uniontown, but to the nearby town of Connellsville. There I had to catch the train coming from Pittsburgh, which went on to Uniontown. There was a four-hour layover in Connellsville. The man who was with me had been in the United States and he was going to Republic. So he went and inquired and says in Slavish, let's go on a streetcar. I thought he meant we would go to a restaurant or something; I didn't know what a streetcar was. So we got on the streetcar, paid our 35 cents, instead of waiting four hours. So I arrived in Uniontown early, I was to have been met later at the station and I didn't know where to go.

But I knew there were other people who had come to Uniontown from my town and I used to write the address for them. It was 8 Pittsburgh Street. So I figured I'd find Mr. Shine at that address. So, I find 8 Pittsburgh Street and it's a little tailor shop with an Italian fellow who looks Jewish to me. I started to tell him my story and he says I don't understand. But he knew who I was. The tailor shop was a gathering place and my cousin Philip Peril had been in that morning and said I was arriving. So he called him up and they sent someone to get me.

My brother lived in Farrell, PA, at that time. So the next day I took the train to Pittsburgh to meet him. He bought me a new blue serge suit, a new coat and a new hat. I did have some clothes with me, two suitcases of stuff, that I had had made for me, but he said you'll wear those later, but I never did.

Seven

Immigrant Life

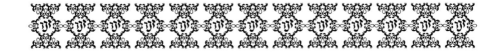

"Between 1881 and 1924, the migration shifted from Central Europe eastward, with over two-and-one-half million East European Jews propelled from their native lands by persecution and the lack of economic opportunity. Most of those who arrived as part of this huge influx settled in cities where they clustered in districts close to downtowns, joined the working class, spoke Yiddish, and built strong networks of cultural, spiritual, voluntary, and social organizations. This period of immigration came to an end with the passage of restrictive laws in 1921 and 1924. Jewish emigration from Eastern Europe to the United States never again reached the levels that it did before 1920."
—*The Library of Congress Exhibitions, 2004.**

Arrival

My father arrived in Pennsylvania in December 1921. In just a few weeks he would celebrate his 18th birthday by the Gregorian calendar. For the first time in his life, he would be living by another calendar and living in another world. Ships, trains, streetcars, automobiles, airplanes, telephones, phonographs, indoor plumbing, electric lights, paved streets, department stores, ordinary houses that looked

---

* The Library of Congress Exhibitions (2004). *A century of immigrants, 1820-1924*, From haven to home: 350 years of Jewish life in America.

like mansions, mail that came regularly, plenty of food on his brother's table, no armed bandits around the corner. His brother Meyer. A new sister-in-law. A young nephew. A language he couldn't understand.

I keep imagining the reunion with his brother. He arrived first in Uniontown and was met by his cousin Philip Peril, and the next day, he took the train to meet Meyer in Pittsburgh. I asked my father if he cried when he saw him, or if Meyer cried. I keep picturing the scene. My father was taller than Meyer when I knew them both. I imagine that he was taller then, too, in 1921. He was thin, and dressed in his old world clothes, and so excited he could barely speak. He didn't cry, he told me, when I asked, maybe Meyer did. Meyer embraced him again and again, he said, and when they got into his house, he did it all over again, and they started talking and they talked and talked for days and nights throughout their lives.

Meyer wanted to know everything, my father said, and he wanted to tell him. Meyer didn't know the details of anything, nothing, since he'd left in the spring of 1911, nearly eleven years before. He didn't know the details of what had happened to his sister Yeta, who died the following year, or to his mother, who died in 1915, or to his father or his brother Paci, who died that June day in 1919. He didn't know precisely what had happened to the town or the people, who was alive or who was dead.

When I was growing up, Meyer was working as a peddler in the hills of southwestern Pennsylvania, and my father was working in what he called "the store," the furniture store across the street from our house in the mining town where we lived. This was in the middle of the last century. Meyer was selling clothing, small appliances, housewares, and the like, in the towns and 'patches' in southwestern Pennsylvania and West Virginia.

My father was also working the towns, as a bill collector for the furniture store. Once a week or so, when the brothers were both in the same territory, Carmichaels or Point Marion or Clarksville, they'd

Motye and Meyer, December 1921

arrange to meet by the side of the road, maybe for a cup of coffee that they'd bring along in a thermos bottle. And when he came home, my father would say, *"I met Meyer on the road today."*

Every week, Uncle Meyer stopped by our house, coming in by the back door, which was unlocked, and appearing suddenly in the kitchen to drop off fresh eggs from Mr. Horn's farm nearby. He didn't stay long. My mother would give him money for the eggs, he'd *kibitz* for a few minutes, tease my sister and me, and then he'd leave. In those years, we didn't socialize much as families, and you didn't talk on the phone either, just to talk. You had to pay for each call. But the two brothers were in touch with each other one way or another, bonded, for the rest of their lives.

All this was later. On that first day of their life together, Meyer took him shopping on the "Strip," the wholesale district in Pittsburgh, for new American clothes, all the fittings, everything, new underwear and socks, a suit, winter coat, hat, and shoes. He had my father change into the new clothes right there and put the old clothes into his suitcase. They got him a shave and a haircut and stopped in a photo booth to take a picture. Here in this photo, taken December 1921, they both look so serious. Neither is smiling. They are both wearing white shirts and striped ties. My father is on the left, his hair freshly parted. He looks much older than 17.

Meyer took his brother home that day. They traveled together by train north to Farrell, and Meyer took the two suitcases that my father had carried with him from Bucharest, and placed them under the front porch of his house, and said, *Ok you won't need these now, you'll use them later,* but when they moved, my father's suitcases were left behind.

When his new uncle arrived from Russia, Meyer's son Berne was five, and my father was almost 18. There were eleven years between Meyer and my father, and thirteen years between my father and Berne. Berne was an only child, and my father was more like a brother than an uncle. In fact, they both married the same year—in 1939. My father was 36, and Berne was 23.

My father had a home at Meyer's and he began to make his own way, to figure out what he was going to do, how he'd make a living and live on his own. Those first years in Pennsylvania were not easy. It was another world, and he was out of place, out of step with the waves of Jewish immigrants who had come before him. He didn't come as part of a large influx of immigrants to a city, where there were networks and social organizations with people of his kind, where everyone spoke Yiddish. Nor did he come with anyone else to the small towns in southwestern Pennsylvania, where he was now. Even though he had

Meyer, he was alone. There weren't others who had shared his experience. In these far-off corners of Pennsylvania, the Jews he met had all come before the First World War, or even earlier. Except for Meyer, no one was really interested in what had happened in Podolia. Everyone was getting on with their lives. They had left the old country behind.

The details of my father's early years in America are sketchy, but there are moments that he talked about from time to time, about what he had to do to find his way. First, there was the language. My father arrived in December 1921, and at some point he was enrolled in the public school—in a third grade class. The seats were too small. And he was completely out of place. How long he stayed in the school—a day, a week—I don't know, but it wasn't long. He was eighteen, and the children were young. He never had a formal education in English. He learned the language on the job, but was always self-conscious about how he spoke—about his accent—which revealed him immediately as an immigrant. Many of the young people he met in those early years were already first-generation Americans. And he was a *greenhorn*. This photo was taken in 1922. It was the first formal photograph he had taken in America.

In his later years, he was able to laugh at the ways he mixed up words and idioms in English, like Leo Rosten's[*] outrageous immigrant, Hyman Kaplan, who botched the English language at every turn. But in the early years, it was hard to laugh.

He got a job delivering flyers, traveling with someone who knew the roads, and he began to learn the language, and realize that the place he had come to was relatively safe. He remembered a moment early on, when he asked his brother where to apply for the permit that would allow him to travel from one town to another. Meyer said you didn't need papers in America. You could go from place to place without a permit. You didn't even need papers if you were traveling from New York to California. It was a free country.

---

[*]   Rosten, L. (1937). *The education of H*Y*M*A*N K*A*P*L*A*N*. New York: Harcourt, Brace.

Moyte's first formal American portrait, 1922

Then, one day, when he was walking along the side of the road, delivering flyers, he passed a young boy who said *hello* and smiled at him. Throughout his life, my father remembered that moment when a perfect stranger greeted him. You didn't walk along the road like that in the old country, without fear. You certainly didn't say hello to strangers, and you didn't speak with gentiles, casually, that way. In America, strangers on the road or on the streets in the towns said hello and smiled at you. Jews might even be friends with gentiles.

So he learned the new language on the road, on the job. He had to learn how to read the flyers. As Berne learned to read, he probably learned with him. And as Berne got his education, so did he. He learned to read as well as speak the language. He read throughout his life. He remained a regular reader of the Yiddish language *Jewish Daily Forward*, educating himself not only in "manners," conventional conduct, through the advice column, "Bintel Brief," but also in history and current affairs.

He read the Jewish classics of the time, and also the Anglo-American classics, including serialized Shakespeare plays. He read the Yiddish writers of the time, including Abraham Cahan, socialist leader and one of the founders of the *Forward*, who wrote short stories and novels in English. Cahan's *Rise of David Levinsky*, a novel about the loss of identity and the lure of riches and success, made a deep impression on my father. And he read more and more in English. He read the local papers and the Sunday *New York Times,* to keep abreast of international news, particularly on what was happening in Israel. He read whatever he could find about the Russian Revolution and the pogroms that he had lived through. But all this would come later.

His first home was in Farrell, Pennsylvania, about 150 miles northwest of Uniontown, near the Ohio border. It was a steel town, and during the war, there had been a boom—perhaps that was why Meyer moved there to start a clothing store, but after the war, things had slowed down, and in 1919, there was a steel strike that turned violent. Things were now quiet, and business picked up, but sometime in 1923, Meyer and his family, with my father, moved back to southwestern Pennsylvania, and my father got a job in his cousin Philip Peril's clothing store in Republic, a few miles west of Uniontown. It was a small mining town, with a few stores. *

In the photo of the store, his cousin Philip is standing on the left, his wife Liza, behind the counter. My father is across the coat rack,

---

Philip Peril's clothing store, Republic, PA, 1922

smiling in his buttoned-up dark cardigan, white shirt and dark tie.
Sometime later, Philip gave up the store and moved to Baltimore,
which was Liza's hometown. They moved along with Philip's mother,
my grandfather's half-sister Beila. She is the one who fell off a table and
died while trying to dust a ceiling lamp to prepare her apartment for
the holiday of Shavuot.

During that first year, my father saved enough money to send a
ticket to his brother Moishe to come to America, but the gates of entry
to the United States were now closed to him. Through Meyer's help,
my father had entered the country under the wire. The immigration
act of 1921 was meant to restrict entry to Jews and other Eastern Euro-
peans, like my father, fleeing from Russian persecution. In 1922, more
limited restrictions were imposed, and in 1924, the Johnson-Reed Act
set the quota for immigrant groups based on the Census of 1890.

The family left in Russia was now prohibited from immigrating to the United States. Moishe made his way to Argentina in 1923, sending for his family the following year, and Duved and his family arrived in Buenos Aires in 1926. Beila and her family stayed in Dunaivtsi in southwestern Ukraine.

Wanderings

In the mid 1920's, my father was living in Uniontown with Meyer and his family, both brothers trying to find work. Throughout the following years, Meyer moved around, too. He tried one business after another. Some were successful for a while, others not. The depression came, and he moved without his family to Ohio and then further west, to try to find work. Then he moved his family to Chicago for a while, and eventually came back to Pennsylvania. How much my father was involved in these business ventures, I don't know. But in the mid 1920's, Meyer was in Uniontown, where he eventually settled for good.

In the 1920's, Uniontown was a prosperous city, with a population of 16,000, and a proud history. Compared to Republic and Farrell, Uniontown was a metropolis. The "Town of Union" was founded on July 4, 1776, and during the late 19th and early 20th century, it was a boomtown, a crossroads connecting the eastern states to the West, through the National Road, Route 40, which went right through the town. That area was dotted with stagecoach inns, and then railroad stops, and was the heart of bituminous coal mining in the late 19th and early 20th centuries. Before coal was discovered, it was a great lumbering area. The town is situated at the foothills of the western ridge of the Appalachian Mountains, a few miles from where Frank Lloyd Wright built his 1937 masterpiece, Fallingwater, for the Kaufman family of the Pittsburgh department store.

I grew up near these mountains, with their shadowy forests, deep-cut rivers and fast-moving streams. We used to picnic at the great falls at Ohiopyle. I remember as a child that my father, sister, and I would splash about in the shallows under the iron bridge at the town site, or try to balance ourselves on the rocks close to shore. You could step-stone across the whole river near the iron bridge.

It was my favorite spot as a child. On the hottest days, the water was cool and clear. Uncle Meyer used to say that the place reminded him of the river at Novokonstantinov. Meyer is buried in the mountains, a few miles further north, in Hopwood.

Uniontown was the 'mother town' to the coal mining company towns and 'patches' in the nearby areas. There are still a few historic buildings left in the center of town, including old Federal style banks, the Romanesque courthouse, and the grand old library. One of the hotels is still standing, as are the mansions that the coal barons built in the surrounding residential streets. In 1912, the downtown had nine banks, thirteen theaters, and fourteen hotels.

There was a thriving Jewish community, and eventually a Jewish Community Center established in the 1940's, where Meyer was a member of the board. He was also charter member of the new Reform Jewish synagogue. He and his wife and son found a home and became part of a stable Jewish community. His wife's brothers and sister and their families lived in Uniontown or close by, and his friend Hymie Fox (Chaim Fuchs) from the shtetl also moved to Uniontown. His cousin Mendel Peril was in Uniontown, with his wife and four children. There were people that my father knew, even cousins. But he felt out of place. He was out of step with the Jewish community that was quickly being Americanized. He couldn't find his place.

The worst for him was the social scene. He was a *greenie*, and the girls didn't want to know him. He spoke with a heavy accent, and he was embarrassed, awkward, increasingly humiliated. He couldn't make conversation. *I finally asked a girl out to the dance, and I didn't know what to do. I didn't know you were supposed to take her dance card and have it filled out by other guys, so she would dance with lots of guys and not just me, nobody told me how to behave, and boy was she mad at me. She never talked to me again.* By now, he was in his twenties and finished with asking girls out for a long time afterwards.

During the next decade, he moved from place to place, job to job. It was time to be on his own, and probably good for him to get out from under his brother's protection. He was strong and capable, and welcomed physical labor. He had experience as a salesman now, and his English was improving. But then it was the depression, and nobody was making a living. My father moved to New York. Then he moved to Chicago to be with Meyer and his family to help them out when they hit hard times. He was at least mobile, and single, so his needs were few, and he was sending money to Meyer and to his sister Beila in Russia when he could.

Then he moved to upstate New York, where he worked on a dairy farm, and then back to live in the Bronx, and work in the famous Automat in Times Square, filling the dessert compartments with fruit pies. He had friends in New York, but they were all settled down, married with children. He went to the Yiddish theatre and to Broadway. He loved going to the Bronx Botanical Gardens and the zoo. He would sit on a park bench in the zoo on a Sunday afternoon and enjoy the fresh air.

But he was lonely. He told me that he was so lonely in his room in the boarding house in the Bronx that he didn't know what to do. So he bought a pack of cigarettes, and figured that at least smoking a cigarette would give him some company. But he choked and coughed and threw up, and never smoked again.

In 1932, he went to Argentina. He was an eligible bachelor, nearing 30, and there were plenty of young people, and there was family, his two brothers Moishe and Duved. Buenos Aires was a thriving Jewish community. He could speak the Yiddish he loved, and he learned Spanish. He opened a little tailor shop on Corrientes Street, and was making a living. His brothers were doing well, their families were growing—the nieces and nephews all loved him, and he had a place there as Tio Motye. He began to gain confidence in himself. He met women, and almost got married. But he had come to know that there was no place like America, and he was an American citizen. He had his papers. So he came back.

Here, in these two photos, is my father setting sail back to America. In the first picture (below), he is on the far right with his brother, Duved, next to him. Next to Duved are his wife Dina, their daughter

Motye, leaving Argentina, 1934, with Duved and family

Anita, whose Hebrew name was Chana, after our grandmother. Their son José, named for our grandfather Joseph, stands in front of my father with his arm around his brother Herman.

In the second photo, my father is standing between his brother Moishe and his wife Rosa. In front are their three children: José, Rebeca, and Anna. José and Anna were also named for our grandparents, Joseph and Chana

Motye, leaving Argentina, 1934, with Moishe and family

Eight

Finding a Place

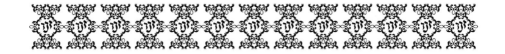

"As for the relatively small number of Jews who settled in small towns. . . that is another story."

      —Irving Howe, Preface, *World of our Fathers*[*]

Becoming American

Motye came back from Buenos Aires to the small towns in southwestern Pennsylvania in 1934. He found jobs in the following years in several towns: Uniontown, Brownsville, and then Fredericktown. I figure that during those years, from 1922 to the end of the 1930's, some 18 years, he moved at least a dozen times. But now, back in a small town in Pennsylvania with a job in a furniture store in Fredericktown, he began to settle in.

And soon after, in the summer of 1939, at his cousin's house in Uniontown where he was visiting, he found my mother. And he created a new identity. He could no longer be Motye or Tio Motye, as

---

[*]   Howe, I. (1976). *World of our fathers: The journey of the Eastern European Jews to America and the life they found and made.* New York: Simon Schuster.

Martin and Bessie Pearl, wedding portrait, 1939

he was in Buenos Aires. He needed to become Martin. And he married a Jewish woman who was born in America.

My mother's large Jewish family came from Hungary forty years earlier. And they were now, above all, assimilated Jews. Both my grandparents had come to McKeesport from the same village—Kolbasov— near Munkacs in the eastern Carpathian Mountains in what was then

Hungary, but they met and married in the United States. My grandfather Louis (1872-1944) and his older brother Max (1871-1940) came directly to McKeesport in 1888 to work in the mills. It was a different time—and history—from what my father experienced almost thirty years later.

The Judkovitzs were an earlier generation of Jewish immigrants; they came to the United States primarily for jobs, for new opportunities, and not as refugees from the Russian Revolution. They were part of the largest wave of Jewish immigration in the nation's history. Between 1881 and when the immigration laws began to change in the early 1920's, one-third of Central and Eastern European Jewry left their homelands. Most in the 1880s came to the large cities, but 25% settled in small towns, particularly in the industrial river towns in southwestern Pennsylvania.[*]

In the late 1880s, the mills and factories were advertising for cheap labor in the rural areas of Eastern Europe, and price wars among ship owners had lowered prices for tickets. At the time, McKeesport and the surrounding towns were overrun with new immigrants, and their families:

> In McKeesport, the newly arrived Hungarian, Russian, Lithuanian and Ukrainian immigrants worked at National Tube or the nearby mills. In Jeanette it was a glass manufacturer and in Butler at a railroad car factory. The pattern was repeated constantly in 44 Western [Pennsylvania] towns, from Aliquippa to Wilkinsburg and Brownsville to Washington. That led to a phenomenon known as 'chain migration,' where 'landsleit', or kin, would immigrate to America and settle near family who had arrived earlier from Europe (Levin, 2).

Jews settled in 38 of the country's 47 states, "but no single state had more Jewish communities of this size than Pennsylvania."[**] In 1888,

---

[*]   Perlman, R. (2001). *From shtetl to milltown: Litvaks, Hungarians, and Galizianers in Western Pennsylvania, 1875-1925.* Pittsburgh: Historical Society of Western Pennsylvania.

[**]   Levin, S. "A Century of Jewish worship ends as McKeesport loses its last synagogue." *Pittsburgh Post Gazette.* May 26, 2000, 2. In Weissbach, L.S. "Small town Jewish life and the Pennsylvania pattern." *Western Pennsylvania history* 83, Spring 2000.

Louis and Max Judkovitz booked passage directly to McKeesport for a job in National Tube Works. Max was 18, and Louis, 17.

By that time, the city was the second largest in the area next to Pittsburgh. It was a quintessential mill town, "filled with the sounds, sights, and smell of steel making and the burning of soft coal—and the news of workers maimed and killed in the course of their twelve-hour days in the mills" (Perlman, *Bridging*,153). A friend's father remembered arriving at that time, and thinking that he had come to a war zone, with bombs exploding all around him.

How long Louis worked in the mill, I don't know, but sometime after he arrived in 1888, he and his brother Max took off for Nashville, Tennessee, to earn a living as peddlers. In both cities, there were substantial Hungarian Jewish enclaves. Nashville's Hungarian Jews had established a place of worship in 1871, and in 1887, they chartered a Hungarian Benevolent Society. Nevertheless, the brothers didn't stay long, and by 1891, they were back in McKeesport. According to his first passport application (1902), Louis was living continuously in McKeesport from 1891 until 1902. In 1892, he married my grandmother, Lena Lefkowitz (1872–1948). The next year, their first son, Samuel—my mother's eldest brother—was born.

The story goes that in 1890, my grandmother Lena, 18, left on her own for America to avoid an arranged marriage to a man from her village. According to my mother, passage had been provided for Lena in exchange for employment in domestic service. She was working for a Hungarian Jewish family in Duquesne, and the next year, she met my grandfather at a wedding of *landsleit*. They were married within weeks of their first meeting. My mother proclaimed that her parents, Louis Judkovitz and Lena Lefkowitz had a blissful marriage, and that her father "worshipped the ground her mother walked on." She further insisted to my father that Louis agreed with everything that Lena said.

Louis and Lena produced eleven children, all born in this country: Sam, Mollie, Sadie, Joseph, Edith, Gertrude, Maurice, Bessie, Sydney,

Milton, and Rose. Joseph and Gertrude died as infants. My mother, Bessie, named after her father's mother, Pessel, who died in Europe, was the eighth child. On the following page is my mother's hand-written family history in my English translation of The Holy Scriptures. My mother, who reminded my father frequently that she was "American-born," also reminded us that she came from a once prominent Jewish family, and that her father had not only done well in America, but also that he had been president of the Hungarian synagogue in 1903.

The synagogue, Gemalis Chesed Anshe Ungarn (literally, Deeds of Kindness Men of Hungary), was founded in 1886, and still exists today. A second synagogue was founded by a union of Galitzianers, Lithuanian (Litvaks), and Russian Jews, but the Russians broke away a few years later, as did the Galitzianers and formed their own synagogues.* Those divisions among the four Jewish groups from varying parts of Eastern Europe—the Russians, Litvaks, Galitzianers, and the Hungarians—persisted for years, so much so that when my father proposed to my mother, her oldest brother, Sam, said that if it weren't for how much they liked my father, they would have had a hard time accepting a Russian into the family. Perlman notes that Jewish marriages were typically discouraged on the basis of class, but in his Hungarian family "intermarriage among immigrants meant marrying a Russian Jew, which was close to unthinkable."**

Life in McKeesport for Jews was a world within a world. While still a minority in the gentile world, where anti-Semitism could surface at any time, they were a significant presence in the city. The Jews in McKeesport built a cohesive family and community life. They became merchants and tradespeople and business leaders—only a few Jews stayed in the mills. Dissension among the ethnic groups lessened in later years, to be replaced by quarrels over religious observance. Although the Orthodox synagogue and the Reform temple were worlds

*   Levin, 2

**   Perlman, R. (1991). *Bridging three worlds: Hungarian-Jewish Americans, 1848-1914.* Boston: University of Massachusetts, 74.

Bessie Judkovitz Pearl
Born Dec. 17, 1905 - McKeesport, Pa.
Louis Judkovitz   1/20/1944
Lena Lefkovitz Judkovitz   1/24/1948
Samuel Judd - July 26, 1893
Mollie Kintner - Nov. 29, 1894
Sadie Judkovitz Sept. 16, 1896
Joseph Judkovitz Died as infant
Edith Judkovitz Nov. 23, 1899
Gertrude Judkovitz Died in infant
Maurice Judd March 11, 1903
Bessie Pearl   Dec. 17, 1905
Sidney Jack Judd Dec 8, 1907 - Oct. 25, 1950
Milton Judd   Nov 8, 1909
Rose Schulhof Jan. 24, 1912

10 - 16 - 57 - Fredericktown, Penna.   - U.S.A.

My mother's handwritten geneology

apart, there was still a tangible Jewish culture, a way of being in the world. As Landesmann put it: "Here on the banks of the Mononga-hela for a time at least, the East European shtetl with its folkways and its religious overtones"* was reproduced. Being a Jew shaped the daily structure of the life. As one of my friends who grew up in McKeesport said, "The Jewish holidays determined our calendar—like religion did our lives."

My grandfather opened a meat market, which grew into a grocery store. Until the depression, Grandfather Louis's grocery business did well, and the family thrived. Lena's parents came to live with the grow-ing family, as did Louis's father, who did not, however, enjoy his life in America, and so returned to Hungary. But Louis had means enough to travel back to Hungary in 1902 and in 1904 to visit his father. He was also able to help bring his other siblings, a brother and three sisters, to America, and to help out family members when need be.

During the good years, my grandfather owned several houses. He had a big new house built up on the hill overlooking the city with one of the first bathrooms in town, and he owned other buildings, as well. I remember when we'd drive into McKeesport every Sunday along the river road, we'd pass the large stone building with the name JUDKOVITZ still visible at the top. The big house was built in 1913, the same year as my mother's sister Mollie's wedding. My mother said that the bride and groom were driven to shul in an automobile, and that the "whole town came to the wedding." My mother was seven.

The Judkovitz children were doing well. Sam, the oldest son, be-came a pharmacist, as did the youngest, Milton. Mollie, the oldest daughter, married a man who worked for a meatpacking firm and later opened his own grocery. Maurice, the seventh child, became a butcher. Everyone worked from a young age, helping in the grocery store. Sadie became a hairdresser and opened her own shop on Market

---

* Landesman, S. (1986). *The beginnings of the McKeesport Jewish community*. McKeesport. Gemilas Chesed Synagogue publication.

Street. By the time my mother was in school, she was encouraged to finish high school—and go on for teacher training in Pittsburgh. The children were all industrious: There were doctors, dentists, and pharmacists among Louis and Lena's children and nieces and nephews. The children's children were going to college. But in the Depression, my grandfather, like so many others, lost everything—including his will to live.

By the time my father entered this large family, the prosperous times were gone, as was the cohesiveness of family life—as well as connections to or even stories about the old world. My mother's eight siblings had all been raised to be Americans, to live conventional American lives. *Judkovitz* became *Judd*. There were traces of the old ways, here and there, in customs and traditions, in holiday celebrations, certainly in food, in superstitious belief, and in language. Yiddish had been the first language in the house.

But, in 1939, when my father joined the family, he was again a *greenhorn.* He stood out as the only foreigner in this Americanized Jewish family. He was described by my mother's family as *having an accent.* And his experiences—his traumas, and ultimately his story—weren't of particular interest to the family he had joined. Everyone was busy with their present lives. The American shtetl in McKeesport was dissolving as the old people were dying and the younger of Louis and Lena's children were moving away, not only from Orthodoxy, but also from McKeesport. And there was another war coming.

Fredericktown, Pennsylvania

When my parents met in Uniontown, my father already had the job at the furniture store in Fredericktown. They met in the summer of 1939 and married in November in the rabbi's study in Brownsville—Louis was very ill at the time. My parents moved into an apartment on top of the American Legion building overlooking Front Street in the town. My mother gave up her hosiery concession in her cousin's hat shop in Uniontown and began to make her life in Frederick-town. There is no doubt that she missed the animated Jewish life of McKeesport, and it took some getting used to, to live in a mining town of 1000 people.

A small coal-mining village in the hills of southwestern Pennsylvania, not far from the West Virginia border, the place reminded my father of the world he had left. Our town was built right along the riverfront, on the west bank of the great Monongahela, with hills rising up on our side of the river and extending far into the distance on the other side. There was the riverfront, the main street, a few side streets and alleys, and the road across the railroad tracks leading up the hill. Basically it was a one-street town, which sometime in the 1950's earned a street sign: Front Street.

There was a coalmine at one end of Front Street, and a coalmine at the other end. In the good mining years, the barges carried coal night and day up river to Pittsburgh. The closest bridge was in Brownsville, eight miles west, but we had a ferry that navigated regular runs back and forth across the river, where there was a small patch of houses and a river road. The river separated two counties, our town was in Washington County, and across the river was Fayette County, named after the Marquis de La Fayette, a leader of the French Revolution and a general in the American Revolutionary War.

It was like a cradle, this little town, built on what eventually became Route 88, the north-south river road in that border country of southwestern Pennsylvania, 25 miles north of the West Virginia border, and five miles south of Route 40, the first east-west national highway. We were 30 miles north of Fort Necessity, where the young Lieutenant Colonel George Washington started his military career, in the first battle of the French and Indian War. The place is steeped in early American history, and there are still traces of the people and the world that had come before, the indigenous Monongahela people.

Our house, Fredericktown, Pennsylvania, photograph 2014

The village—it was not even large enough to be considered a town—was patented in 1788 as "Sugar Tree Bottom" by Major Frederick Wise, who received what was known as a *bounty land warrant* from the government for his service in the Revolutionary War. That was the site of our town. In 1790, the place was named Fredericktown,[*] after him. In its heyday in the last century, the main street was a stretch of four blocks, with several dozen stores and houses. A traffic light was

---

[*]   Bowers, W.S. and Crowthers, L. (1990). *Fredericktown: 1790-1990: East Bethlehem Township, Washington County, Pennsylvania and its neighboring communities.* Fredericktown Book Committee Distributed by the First National Bank & Trust Co. of Washington, Pa., Fredericktown Branch.

installed in the center of town around 1950, before the beginning of the decline of the mining industry.

When I was growing up in the mid-20th century, the town was flourishing, with two banks, two movie theatres, the post office, an A&P, two small groceries, two clothing stores, a couple of beauty shops, a barber shop, shoemaker, two drug stores, both with soda fountains, the jewelers, the "five and dime," and the mine's "company store" at the south end of town. There were several taverns, a liquor store, the old hotel, the American Legion building, and the First Methodist Church at the north end of town. There was plenty of parking on the riverbank, and in the 50's, the town installed parking meters on Front Street.

On this side of the river, if you were traveling south on 88, and turned right at the stop light in town, you'd head up "The Hill," past the fire house and up over the railroad tracks into the residential section. There were a number of big beautiful houses on top of The Hill, and also the Catholic Church, and the little two-room schoolhouse, with two grades in each room. And a mile down 88, in Millsboro and Vestaburg, there was a Baptist church and a Presbyterian church, and also the middle school and high school. There was a Russian Orthodox Church in Brownsville, and also the Hungarian synagogue, where some of the Jews in town went to *shul*.

We lived in a house that was on the main street in town, across from the furniture store where my father worked for 47 years. We were the four of us, my father, mother, little sister, and me. The house was a fulfillment of my father's American dream—that he would own his own house. It is still there, a 1910 two-story wooden frame house with an ample front porch right on the main street, in a town that felt safe. Never mind that we needed to turn the second floor into a rental to pay the bills.

My parents were proud of our home, of the front and back porches, the lilac bushes and the immense hickory nut tree, whose roots, we discovered when lightning struck it, had grown along the side of the house, across the main street, and all the way down to the riverbank. The backyard extended uphill to the railroad tracks and gave my father the space for growing tomatoes and eventually building a garage. Because he worked in a furniture store that also sold appliances, we were one of the first in town to have a television, a dishwasher, and an automatic washer and drier, and in the basement, my mother had an extra refrigerator and freezer.

The town was such a mix of people: there were descendants of the pioneering families, the Crocketts, Bowers, Crumrines, and Hawkins, who had come from England, Scotland, and Ireland, and then the later immigrants came, from Italy and Eastern Europe, particularly the Poles, Czechs, and Slovaks. There were African Americans and a family of Muslims. When we were growing up, there were ten Jewish families in the town, about twenty people in all, in a town of about 1000. They owned the two clothing stores, the jeweler's, the Five & Dime, and the furniture store, where my father worked. All the men, except for one, were foreign born. All the women were American born. There were six of us Jewish kids, all in different grades, except for my grade, where there were two of us.

My mother hosted a little circle of Jewish women friends for her mahjongg and bridge games, and because they had to pass our house every day on their way to pick up their mail at the post office, you'd often find one or two of her friends sitting on the front porch or in the kitchen with her. The Jewish men of the town occasionally had a pinochle game, but, mostly, they were working, and didn't congregate with each other. My father felt at ease with the people in the town, who were immigrants from Eastern Europe, just as he was. He had found a steady job in the furniture store, and the people in the town were welcoming.

But the Jews in the town did not cohere as a community—perhaps because we didn't want to draw attention to ourselves. There was no synagogue or house of prayer or any kind of social organization—except for the women who had their card playing. Whatever the reasons, we didn't congregate as families. We didn't celebrate the holidays together—or the Sabbath. Coincidence had brought us together, but our roots were elsewhere. Jobs arranged for by family or friends or ads in the newspapers in New York, in one case, had brought us to this place.

Everyone had come from someplace else. Although we all lived in the town, all of us had roots in the little towns or big cities somewhere else in the area. We all had grandparents or relatives in the neighboring towns, and we had things to do in these places that we didn't do in the town. In many ways, it was a peripatetic life. All of us were travelers—every weekend, traveling to family in neighboring towns or cities. Mostly, Pittsburgh, but also McKeesport, Washington, Roscoe, Monessen, Charleroi, Wilkinsburg. Ambridge, Masontown. Uniontown. Morgantown, West Virginia. Cleveland, Ohio.

Our family was connected, on the Pearl side, to Uniontown, to Uncle Meyer and Aunt Fan. Their son Berne had moved with his family to Chicago. And Berne died young, his wife and children staying on in Chicago. The family my father longed for was in Buenos Aires.

On my mother's side, there was family, and every Sunday when I was young, we'd be in McKeesport, with my grandparents. Even in bad weather, my father would put chains on the tires, and we'd wind our way north on Route 88 to get to their house on Jenny Lind Street. Louis died when I was two, and Lena when I was six, but we still went to the house in McKeesport for a long time after, every Sunday afternoon to see my mother's two unmarried sisters, Sadie and Edith, who was ill most of her life.

In the years when I was in high school, we'd drive to McKeesport, pick up Aunt Sadie and travel to family in Pittsburgh. We'd shop on Murray Avenue for kosher meat and baked goods, and the Sunday *New York Times* for my father. Some Sundays Aunt Sadie would open her beauty shop on Market Street to give us all haircuts.

Other Sundays we'd stop at Uncle Sam's drug store in East Pittsburgh, right near the Westinghouse plant, or at Uncle Milton's pharmacy in Homewood. Or for a dinner at Aunt Mollie's or Uncle Maurice's. If we were there during the week, we'd stop at Sammy Judd's hat shop or Ruthie Feldman's lighting shop. At times, one of the cousins would have the whole family over for a holiday or celebration. For many years, my parents attended the Judd family 'cousins club.'

Other Jewish families in Fredericktown traveled to the metropolitan Pittsburgh area on Sundays, to visit relatives, as we did, or, if they were merchants, to shop at the wholesale stores in the garment district. As I now know, this itinerancy was a recreation of the life in the towns of the shtetl, with the little villages, in both Hungary and in Ukraine, all connected to their families and to shopping and other business in the neighboring "mother towns." It seemed a re-creation of the life my father had led in Novokonstantinov, with his mother travelling from place to place to visit her family and also to buy supplies for her store.

The Orthodox synagogue in Brownsville was also a part of our lives. Some of the Jewish families in town went to synagogue in Pittsburgh, but we went to the synagogue in Brownsville, which was founded by the Hungarian community in the town in 1889. My sister and I went to Sunday school every week, and stayed on after graduation to teach the little kids. My father would drive us to the synagogue and take a walk or wait in the car reading his paper while we were inside. We studied Jewish history, the great Old Testament stories, and the early history of the Jews. But we learned nothing of the history of the worlds that our own families had come from, even though most of us had at least one parent who was an immigrant from Eastern Europe.

My father didn't mingle with the men of the congregation, and he wasn't involved in social activities. I know that he felt that he couldn't make the kind of financial pledges that the wealthier men of the community were able to do. And he was not, as far as I know, called for *aliyah,* the honor of reading from the Torah or reciting a blessing during services. During the year, he worked on the Sabbath, but he honored the High Holy Days. There was much discussion with my mother about his taking off two days for Rosh Hashanah. His boss, though a Jew, preferred that he take only one day, but my father remained adamant that he attend services on both days of Rosh Hashanah, and, of course, on Yom Kippur when we all observed the fast.

I remember him on those days—the solemnity of his taking the *tallis* out of the box in the drawer in his bedroom and dressing in his good blue suit to go to *shul*. They were quiet, serious days that I know he looked forward to every year, marking a new beginning, being inscribed for another year in the book of life. What he was calling up in his memories, I don't know. But there was something wistful and melancholy in the house—a silence that was unusual for him and also for my mother. Observancy had waned for both of my parents, but it was clear that these days were sanctified, when we stopped our ordinary lives and entered another place. When we got home from synagogue, my mother was waiting with the holiday meal, and a peacefulness that marked a change in the day-to-day.

These exits and entries into the varied places that we traveled as part of our Jewish lives were complicated. Even though we lived, comfortably, in our house in the town, it felt at times as if we were always driving somewhere, searching for something. Just as my father had wandered by himself for nearly twenty years, so were we still wandering about. My sister said that sometimes it felt as if the four of us, my mother, father, and the two of us, were suspended in mid-air. Untethered. Traveling from place to place.

It also felt as if we needed to be careful about what we said and did, and I began to question what I saw as my father's reticence about taking a stand, speaking up for his beliefs, railing against injustice. The traumas of his life, the oppressive era that we lived in after the Second World War, his concerns that one day someone might discover that his immigration papers were in error—these fears haunted him. He cautioned against standing out, making a fuss, or signing our names to documents that might jeopardize our lives. *Shhhhahh* was the mantra in our house. Be quiet.

In the school in the town, there was one Jewish boy who was my age—Toby. The two of us grew up together from infancy, and he was the closest I had to a brother. We irritated each other as siblings often do, and by the fact of our presence, as a pair of Jewish kids, we brought attention to ourselves. One day in fourth grade, I wore a silver Star of David that my mother's sister Edith had given me for my birthday. I remember Toby pushing me against the blackboard in the back of the classroom, saying, "Take it off. You don't have to remind everybody you're Jewish." I wasn't going to take it off, I said, I was *proud* to be Jewish. I'm sure I said that as a pat response, but I'm also sure that we were both desperate to fit in.

In the end, though, we did have a place in the town. It was the place that my father had found after years of wandering, and he made it our home. He grounded us all in the present, where we lived our daily lives. One day, late in his life, when he was telling some of the story to one of my friends, he said, *"I found a wonderful place—that little town. I have no complaints."*

It was possible to live in that world relatively unafraid. It was possible for him to have a steady job and support his family, to move from blue-collar work (delivering furniture) to working in the store as a salesman—and proudly wearing a white long sleeve shirt (even in the summer) and tie. It was possible for him to buy a house and grow his garden, have plenty of food on the table, and send his two girls to college. Everyone in the town knew my father: he was a joyful gentle spirit, a man unafraid of hard work who relished his life, and his family. He could walk into the bank and get a loan when he wanted to buy the house. He could count on Doc Morgan—who was also our congressman in Washington—to sit with him during the long nights when he had pneumonia until the fever broke. He could buy a car from the local dealer at what he thought was a fair price—and not be swindled when he had to take the car in for repairs. He knew everyone in town and the neighboring areas he needed to know, whenever he needed anything. And he could be counted on to help others, when they needed him, no matter what.

It wasn't a Jewish community, but there were so many immigrants from neighboring countries in Eastern Europe, that he felt at home, and he was able to understand the customers in the store, no matter the language they spoke. This was his place. With his children in school, his world expanded. I figured my father could do anything. He provided big cardboard boxes from the furniture store whenever we needed to build some kind of prop for a school play or for the Girl Scouts troop.

Years later, when I came back to the town to visit old friends, one of our favorite elementary school teachers joined the group. She remembered my father bringing a refrigerator box for the crèche. "My kosher girl," she said, "will you ever forgive me for making you take part in the Christmas crèche?" She reminded me that I was the narrator of the story of Joseph and Mary and the birth of the baby, Jesus. There was nothing to forgive, I told her. We were all included in each other's worlds. This was America. It was a place where Jews could live and not be shot at. This was the triumph, the gift, and I think my father celebrated that every day of his life. He had escaped, and he was safe.

And later on, when my little sister was growing up, he allowed himself to speak. Janet, who is several years younger than I am, remembers an incident when she was in middle school. A student in her eighth grade Latin class was being disruptive, and the teacher said to him, "You are as bad as the Jews who killed Christ." My sister was upset and told our parents. My father made an appointment with the school principal to complain about the incident, and the teacher subsequently apologized to the class. My father had come a long way from Novokonstantinov.

In recent years, my childhood friends and I have talked about what it was like living in the town when we were growing up. These are the friends who came to my confirmation at the synagogue in Brownsville, and I went to their churches for special events. We learned about each other's traditions, holidays, and beliefs. Carolyn remembers the matzo sandwiches that my mother made for her at Passover, and years later, when she was teaching elementary school in Ohio, she brought an ecumenical curriculum into her classrooms.

It was a remarkable moment, we agreed. There was a democratic fervor after the War, and we all felt it. There was a strong belief in the family and in being able to live together and accept difference. We felt that we were all part of something larger than ourselves. And with Doc Morgan, as our doctor and congressman, we had a direct line to Washington, D.C. In fact, Doc Morgan, himself, assisted Janet in getting a summer job after high school as an elevator operator in the House of Representatives. As my friend Carolyn said, "I think it was a time when war-weary adults came together to live in harmony with their neighbors from many different backgrounds. They were all the town's people and we were all the town's children. People looked out for each other and all the adults looked after us. We were fortunate to have been in that place at that time."

The town is now pretty much gone—as are the city of McKeesport and the shtetl in Novokonstantinov. These are places that have seen their time. But for my father, the shtetl, and later, the little town in southwestern Pennsylvania, were home.

On a trip to Fredericktown last year, one of my classmates gave me an article that she found in her mother's scrapbook, dated May 26, 1949, and entitled, *Jewish Families Donate Windows for Methodists*:

> Five stained glass windows in the Methodist Church of this little town in Washington County tell a story that is more than Biblical. Or maybe one that is truly

Biblical. They are "Old Testament" windows, dedicated by 10 Jewish families because of their affection and respect for the Methodist minister, the Reverend John B. Warman, who is working to establish brotherhood in the town.[*]

Reverend Warman had served in the Pacific as a Navy chaplain. It was there, he said, that he came to understand that faith must be inclusive. He was born and raised in Uniontown, and after the war, he took the position at the Methodist Church in Fredericktown. He was determined to build a cohesive community that would embrace all religions. He called it a "Family of God," a brotherhood of understanding. He held services with members of the community from the different religious communities. To celebrate the effort, the Jews in the town contributed five stained windows, all depicting stories about Old Testament Patriarchs, Abraham, Moses, and Issiah. They are part of the same story, he said. The plaque beneath the five Tiffany windows reads: *Our Brotherhood Windows: A gift of our parent faith.* My father was one of the volunteer workers who helped install the stained glass windows in the Methodist Church in Fredericktown.

He also helped to dig the foundation for the new recreation room in the church. Years later, he told my friend Carolyn that he had accepted an invitation to a church dinner for the volunteers. They served pork chops, he said, but he couldn't bring himself to eat them. No doubt he was reminded of the ham sandwich he had tried to eat on his journey to America.

Although most of the stores in the town are gone now, the Methodist Church is still open. There is an itinerant preacher who comes in once a week, and officiates at funerals and weddings. Several years ago, when Carolyn's mother died in the town, I phoned the local florist, one of the stores still open, and placed an order for flowers to be sent to the funeral home up on the hill. They didn't take credit cards. But when I said that I had lived in the town, that my father was Martin

---

[*] "Jewish families donate windows for Methodists, *Pittsburgh Post Gazette*, May 26, 1949.

Pearl, they said, "Oh, sure, I remember him. What a nice man. No problem. Just send a check."

We grew up knowing that all of us had histories. I knew that Ann and Ellen, who are Catholic, were descendants of Davy Crockett, and that Carolyn, who is Methodist, had Scots-English roots, and that her grandfather, who had been a union organizer, died as a result of an accident in the mine. (The total death benefit, she later told me, was $65, and there was no pension for her grandmother. Her grandmother lived in the house with Carolyn, her parents, and brother for the rest of her life.) I knew that there was a history connected to the Bowers family down the street. They were from an early pioneering family in the area. I knew that the Moschettas were from Italy and the Moskowitzs from Poland, and the Saladnas from Czechoslovakia. I knew that there were descendants from the Eastern European towns where my family was from. It was an education that taught me how to live in the world.

And as my father kept telling the stories, he brought the past to life. My sister and I came to know that there was a real place that he had come from, a way of living and being alive in a world that was gone, but that lived on in his memories. There had been terrifying times that he lived through, murders, close calls, anti-Semitism, pogroms, and revolutions, but there was something wonderful about the daily life itself, the family, the community, and a sense of belonging that he wanted us to know.

Nine

Holding onto the Past

"Maybe all exiles try to re-create the place they've lost out of their fear of dying in a strange place."
 —Nicole Krause, *Great House**

Reunion: Meyer, Duved, Moishe, Motye (1965)

What was missing from my father's life—and ours—were the brothers and their families in Argentina. The four brothers, Duved, Meyer, Moishe, and Martin, kept the connections strong throughout the years, through letters, wedding and birth announcements, and occasional phone calls. There were gifts sent through *landsleit* in Buenos Aires coming to New York. I remember one year my father traveled by bus to New York (375 miles) to pick up a watch that his brother Duved had sent through a friend.

In the 1960's, my father traveled again to Argentina. It had been thirty years since he'd been there. But he was still Tio Motye, the American uncle, and greeted with open arms by a large growing family. A few years later, Duved and his wife Dina came to Uniontown

---

* Krause. N. (2010). *Great house*. New York, NY: W.W. Norton & Company.

and Fredericktown, and they all traveled to see *landsleit* in Philadelphia and New York. In a letter that Duved wrote to his son in Buenos Aires, he describes my father as working long hours, six days a week in the furniture store in Fredericktown. It wasn't easy, he said, but my father seemed content with his life.

Then in 1965, Moishe and his wife, Sonia, and Duved came, too. It was 54 years since the four brothers had been together—in Novokonstantinov. It was 1911, when Meyer left for America. My father was seven, Moishe, was eight, Duved was 20, and Meyer was 17. Their seeing each other after more than fifty years was newsworthy. This photo, along with an article appeared in the local newspaper.

Meyer, 72, is far left, then Sonia (Moishe's wife), Moishe, who is 64, is in the middle, then Duved, 74, and my father, 62

My sister and I had been schooled in genealogy, in who belonged to whom: Duved's family and Moishe's family and their children and grandchildren. Now that we had met our uncles when they came to visit in 1965, we had a sense of who they were. Duved had been here a few years earlier, but Moishe and Meyer hadn't seen each other since 1911.

Meyer (on the left) and Moishe, 1965

I remember that meeting, the four brothers embracing, and talking and talking and talking in Yiddish, at times their voices rising or lowering, sometimes whispering. Spilling stories of their lifetimes. They argued over memories and settled old disputes, my father said. They tried to make up for the lost years, and they vowed to have the children know each other. This was the summer of 1965, and by fall, Meyer was gone. Moishe's first grandson was named after him a few months later.

In 1957, eight years before, Meyer's son Berne died at the age of 40, and my father said that Meyer never recovered. His first heart attack happened shortly after that. He had been sad for many years. When Meyer died, it was my father who was called. Meyer had been working in the mountains, and stopped at a customer's house in the nearby town of Carmichaels to have a cup of coffee. He was sitting at the kitchen table talking with his friends, people he had known for a long time, when he collapsed. He died immediately, they said.

At the funeral home in Uniontown, although our Pearl numbers were few, the room was filled with Meyer's friends from Uniontown and his customers from all around the area. People who knew him came from far and wide to pay their respects at the funeral home. A Mennonite farmer, one of Meyer's customers who had known him for years, told me: "When your uncle came into the kitchen, the sun always came in with him." Meyer was buried in the mountains he loved, not far from the spot that reminded him of the river at Novokonstantinov, above which his family was buried.

My father felt the loss, deeply. Now, with both Berne and Meyer gone, he was even more determined that my sister Janet and I know the family in Argentina. My father's first grandchild was born in 1966, the year after Meyer died. My daughter, Sharon. Her middle name is Myra. My father sent her photograph to the family in Argentina. He was so proud of her and the three grandchildren who followed. The next generation was growing.

He went back to Buenos Aires the next year, and again in 1970, a few months after Duved died. In the late 1970's, there were the two youngest brothers left, Moishe and my father, when he bought tickets for Janet and me and our families to travel to Buenos Aires. The two of us bridged the generations: we are the youngest of Chana and Joseph's grandchildren, born decades after the first of our generation. Malka was born in 1912. Janet was born thirty-five years later, in 1947. The oldest of the next generation, the great-grandchildren, was born in 1939. We spent several weeks in Argentina, meeting more than sixty cousins, and over the years, the bonds between us have grown. The next generations want the stories and the history.

In the 1970's, my parents were still in Fredericktown. My father worked in the furniture store in town six days a week until he was in his late 70's. All the time, he kept reading, studying, and talking about the past. By then, I was taking notes, and also arranging taped interviews with him. He kept busy, with his garden, the house, and taking care of my mother, who was not well. He was still painting the exterior of the house and doing repairs. He was always fixing or building something, the garage or the shed behind the house, or a broken pipe. What materialized was often not the most aesthetically pleasing, but it usually worked.

As my father grew older, it seemed as if the past grew nearer. He was preoccupied with what had happened in his life. There were parts of the story that he obsessed over—the day his father and oldest brother were killed in the house and he ran out the back door. What happened that day? He went over and over the details in his mind. The question of who killed his father—the Bolsheviks or Mensheviks or the local peasants? He kept reading to find mention of the pogrom in Novokonstantinov in 1919—new details, in new histories in Yiddish and English that might shed light on what had happened. Something was always coming up from somewhere.

He obsessed over not having found a way to bring his sister Beila and her family here to this country. He might have saved them. He still worried that one day someone would find something out of order with his immigration papers, and that, even five or six decades later, he would be sent back. Throughout our lives, Janet and I heard new details that he added to the stories, the truths he now saw fit for our adult ears. We heard more and more of his obsessions, the ghosts that would not lay quiet. When he got something in his head from the past, or the present, he would increasingly worry it to death—and drive us to distraction.

Valhalla, New York

Duved had died in 1970 in Buenos Aires, and Moishe died there, too, in 1982. They are both buried in Argentina. In 1982, at 79, my father retired from the furniture store in Pennsylvania. When he and my mother resettled into the apartment in my town in New York, he set about, almost immediately, to shop for a burial plot. Every visit to their apartment, I found him studying newspaper advertisements and brochures, or talking to salesmen on the phone about cemeteries. He talked and talked about the options. Perhaps the cemetery of the burial society of Novokonstantinov in Long Island would do. But all his connections, his *landsleit,* were gone, and the cemetery was far away. How would anyone come to visit? My poor mother was trying to adjust to the new apartment and the new surroundings, and here was my father obsessing over burying her. She would shake her head. We toured a couple of local cemeteries, but they didn't suit him, and he kept on looking.

He finally found the Kensico cemeteries in Valhalla, a few miles north of our town. The cemetery is a sprawling 460 acres of sloping hills in Westchester County, founded in the late 19th century to accommodate the overcrowding of Manhattan's cemeteries. The Jewish section, Sharon Gardens, some 76 acres, was founded much later, in 1953, and that is where my father found his burial place.

The day my father, sister, and I walked through the cemetery to choose a spot, it was clear he was looking for something in particular. He moved quickly, as he always did, inspecting the grounds, and walking to the open spaces in the last rows of the cemetery. Row Z. There was a border of willows along the bank of a stony creek, and he found a spot that he liked. *He liked the view*, he said. There was an elevation there, and you could feel the breeze on this warm summer day and see the willows along the river. He bought a burial plot with room for four graves, and now that I have been to the cemetery on the hill overlooking the river in Novokonstantinov where my father's parents and four siblings are buried, I think I know what he was looking for.

My father had no intention of ever going back to Ukraine, to the shtetl, although that was the place he had come from, and it was always on his mind. He knew that what had been there was gone, and he knew more than he said about what had happened. But in his later years, he began to tell me. I asked one day what had happened to the town, and what had happened to the Jews of the town. He said that they had all been murdered in the Holocaust. There was not much left of the town. He also knew some of what had happened to his sister Beila and her family in Dunaivtsi during the Holocaust in 1942. In the 1960's, he located the cousin who had grown up in the house next to him. They began to write to each other. He was living in Moscow and able to track down records of the killings of the Jews in Ukraine, and told my father what he knew. Going back was not an option.

But he was in a new town, and he still had work to do. He bought a stationary bicycle, so that he could keep his body fit. In those years, he developed a regimen that kept him active. He was doing "revolutions," as he called them, on his stationary bicycle. He kept up his reading. He was cooking now, for the first time. My mother decided that if my father had retired from the store, she would retire from the kitchen. So he was making the meals: soup, stew, burgers.

My daughters were spending time with their grandparents, and once a week, he was making a meal for Lauren, his younger granddaughter, making sure that she was eating well. He was taking his daily walks—he loved being outside in the fresh air. He managed to walk to the supermarket nearby—with his shopping cart—and my mother's store coupons. Occasionally, he would be sent back to the store if he turned up with the wrong item. My mother was very particular about sliced peaches in *light* syrup, and *unscented* soap powders. And he wanted to please her.

One day, as I was driving up the main road near his house, I caught sight of a man sitting in a lawn chair on the side of the road. He was wearing a rimmed hat, and it looked as if he was selling vegetables—or something. I couldn't quite see. The man looked very familiar, and as I passed by, I recognized him. I backed up the car to where he was sitting, and there was my father, on his way back home from the supermarket. He had built himself a perfectly reasonable contraption: onto each handle of a portable shopping cart he had attached a metal clasp and fastened a broom handle to serve as an extension, making the cart easier to push. He attached a folding mesh lawn chair to the shopping cart. He figured that when he got tired pushing the cart back up the hill to his house, he could stop and take a rest. That's where I found him, sitting on the lawn chair on the sidewalk of the busiest street in town. I helped gather the heavy shopping bags that he was pushing, folded the chair and the cart, put all into the car, and drove him home. Nothing, it seemed, was going to stop him.

Sabbath Shuvah

My father wanted to live until he was 90. That became his goal. He wanted to see his grandson Michael a bar mitzvah. He did everything he could to stay alive, and to stay buoyant. We were talking more and more about the old country—his memory was as sharp as ever. He was filling in gaps—telling me more and more of what he hadn't told me as a child. These were not stories for children. I learned the specifics of the day my grandfather and his eldest son were killed. And how my father almost didn't make it to America. Every time I visited my father, who lived around the corner, he told me something else that came to mind. Something that I'd not heard before. He had time now to think. He was re-reading the books that he had. While in the hospital, during the last six months of his life, he asked for Gorky's *Mother*. He was watching what was happening that summer of 1991 in the Soviet Union– the changes that were taking place in the world that he'd left. It had taken all this time for the Russian Revolution to be over.

My friends who visited came often to see my parents, too, and he would invariably begin to talk, to tell his stories. As always, there was something that came up that he used to start the stories. Anything. A loaf of bread that reminded him of the Russian rye he loved. A beautiful winter's day that reminded him of the day that he took the horse for a sleigh ride. Something that reminded him of something that had happened nearly 70 years before. Something informative, usually. He was an astute rhetorician: he didn't tell sad stories to strangers. He was painting pictures, drawing images of the way things were, bringing his audience into the world that he was calling up in his memory. My poor mother had stopped listening years before, but now she might tune in, and quibble over a detail.

You never knew where the conversation would take you. He mentioned one day that his mother had sold canned sardines in her store in the market place in Novokonstantinov. And my mother insisted that there couldn't have been sardines sold in cans in the marketplace in the shtetl in those years. How could there be canned goods in such a primitive place? I had come to see these as their Hungarian-Russian disputes. Although she had no actual knowledge of the world of the shtetl, she insisted that she knew. And they were still at it all these years over the languages: she was still correcting his pronunciation and grammar in English, and he, correcting her Yiddish.

Once, after having seen a documentary of the life of Tolstoy and footage of his elaborate state funeral in Kiev, I came to visit. I was struck by the images of the golden domes of Kiev, and asked my father if he had ever been to Kiev. He told part of a story I hadn't heard. I knew about his sister Yeta's death, how she died in childbirth, but I didn't know that her parents had taken her by train to a specialist in

Kiev, some 200 miles away, and that their daughter died in the doctor's office, and they left her body there to be buried. I had come to visit on a sunny afternoon—to make conversation—and there, suddenly, was a bruising image of the past, of my father's sister's death, and his parents' suffering. He was living with the images—the memories—all the time. And now that he was retired, he had the time, as he said, to turn things over in his mind. I became his amanuensis in those years.

My father died as he had lived—in touch with the past. In those last six months, as his heart was giving out, and he was still struggling to stay alive, he was in and out of the past. On one day, when I would come to the hospital, he would be far away in the shtetl, talking to his mother. On another day when I came in, he was talking to me as if I were his sisters, Yeta or Beila. At other times, he was talking to Duved, Moishe and Meyer. Or my mother. He was worried about her—he had taken care of her for so many years—and he knew that she was unable to care for herself.

At other times, he was perfectly present, attuned to our lives, my mother, sister, and grandchildren, and he would recite his list of worries about us. What would I do if such and such happened? What would so and so do? What, I wondered, would I do without him? As he lay dying, I dreamt that I could keep him alive, that he wouldn't die, that his doctor would find a way to keep him alive. There was good reason to think that. He had had close calls in the years before, and Dr. Leblang had always helped him come through. My father, the etymologist, had recognized Dr. Leblang as *landsleit,* and he translated his name the·first time he met him. *Leb is life, and lang is long,* he explained to me. *Long life. Dr. Longlife.* I think that Dr. Leblang also thought that Motye would survive, that he would keep on being alive. The nurses did, too. When he could, of course, he was talking to them, and they would tell me when I came on the floor what he was saying. "Where was he from?" they wondered. "What a gentle man," they said. "What a beautiful soul." One of them, who was in touch with

Native American beliefs, said that he was an *old soul,* that he knew things, he was in touch with truths that few knew.

When it was time, he was ready. I came in that Friday morning, September 13, and he was breathing heavily, but he was present. He told me in a voice that was clear and certain that his soul was leaving. "*My neshumeh,*" he said, "*my neshumeh is leaving me now.*" Neshumeh is soul. I should have known that it was the time, but I didn't. That Friday night at sundown, Dr. Leblang phoned, to say that he had died. It was Friday, the start of the Sabbath. It was the Friday night between Rosh Hashanah and Yom Kippur, the holiest Sabbath of the year. It is known as *Sabbath Shuvah,* the *Sabbath of Return.* Belief has it, among some, that the gates of Heaven are open on Sabbath Shuvah, and that all who die then may enter, without question.

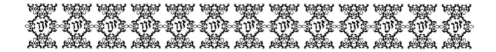

Ten
Return to the Old Country

We were persuaded to make the long journey to Novokonstantinov by my cousin Silvia. She is the granddaughter of my father's brother Duved. She grew up in Buenos Aires, but left during the height of the years of state terrorism in the 1970's, and since then has lived in various parts of the world. In 2010, when she was living in Budapest, she found her way to the shtetl in Ukraine with her husband and son, who was about to be bar mitzvah. Her father (Duved's son, José) was born in the shtetl, and she wanted her own son to be connected to the past.

With my father's descriptions of the town, of where things had been, she was able to find the remains of the Jewish cemetery. In that same year, my husband and I traveled to Buenos Aires for her son's bar mitzvah, and talked to many in our family about Silvia's trip to the shtetl. It was because of her effort—and her insistence—that I went the following year.

Silvia made all the travel arrangements for drivers and guides, lodging and routes. With a command of six languages and years of international experience, very few borders or barriers are closed to her. Four of us, Silvia and I and our husbands, made our way from Budapest to

Kiev. Silvia's husband, Mark, who works for an agency of the United Nations, had meetings there. Then Silvia, my husband, Phil, and I were driven deep into the far southwestern reaches of Ukraine to explore the places my family had lived. I was equipped with my father's voice, his stories of the past, descriptions of how and where things had been, my father's rudimentary drawings of the shtetl (on graph paper), and even a detailed description of the house they had lived in.

We had photos and other artifacts. I wanted to go to Novokonstantinov. I wanted to know the roads that my father had walked, from Novokonstantinov to the neighboring towns of Letichev and Khmelnick, where his aunts lived, and to the cities where he had fled, Proskurov, and then Dunaivtsi. I wanted to go to the Romanian border, where he had run across the frozen river. I had an itinerary in mind, of people and places and events, from my father's stories. I intended to find the burial places of my grandparents and aunts and uncles, and to place stones on the graves, a Jewish ritual signifying the permanence of memory and legacy. I brought a handful of stones from where my father lay buried in the cemetery across the world.

Kiev: Yeta, 1912

We began in Kiev on a Sunday in late June, 2011, a hundred years after my Uncle Meyer left Ukraine for America. I was looking for Yeta's burial place. My father's two sisters, Yeta and Beila, were both beloved figures in his life: Yeta, in his early years, and Beila, in the later years, before he left for America. I knew that Yeta had died in childbirth. This was one of the stories that my father told me many times, how hard the childbirth was, how much pain she was in, there was no doctor in the town. I heard the same details over the years. It was 1912, Yeta was 26, and my father was eight. I assumed that Yeta was buried in the Jewish cemetery in Novokonstantinov.

Near the end of my father's life, he filled in details about her death. No, she wasn't buried in Novokonstantinov, she was buried in Kiev.

Chana had taken her by carriage to the nearest train station where Joseph met them, and the three traveled by train to Kiev, some 200 miles away, to see a doctor. Yeta died in the doctor's office, my father said, and she was buried in Kiev, *because you wouldn't bring the body back.* My father also told me that the Jewish cemetery where Yeta was buried had been on the outskirts of the city, but that the cemetery was no longer there. It had been razed to build a road, a highway, and then a monument, perhaps. He wasn't sure, but he knew that the cemetery had been paved over. I found it curious that he knew that.

At the hotel that first morning, we met our driver, Vilodin, who was to be with us throughout the trip. He was a retired military fire truck driver, a man who knew his way around. His wife, he told us, was a major in the army. Silvia had arranged for his services and for all the guides. Yuri, who had come with Vilodin, was the tour guide for Kiev. He was a college teacher, and proud of his city. Although he wasn't Jewish, he knew that we were, and tried to provide a Jewish slant to the tour. He organized the route and offered commentary at each place we stopped.

Yuri told us about the architecture of Kiev, which, like many Eastern European cities, is a study in contrasts, of old and new, a mix of styles that reflect the dramatic changes and upheavals in Ukrainian history. There is an overwhelming presence of religious iconography, the golden domes of Kiev peering over scarred buildings and traffic jams and urban renewal of the 21st century city. The juxtapositions are jarring: the stark Soviet buildings next to Victorian mansions, next to Ferrari dealerships and international hotels. The upscale shops alongside the old world markets; and the overcrowded streets leading off open squares with their enormous Soviet and Ukrainian monuments.

The monument commemorating Boghan Khmelnytsky stands in the city's central square between the oldest building in Kiev, the 11th century Cathedral of St. Sophia and the 18th century Church of St. Andrew. Both buildings are architectural tributes to the Slavic found-

ing of the city—known as Kievan Rus. Khmelnytsky's monument cel-
ebrates the 17th century Cossack leader as heroic warrior in full rega-
lia, astride his rearing stallion—the horse and rider are set imperially,
upon a massive stone pedestal.

Yuri explained that the original plan for the monument, in the late
1880's, called for three figures—a Pole, a Jew, and a Catholic priest—
to be vanquished under the hoofs of the horse, but a wiser voice prevailed when the monument was installed, and there are no trampled
figures under the stallion's hoofs. Another controversy arose about the
placement of the horse's rear end—and the statue was positioned to
make certain that the horse's tail did not fly in the face of St. Sophia's
Cathedral.

In the Russia of the 19th century, Khmelnytsky was hailed as national hero of all Russia, unifying Ukraine and Russia. Now, in the 21st
century, Khmelnytsky is re-positioned as national hero of the Republic
of Ukraine. The brutal history of the pogroms of the 17th century is
virtually erased, as is most evidence of the Jewish world of the following centuries. There are few markers of what was once a thriving Jewish life in the city in the years before the Second World War.

In the late 1800's through the mid 1900's, the Jewish middle class
of professionals and merchants, doctors, lawyers, artists and writers,
civic leaders and philanthropists made their mark. More than a quarter
million Jews lived in Kiev before the Second World War, more than
12% of the population. Sholom Aleichem, Isaac Babel, Osip Mandel-
stam, Ilya Erenburg, Golda Meir, all lived in Kiev. Yuri pointed out
the great houses that once belonged to the Jewish "sugar beet kings."

Most of the Jewish population fled before the Nazi invasion, but
those who remained were killed. In the post-war era, a Jewish culture
again surfaced, only to be squelched by a virulent anti-Semitism, and
mass emigration of Jews to Israel. Now there are a few vestiges of that
life: a plaque on Meir's house, a statue of Sholom Aleichem, a restored
Great Synagogue. The building was nearly destroyed by the Nazis dur-

ing the Second World War, then used as a puppet theatre during the Soviet era, and reconstructed by the ultra-orthodox Chabad, as the Central Synagogue. It is now serving as synagogue and Jewish community center, particularly for the elderly Jews of the city.

In the Old City, another synagogue was being restored, and a yeshiva built. There were two other synagogues, an Israeli Cultural Center and a Jewish theatre. Yuri told us that there are once again Jewish merchants on the street near the synagogue in the Old City. He also told us that there were now ten Jews in the Ukrainian Parliament, out of 450 members, a sign of a renewed Jewish life.

It was raining hard, but it was a national holiday, so the streets we learned were relatively empty. Now we were driving to Babi Yar, the site of one of the largest massacres carried out by the Nazis in the Holocaust of the Second World War. We knew some of the history: it had been brought to international attention in 1961 by Yevgeny Yevtushenko's poem, "Babi Yar." In fact, my father had read the poem when it was first published, and he hoped that it was the beginning of a change in Soviet policy that would allow truths to be told about what had happened to the Jews and others in Russia during the Holocaust.

We knew that it had taken another decade before a monument of any kind was built near the killing fields that became known as Babi Yar. Now we were trying to connect what we knew with what we were seeing. The rain made it more difficult. In the middle of a grassy field, we saw a massive black granite monument of writhing figures on top of a stone pedestal. A deep ditch surrounded the monument.

The site was situated between two boulevards next to an old Ukrainian cemetery, which was still being cared for. In passing, Yuri told us that the Soviet monument stands on ground that had once been the old Jewish cemetery. The monument is dedicated to the "Citizens of Kiev and prisoners of war." There was no mention of Jews, until a plaque in Yiddish was added to the monument in the 1980's.[*]

This was not the actual site of the *Babi Yar* massacre, he told us. *Babi Yar*, which literally means "grandmother's ravine," refers to the deep chasms nearby where the killings actually took place. The ravines were several hundred yards away from the site of the Soviet monument near the two boulevards. We left the Soviet monument, and Vilodin drove us down a long narrow asphalt road, past an old stone building that Yuri told us had also been part of the old Jewish cemetery. All the ground here had been part of the Jewish cemetery, he thought, and the road looked as it might have been part of the cemetery, too.

At the end of the road, we stopped near the Jewish memorial, a large stone Menorah that had been erected through a joint effort of Jewish and Ukrainian groups, and sponsored by the new Ukrainian republic in 1991. It is a marble monument, with eight steps leading up to the menorah. The ravines are behind the monument, hidden by dense woodland. There are paths leading down to the ravine. The whole area is a park, with stone walkways and benches and playgrounds.

Behind the park is the site of the massacre, the gravesite for 100,000 people, mostly Jews, who were thrown into the ravines, dead or alive, child or adult, during the Russian Holocaust. More than 70% of the quarter million Jews of Kiev fled before the occupation, but on the eve of Yom Kippur, September 29, 1941, approximately 34,000 of those who remained were murdered at Babi Yar. Mostly, they were the elderly, the ill, or children. The others, another 70-80,000 were killed in the days following. Their bodies were buried—or burned—in the ravines, here in what is said to be the largest killing field of the Second World War.

It was raining so hard that we stayed in the van, but Yuri removed his hat, pressed it to his chest, and recited Yevtushenko's poem,[**] first in Russian and then in English. He also knew it in Hebrew, he said. I

---

[*]   Gruber, R.E. (2007). *Jewish heritage travel: A guide to Eastern Europe.* Washington, D.C.: National Geographic Society.

[**] Yevtushenko, Y. (1962). "Babi Yar." *Selected poetry.* London, UK: Penguin.

told Yuri that I had heard Yevtushenko, himself, reading the poem to students at the college where I taught.

Today, I am as old
As the entire Jewish race itself
I am Anna Frank. . .
How little one can see or even sense. . .
I'm every old man executed here
As I am every child murdered here. . .

It was impossible to see, yet alone make sense out of what we were being shown. We hadn't seen the spot where the killings took place. The burial places are still hidden. The ravines were somewhere in the woods behind the menorah. The Soviet monument was dedicated to Soviet citizens killed in the Nazi occupation, and there was a ditch dug there to resemble Babi Yar. The monument was built on the grounds of a Jewish cemetery. We could see what looked to be old tombstones along the asphalt road we traveled to get to the Menorah. If we had followed the paths in the woods, we would have found the remnants of the ravines. But we left without doing so.

We were drawn back to Babi Yar after our journey to the shtetl, to try again to make sense of what we had seen. We went back to the location of the Soviet monument and to the adjacent Ukrainian cemetery, still intact, and saw the site of the Nazi labor camp for Soviet prisoners. The prisoners had been forced to burn the bodies of the dead at Babi Yar and rebury them in the ravine. The sight, apparently, had been ghastly. Now there was a gas station built close to the spot of the prisoner camp. We tried to piece together the parameters of the old Jewish cemetery, but there were no signs or markers here.[*]

I am certain, though, that my father knew what had happened here. He knew that in these places on the outskirts of the city, under

---

[*] Bartow, O. (2007). *Vanishing traces of Jewish Galicia in present-day Ukraine.* Princeton, NY: Princeton University Press.

the paved roads, the boulevards, the gas station, and the Soviet monument are the remains of the old Jewish cemeteries. I knew, though, that somewhere here at this place in 1912, my father's sister Yeta was buried here. I am here a century later, in June 2011.

I say a prayer for her: *May her soul rest in peace.* And I say a prayer for all the souls who were buried and reburied here, whose resting places were disturbed, and for those who died without a proper burial. *May all their souls rest in peace.* I leave a stone on the steps of the Menorah monument, one that I had brought with me from where my father is buried in America.

There was another monument that Silvia insisted we find before we left. It is a Holocaust memorial to the thousands of children who were thrown into the pits at Babi Yar in September of 1941. The monument of *Broken Toys* is a bronze statue of three child-size figures: A little-girl doll, her arms outstretched, her eyes are closed. A boy-doll, without clothes, his neck broken, is leaning against the girl-doll's back. And a puppet clown, his body slumped over, leans against her side. The monument was erected in 2001. There were no signs or plaques here in this urban park. There were people sitting on benches, children running around in the playground. Before we left, we stopped at the Menorah once more and saw that someone had placed half a dozen blue-ribboned wreaths with white flowers next to the monument.

Podolia

"Ukraine had been seared into Jewish historical memory as synonymous with 'suffering.'"
    —Ben G. Frank, *A Travel guide to Jewish Russia and Ukraine*[*]

For us Americans, the metaphor of the *West* conjures up images of a vast unsettled territory—a land, with its own language, culture and laws. That image was in my mind as we were driving southwest from

---

[*]   Frank, B. (2000). *A travel guide to Jewish Russia and Ukraine*. Gretna, LA: Pelican.

Kiev. We were leaving the city behind, and entering a country that is less traveled. It was called Podolia in Tsarist Russia. That is where my father said he was from, Podolia *gubernia* (district).

Now it is in the province (*oblast*) of Khmelnitsky. The area is bordered by Romania and Moldavia to the southwest, Poland, Slovakia, and Hungary on the west, Belarus on the northwest, and Russia on the east and northeast. This Ukraine has been a new republic only since 1991. The country is still charting its course. It is a land with a troubled history, where wars were fought over these abundant fertile plains.

This is the black earth of Ukraine, the breadbasket of the world, and this June, it is *green as green could be*, as my father always said. My husband, who spent his youth in the American mid-West, said that the green rolling fields and immense sky, the woodlands and streams, deeply cut rivers and glacial outcroppings reminded him of the wide open spaces of Iowa. For me, the place felt ominous. There were unfenced cows and horses grazing on the grassy verges of the road, as well as goats and chickens. The hedge rows were high, and every few feet there were people, Roma perhaps, sitting near their vans, selling mushrooms or flowers or what looked like jars of preserves.

Many of the houses that we saw along the road, typical sand-colored flat-roofed Eastern European dwellings, looked to be in a state of disrepair. They were fronted by unpainted wooden fences and ornamental gates. In the distance you could see larger settlements of buildings, with the eggshell blue domes of Orthodox churches dotting the skyline. The two-lane roads were in poor condition and rough riding, full of hazardous potholes. Speeding cars swerved in and out of the lanes, overtaking the horses and carriages that were traveling on the same roads. It was a long, uneasy ride from Kiev to the west.

Vilodin knew the roads well. He took great care of us and his new eight-passenger Volkswagen van. It was white, and immaculate. Every time we stopped, he would take out a cloth to clean the spots on the exterior, and once when we tracked a bit of mud into the car, he pulled out a bottle of water to clean it up. He drove fast, even along the back roads, and he knew what alternate routes to take to move us safely from place to place.

But it felt like an alien world, and I wasn't sure that it had been a good idea to come. There was a psychic border that I'd never wanted to cross. Although I am a student of history and literature, there is a limit to what I want to know. I have no illusions about what we, humans, are capable of doing to each other. And now that we were here, I wasn't sure that I wanted to know what had actually happened to the people who lived and died here, particularly to those who remained in Ukraine and were killed in the Holocaust of the Second World War. I also knew that what happened here is largely uncharted—or erased—given the suppression and rewriting of history still taking place in Eastern Europe, particularly in Ukraine. But we were heading into the territory, and I didn't close my eyes.

Letichev

It took much of that first day driving to get to the far western regions of Podolia, which had been a crossroads between the Polish-Lithuanian, Russian, and Ottoman Empires. Until the end of the life of the shtetl, it was home to more Jews than any place in the world. Jews lived mostly in the shtetlach. There were the *shtetl* (singular) and the *shtetlach* (plural), my father instructed, the villages and towns of the Pale of Settlement, where Jews were permitted to live. What defined the shtetl was that the majority of the population in these villages and towns were Jews. This was also the home of Chassidim, the 18th century Jewish spiritual movement that took root in Eastern Europe, particularly in Podolia.

We came first to Letichev, one of the "mother towns" for the surrounding smaller shtetlach. At the turn of the last century, there were more than 4000 Jews in the town, more than half its population. It had been the second largest town in Podolia and a thriving center of Jewish life until the Second World War. It was a market town, built at the confluence of the Southern Buh and Volk Rivers.

My grandmother Chana came frequently to Letichev to buy goods for her store. My father's closest aunt, Bessie (Joseph's sister), a widow, raised her four daughters in Letichev, and my father frequently walked the nine miles southeast from Novokonstantinov to visit his aunt and cousins. At one point, it was thought that my father would marry one of Bessie's daughters. She wrote to him herself to put forward the idea, but he never wrote back, he told me one day. She, apparently, stayed in Podolia.

It was the town where my father's oldest brother, Paci and his bride Hutka had been married. The wedding was one of my father's first memories. He remembered the sequins on his Grandmother Sur's dress and the wedding entourage walking down to the river to toss coins into the water for good luck. The town was also where Beila's husband was born and raised. The town had been destroyed in the 1648 Khmelnitsky pogroms and badly damaged in the pogroms of 1881-1882 and 1905-1907. Its network of hiding places under the houses saved many of the Jews of Novokonstantinov who fled there during the pogroms of 1919-1920.

My father remembered the family going to Letichev during that terrible year of 1919, when his father and brother were killed. But Yosel refused to go. He stayed in the house, presumably by himself. Duved's oldest child, Anita, born in 1919, remembered how everybody ran to hide in her parents' basement in their house in Novokonstantinov. When Silvia interviewed her about her early years in Novokonstantinov, Anita said that for her whole life, she could still hear the sounds of the pounding horses' hoofs on the earth above her head.

At the bus station in town, Anna, our guide was waiting for us, and with her, a friend, Zina. They are both natives of the area. Zina, who lives in Letichev, is a high school history teacher, and Anna, who lives some 80 miles west in Dunaivtsi, is a high school English teacher. Zina knew very little English, so Anna became the translator for all of us for the days that we were together. Later, I would find out that they lived in Ukraine because their grandfathers had been exiled to Uzbekistan for political asylum before the Second World War, and when they returned, they found their worlds shattered. Their grandparents stayed and tried to build a life in the area.

Both Anna and Zina were in their 50's. Zina's two children lived in Israel. Her son was married to an Ethiopian Jew. Anna's children were in Ukraine. Zina was the Jewish "community leader" for Letichev, and they both served as guides to the area as members of an organization of local Jewish communities. In their own communities, there was a handful of Jews. In most communities, there were none. As this wasn't her home territory, Anna invited Zina to be our local guide. Silvia had told Anna that I wanted to explore the area around my father's shtetl, Novokonstantinov, and we asked her to lay out the route. As I was to find out during the next few days, we often didn't know where we were being taken until we arrived there.

Now that Anna and Zina were in the van with us, Vilodin drove to the outskirts of town, past a number of farms and onto a dirt road. He stopped at an isolated spot that seemed to be private property belonging to the farm nearby. There were no signs anywhere, and no one was around. There were a few cows grazing in the pasture. Vilodin parked the van, and we got out and walked along the dirt road. The road stopped at what looked to be a thicket of bushes and trees. We pushed aside the low hanging branches to make our way. There was no path, and it was threatening rain now. We climbed a hill and came to an iron gate hanging from its hinges, half open. We came shortly to a clearing in the woods, overgrown with high grasses and wildflowers.

In the center was a grassy hill that reminded me of a pre-historic *tell*—a hill that appeared to be man-made. On top of the hill was a

Letichev memorial, mass grave site

stone monument. As we got closer, we could see that there were two parts to the monument: a six-step pedestal supporting a narrow stone column, perhaps 30 feet high. There was a Star of David etched into an iron plaque at the top. It was a beautiful spot, high on a hill over-looking Letichev. Wildflowers were growing between the steps, and the top of the monument was badly weathered—perhaps vandalized. It looked as if there had been an obelisk at the top of the monument, but it was gone, and perhaps someone had also tried to chip away at the stone and rub out the letters on the plaque.

No one, it seems, had been tending the site for a long time, but someone had been here not too long ago: there was a little white flower pot with artificial pink flowers and two glass *yahrzeit* jars, which had held candles to be lighted on the anniversary of the death of the deceased.

It was, in fact, a burial mound, a mass grave for the approximately 7200 Jews who were killed by the Nazis in the early 1940's. We stood in the clearing by the monument while Zina told us about Letichev, and Anna translated. The story of the mass killing at Letichev is part of a larger history of the Second World War, as it was carried out in what the historian Timothy Snyder[*] calls, "the bloodlands," the vast area of Eastern Europe that includes Poland, Ukraine, Belarus, Russia, and the Baltic states. These lands were subject to horrific policies carried out under both Hitler and Stalin, at first, as collaborators and then enemies.

Ukraine was critical to Hitler's plan for world-domination, which included his Final Solution. The black earth of Ukraine would grow the crops to feed the world, and there would be fuel enough for his empire. The land, itself, once removed of the Jews and the entire Slavic population, would give Germany ample room to grow its Aryan culture. Tactically, Letichev was important because it was situated on an important east-west road from Proskurov (west) to Vinnytsia (east). Hitler's own headquarters in Ukraine was in Vinnytsia, where the Nazis engaged special killing units, the *Einsatzgruppen*, to carry out the mass killings of the Jews.

To build the road, the Nazis needed laborers, and the Jews could serve this purpose. The able men would work on the highway. The women would help, domestically, to feed and clothe the workers. In the first stage of the Letichev mass killings in fall 1941, the Nazis rounded up the Jews from three neighboring shtetlach, including my father's shtetl, Novokonstantinov, and marched them to a newly constructed ghetto (in the Letichev 'castle') to take part in building the road. In September 1942, 3000 Jews were brought to ravines on the outskirts of Letichev and shot. Their bodies were thrown into the ravines. In November 1942, another 4000 Jews from the surrounding counties, including Vinnytsia, were brought to the ravine and killed. In November 1943, with the road now complete, the final group—200 slave laborers—was killed.

---

[*]   Snyder, T. (2010). *Bloodlands: Europe between Hitler and Stalin*. New York, NY: Basic Books.
    See, also, Desbois, P. (2008). *The Holocaust by bullets: A priest's journey to uncover the truth behind the murder of 1.5 million Jews*. New York, NY: Macmillan.
    See also Desbois web site: http://www.yahadinunum.org/?lang=en and the Jewish Gen Holocaust database: www.jewishgen.org/
    Brandon, R. and Lower, W. (Eds.) (2008). *The Shoah in Ukraine: History, testimony, memorialization*. Bloomington, IN: Indiana University Press.

In Chapin and Weinstock's remarkable two-volume Yiskor (memorial) book, *The Road from Letichev: The History and Culture of a Forgotten Jewish Community in Eastern Europe,* Pinkhas Michelson, who was born in Letichev, describes what his father-in-law, Froim Burshteyn, saw at the site when he returned after the war:

> In Zaletevichka (outskirts of Letichev), there are deep ravines. In these ravines the Jews were shot. When Froim came to this place, he was horrified. There were three big graves. In one grave there were children, in another women, and another the men. The graves were poorly covered with earth. Bones stuck out from the graves. After a strong rain, the Ukrainians said to Froim Burshteyn, 'The bones of the Jews swim in the puddles.' (Vol. 2, 782-283)

Froim Burshteyn worked with an engineer and the town authorities to have the bones properly buried. He raised money from people all over the U.S.S.R., who had relatives in Letichev, to build the monument. It took years for the work to be completed.

This was the first of the Nazi killing fields in western Ukraine that we were to see during the next few days. There are more than 3000 mass killing sites in Ukraine, each site tailored by the Nazis, often helped by local collaborators, to fit the needs of the particular time and place. I did not know that here in Letichev were also the dead of my father's shtetl. I don't think he knew. What he told me towards the end of his life, when I asked what had happened to the shtetl, was that the Jews were taken to the woods outside the town where they dug their own graves. That is why there was no need to return. *There was nothing there*, he said.

At that time, before the end of the Soviet Union, there was little knowledge in the west or anywhere else about the extent of the mass killings of the Jews of Ukraine—or of the details of each site. I know that my father no longer had hope that any of the people had been saved. And as a wise storyteller, who knows what his audience can

---

* Chapin, D. A and Weinstock, B. (2000). *The Road from Letichev: The history and culture of a forgotten Jewish community in Eastern Europe.* Lincoln, NE: Writer's Showcase.

bear, he always protected me when I was young from what he knew about the way the lives of the people of the shtetlach ended.

On the hill—this unnatural earth-mound—overlooking the blue domes of the churches of Letichev were the Jews of Letichiv and Novokonstantinov and other towns nearby. My father's Aunt Bessie, if she had been alive, and her daughters, their families were here; my cousin Rosita's mother's parents, who did not escape to the United States or Argentina, as her grandfather and my father did. And all the others. All here. I took several stones that I had brought with me from the new world and laid them on the pedestal of the monument next to the white pot with the artificial flowers, and said the prayer for the dead. May all their souls rest in peace.

We left the site and drove through the town, with Zina pointing out the traces of the Jewish life that was gone. We passed the remnants of the Letichev castle, a reminder of the Lithuanian lords who had owned Letichev in the 14ᵗʰ century. This had been the site of the ghetto, the holding pen for the Jews, all of whom were to be killed. The town is filled with such historic markers of its conquerors: Poles and Lithuanians, Tatars, Russians, Ukrainians, Austrians, Germans. There is virtually nothing left of the Jews. They were never the conquerors. We passed a ramshackle boarded up old wooden building that looked beyond repair. That was one of the old synagogues of the town.

We saw a dairy, a construction plant, a brick works, and the large two-story Soviet-style cement-block school, for both elementary and secondary students in the one building. Zina graduated from this high school in 1972, and now she teaches history in the same school. She took us into the building, where we met one of her colleagues, another history teacher, who was working that day on the local history project that Zina was also a part of. In one of the classrooms, they are creating a museum of local history, collecting artifacts to display. The focus seems to be on the rise and fall of the Soviet regime and the birth of the Ukrainian republic in 1991, and the museum will serve not only the school but also the community.

From Letichev, we headed towards Khmelnick, where we were staying for the night, but stopped first in Medzibohh, which had been the largest town in Podolia at the turn of the last century. We stopped at the grave of Rabbi Yisrael ben Eliezer, known as the *Baal Shem Tov*, often translated as "Master of the Good Name." He was the 18th century Jewish teacher who is credited with the founding of the spiritual movement, *Chassidism*, the word *Chassidic* meaning piousness, devotion, or loving-kindness. The grave has become a shrine, a place of study, and a sanctuary for Chassidic Jews all over the world. The 18th century synagogue has been reconstructed, and a study center built.

It was now late in the afternoon when we decided to stop at Medzibohz Castle, a 16th century Polish fortress that overlooks the confluence of the Southern Buh and Buzhok rivers and the town itself. The castle houses a newly renovated Orthodox church, and, most significantly, the Famine Museum memorializing the victims of the Soviets' determination to starve the local populations who resisted collectivization in the early 1930's. The famine is known as the *Holodomoror*, that is, death or killing by starvation.* The museum, which is housed within the walls of the castle, displays artifacts, photographs, personal effects, maps, and farm equipment, representing the victims' lives, as well as their chilling deaths. Although the numbers killed in Holodomoror are still in dispute in the annals of Soviet and Ukrainian history, Snyder claims that at least five million people were killed by the famine. At the museum, they spoke of ten million killed.

The last stop for the day was Khmelnick, where we stayed for the night. My father came here as a boy. His father's sister Zilpa lived here with her four sons and daughter. She, like her sister Bessie, was a widow, and had a hard time making ends meet, my father said. His first cousin, Yosel, left for American when my father did, but he came

---

* Reid, A. (1997). *Borderland: A journey through the history of Ukraine.* Boulder, CO: Westview Press.

back to Khmelnick after he exhausted all avenues of getting his papers. Meyer had tried to help him, and so did Mendel Peril in Pennsylvania, but to no avail. 3000 Jews are buried in the mass grave in Khmelnick. Perhaps Zilpa is here. Perhaps her son Yosel who didn't get to America is here with his family. It was late afternoon, and Silvia wanted us to save our journey to Novokonstantinov until the start of the next day.

Eleven

The Place Itself

"There is a house that is no more a house. . . . And in a town that is no more a town."
—Robert Frost, *'Directive**

We started early in the morning from Khmelnick, the five of us: Vilodin, Phil, Silvia, Anna, and myself. We stopped in Letichev to pick up Zina and Vladimir, who had been a librarian in the school in Novokonstantinov. He was invited along because he was doing research on local military history, and Zina thought he would be helpful. There were seven of us in the white van. Vladimir sat in front with Vilodin.

We rode along the old road from Letichev to Novokonstantinov, the road that my father had walked countless times. It had been bypassed by the main road, the Nazi highway. The old road was empty. There was no traffic for the nine miles from Letichev to Novokonstantinov. As soon as we started out, the military historian turned around in his seat to face the five of us in the back and began to describe the tactics of the Germans in the Second World War. He spoke rapidly in

---

* Frost, R. (1995). "Directive." *Robert Frost: The collected poems, prose, and plays.* Poirer, R. and Richardson, M. New York, NY: The Library of America.

Russian for several minutes and then paused to allow Anna to translate. He explained how the Nazis had planned the invasion of Ukraine in 1941, and how the new road had been built by slave labor. It was clear that he had given the lecture before, and I understood that he was organizing the details of the military history, so that they could be included in the local archives. I told him that we were also interested in the history of the First World War. He looked confused, but went on with his lecture.

When we got close to the turn off for Novokonstantinov, he pointed out the Soviet bunker on the grassy verge. It was a relic of the "Stalin line," the extensive system of fortifications constructed by the Soviets beginning in the 1920's to protect the Soviet Union against attacks from the west. The defense system consisted of concrete bunkers such as this one at Novokonstantinov, and others like it along the road to Letichev. The Soviets were in the process of constructing a new line farther west when the Nazis attacked in 1941, but the old bunkers were never demolished.

We stopped along the side of the road to take a photo of the sign for Novokonstantinov. We passed a boarded-up cement building that had been used to house the Jews of the town in 1942. We learned later that the whole Jewish section of town had been hedged in to form the ghetto.

We arrived first at the school, where Anna had arranged for us to meet with Ivan, the director of the school, who was waiting for us. He and his assistant director, Nadia, came out to welcome us. Nadia was a teacher of history in the school. As in Letichev, the building had been constructed during the Soviet era, and in need of repair. We were led through the main school to another building undergoing renovation, and into a space where the teachers are creating a local museum—just as in Letichev. There were poster boards on the floor, with old photos and newspaper clippings, and on the wall there were photos of partisans from 1919, and a sign detailing safety regulations

Novokonstantinov road sign

during the Soviet era. There were unsorted photos in piles. At the rear of the room were displays of traditional Ukrainian peasant costumes and housewares. We learned that there were now about 600 people in Novokonstantinov, and 120 school children from Novokonstantinov and several surrounding villages.

We began to talk with Ivan and Nadia about why we had come. Silvia showed Ivan the family photos that she had brought with her. He asked if he could make photocopies for the museum. They had

Site of marketplace and synagogue in Novokonstantinov

not met any Jews who had lived in the town or who knew about the town. There is no recorded history of the Jews in the town prior to the Second World War, they told us, and they wanted to know what we could tell them about the Jewish life of the town. They told us that they would take us to where the Jewish neighborhood had been.

We walked to a large open area behind the school, where the ground was uneven under our feet. This was presumably where the marketplace had been, which my father had said was the center of the shtetl. There had been 100 stores in the marketplace, he said, but there was nothing left. We were told that the entire area had been burned and then razed by the Nazis, and what were left were these broken mounds of earth. There were bricks and foundation stones lying in a heap. And we felt jagged pieces of rock and stone as we walked through the area. Ivan pointed to a place farther behind us and said that had been where the main synagogue had been. But this area was overgrown with bushes and trees. There was an old barn, and nearby a beautiful horse, with a chestnut mane, feeding on the grass. I thought of Mutlick, my grandfather's horse, and the night my father and his friends stole him away for a ride in the snow.

The whole area behind the school and where the synagogue had been was a huge expanse, perhaps six or seven acres. There was a section that was used for farming, but most of the area behind the school was essentially an archeological dig. This is where the marketplace and the Jewish houses had been. The grasses here were kept low, so that you could walk over the area. The school children used this section for sports. But we saw no play equipment. It was an empty space. Where the synagogue had been—the land was turned over to the elements, it seemed. Perhaps the villagers who remained saw it as a sacred place. Or perhaps they were too few and too poor to rebuild.

We talked freely with Ivan and Nadia. Nadia told us that a Jewish neighbor had helped her grandmother by giving her a job in the distillery in the town during the famine. They themselves know virtually nothing of these Jewish neighbors, except what the old people told them.

They wanted to know what I knew. I told them that my father loved the town, and that he wanted me to know about the place that he had come from a long time ago, at the beginning of the last century, so he told me stories, and he drew me a little map. I took out a copy of the map for them to see. Ivan wanted to look at it closely, and to make a copy for the museum. He took us back to his office, a small room with a wooden desk and bookshelves. The desk was covered in a gold cloth, and there we lay my father's rough drawing, as if it were a treasure map. I also took out the pages of my manuscript where my father described their house. I began to read a few lines from the manuscript, the section about the house and its location. My father had indicated two rows of houses on his map—across from the marketplace—where his house had been. Nadia gestured towards the window. She closed her eyes for a moment, and put her hand on her head and said that she knew where it was, where those houses used to be.

Ivan requested a copy of the map—and I gave him the copy that I had brought with me. They also wanted a copy of my pages, and I said that I would send them the edited manuscript. They also wanted to have my father's story on the tape that I told them about. I promised to send him something for the museum. Nadia told us again that her grandmother survived through the kindness of the Jewish neighbors. Ivan encouraged Nadia to go with us to explore the town.

We headed across the street, with Nadia as our guide, and we entered a wooded area, so dense that we had to push the branches out of the way to get through, but we could see that there was still a narrow road under our feet, through the middle of the undergrowth. Nadia pushed away the leaves on one side of the path, and we saw what was undoubtedly the foundation of a house among the brush, and she told us that there were two rows of houses, with the road running down the middle, just as my father had said.

Our house was at the far end according to his map, farthest away from the street where the marketplace had been, the last in a row on our right, beyond which were open pastures. We walked to the end of the path, and there, still, were open pastures, just as my father's map had shown. The rubble of this last house was still there, buried under the trees and brush. We pushed back the brush to find the foundation stones and pieces of old pottery. I felt sure that this was the place where the house had stood, just as my father described it.

Here in this spot was my father's childhood—and his sense of the world. The road right outside the house that turned into a little creek in the rain, where he splashed about, sailing his home-made boats, running barefoot through the open fields to the river he loved. Phil and I searched about in the rubble and gathered a few more pieces of pottery—archeologists, now, putting together pieces of the past. I brought the shards home with me. The fields are still there, part of a carefully manufactured collective farm. The peasant farmers are gone, though. On the main road to Letichev, we saw a caravan of enormous bright red threshers, the machines being driven to field after field to collect the rich Ukrainian wheat. The Ukrainians who loved and worked this land also fared poorly in the past century.

I have no illusion that any of the shards of pottery we found come from my grandmother's house—my family was all gone by the time the buildings were burned in the early 1940's. But in 1905, when the town census was taken, there were probably seven children living in the house. Eleven were born in this house, between 1882 and 1903, when my father was born. Twenty years for growing children. Three little ones had died early on. Chana and Joseph were there, and the children. Paci, Yeta, Meilach, Meyer, Duved, Moishe, and my father, Moyte, were all there. Beila was living with her maternal grandmother in another village. Grandfather Labe Perel lived with the family part of the year. Sofia, who lived with the family for thirty years, was there, too.

The house was alive with all the comings and goings of daily life— the sweet smells of ordinary life—my grandmother's rye bread on Mondays, and the challah every Friday, her chicken soup and dumplings, the roasted chicken and potatoes, the samovar always hot. I see the kitchen over there, with a window open to the back garden. It is spring, and the lilacs are in bloom. There was enough of everything in the family: food, enough to share with the poor, clothing, shelter, and the benevolence that I know instilled in my father his love for life, and the hopefulness that he held onto throughout his life.

This is the house, too, where my grandfather and his son were murdered. Joseph and Pesach, and the place, two decades later, that was plundered and leveled. There has been no building here on my father's road—or in the empty green space that was the marketplace. The market town is gone. There is no town center, just the old roads through the green spaces. What once was a thriving market town, a shtetl, with a hundred shops, churches and synagogues, is gone. There are now two little grocery stores and a café. The synagogues are gone. The Roman Catholic Church is abandoned. The Russian Orthodox Church stands, freshly painted, the traditional eggshell blue. The garden wall is still there, as my father described it. The only building standing in the old shtetl is the Soviet-style school building. Next time we come—if we do—I would like to see the children.

To the River

Nadia agreed to continue on with us to the river and the old Jewish cemetery. There were the seven of us: Vilodin, Nadia, Anna and Zina, Phil, Silvia, and me. We drove along the main road of the town, past the two churches, and the post office with the traces of old Soviet signs still visible, past the turn to the ford in the river, and up a narrow wooded path. Vilodin stopped the car at the end of the path, and we all got out. We again found ourselves pushing aside branches and brush to make a path, and now stepping over jagged rocks into a clearing.

Remains of Novokonstantinov Jewish cemetery and fallen tombstones

What opened before us was a quiet scene, in soft muted colors, like a 19th century Corot river painting—the rocky bend in the river, a sliver of green island in the middle of the water, a steep grassy hillside, rising thirty or forty feet above the river, with cliffs dropping off at the river bend, and a wide open sky. There is a settlement of houses on the other side, and none on this side, just this clearing. What we see appears to be a natural amphitheater, a grassy, rock-strewn slope overlooking the river. There is green everywhere this early summer.

When I asked my father if it was a hilly land, he said that there was only one hill in the town, and actually it wasn't really a hill, it was an *elevation.* His words had guided Silvia to this place last year. She knew how to find it again. Nadia knew too where it was.

That day in June, we saw that there were half a dozen cows grazing among the wildflowers and rocks. This grassy *elevation* is their pasture. The birds were in abundance—white storks swooping over the rocks, snowy egrets, swallows, a flock of black birds, I couldn't tell what they were. And the rocks appeared to be limestone outcroppings, until you looked closely. If you didn't know, you might not realize that these were gravestones, that here are the graves of the Jewish cemetery.

The graves were in various states of decay, and it was hard to tell what belonged to what. The graves had been a two-part structure: a long stone burial vault attached to a tombstone. But none of the graves were intact, the vaults and tombstones have been separated, some vaults toppled over by the weather or erosion or vandalism, some were lying at the foot of the hill on the riverbank, and some were so badly worn that they were hardly recognizable as cut stone. But a number of tombstones still had visible Hebrew markings, and Silvia walked off by herself to examine and photograph the Hebrew letters. The others wandered off together or alone. Phil was off by himself with his cameras. I sat down on the slope overlooking the river and tried to make sense out of what I was seeing.

It was one of those moments of dislocation that many of us feel when the present and the past are merged, fused together, and you're not sure where you are, or whose eyes are doing the seeing. I was seeing these fragments of the past, with both my father's eyes and my own. Somewhere here on this hill are the graves of people who shaped my father's life—and mine, too.

There are no Jews in the town now. The villagers we talked with told us that in their lifetimes none have returned, and they hadn't heard from their elders that any Jews at all had ever returned. The Nazis had exiled the town's Jews to the ghetto in Letichev in 1941, eventually killing and burying them together in the mass grave that we had seen the day before. In my father's town, before the First World War, there had been 3000 Jews, and this cemetery, presumably, had been the resting place for many of them and their forebears. Now, seventy years later, the field remains, this *elevation* that my father described, a rocky incline formed by the river cutting through the glacial sediment. It had somehow survived, an accident of topography. This sliver of rocky cliff is unfit for growing crops. But it is good for the cows to pasture—these strange creatures, an old breed, with long faces reminiscent of a Dutch Renaissance painting. They are the guardians of the site now, grazing this tangle of grasses and wildflowers, watching over the graves.

Silvia found a decipherable tombstone, with a date, 1899. It could be one of Chana's children. The baby Shmuel/Samuel could be buried here. It could be that the other members of the family are all buried near this spot. Chana and Joseph and five of their eleven children. Their son, Paci, the eldest, killed in 1919, along with his father. Both were buried at night, my father told me, because it was too dangerous to do so in daylight. And their infant daughter, Brucha, and two small sons, Shmuel, and William, along with their daughter Yeta's child, Malka, who died at three in 1915, in the typhoid epidemic that killed Chana.

Remains of Jewish cemetery at Novokonstantinov

Their son, Meilach, is no doubt somewhere outside the boundary of the cemetery. Suicides make one an outcast—their bodies are not permitted within the cemetery itself, but Meilach's remains are no doubt close by. I say prayers for the souls of each of my family, the three generations, my grandparents, Chana and Joseph, and their five children, Paci, Brucha, Meilach, Schmuel, and William, and granddaughter, Malka. Malka, born in 1912, is the first of my generation. I say all the names. My grandparents and aunts and uncles and cousin. *May all their souls rest in peace.* Before we leave, I place several stones I'd brought with me from my father's gravesite in America on some of the tombs. I had left stones at Babi Yar in Kiev, the place where the old cemetery had been, where my father's sister Yeta was probably buried, and at the mass grave in Letichev, where the Jews of Novokonstantinov were buried, and now here in Novokonstantinov where my grandparents and their children lie. I have yet to find Beila, my father's sister, who remained in Ukraine, and perished during the Second World War. But I will try.

Hebrew inscription on tombstone at Jewish cemetery

We walked to the van and Vilodin drove back down the hill and made the turn to the ford in the river. This overgrown path had been the main road to the riverbank—and the crossing at the ford. And, again, the scene opened up before us. The water was even with the bank. It was clear, and sparkling in the sun, and filled with rocks, large flat rocks that you could easily step on, along the riverbank, or in some places, you could cross the river, rock by rock. It's a quiet place now, made it seems for solace and tranquility, where you can bring a lunch or book or sketchpad or a fishing rod. It is one of those visions of water and rock and sky, a secluded spot, hidden by the trees. When my father was growing up, this river was a center of their lives, where the townspeople got their water and did daily chores. They bathed and washed clothes, and fished, they swam—and the children played games. Nadia told us that the river is a still a popular spot for swimming and fishing.

The tranquility of the place in this 21ˢᵗ century masks its history: this was a vital thoroughfare for centuries, an east-west passageway for commerce, for locals and travelers, and for successive waves of troops, nationalists and revolutionaries, conquerors and defenders, who made their way back and forth across the river, right at the ford where we were standing. This crossing is what made Novokonstantinov a thriving market town. My father remembered the thousands of cavalry who rode through the town during the wars and revolution that he lived through as a boy. They came up the road to town from this spot. Some of them garrisoned at his house.

It was this place of my father's childhood, where the land is still green as green could be, and the river still vital, that fed his memories—and perhaps his determination to survive. Perhaps he learned here that he wasn't land-locked, that there were rivers and oceans to cross to get you to the other side. This was a place where he learned how to swim and fish and steal off by himself, and where he escaped to, whenever he could, in the years after his mother died. Even though there was sorrow in the house early in his life, the early memories of this place sustained and nurtured him, feeding his creative impulses, infusing his huge spirit with joyfulness and hope. I know that he needed—and most likely chose—to be close to rivers in the places he settled, in the Allegheny hills, New York or Buenos Aires, our town in southwestern Pennsylvania, or by his gravesite in Valhalla. And I think that, despite all that happened to this place, he would still feel these gifts, offered up by the rocks and trees and water and air, as blessings.

Zina's House

Vilodin drove us back into town, and we parked by the two churches, the abandoned Polish Catholic Church and the Russian Orthodox. Nadia offered to look for the priest, so that we could talk with him.

But he wasn't home. During the time we were standing in the street, an elderly woman approached Vilodin. She wanted to know who we were and what we were doing in the town. She was small, not quite five feet tall, and elfin. She was wearing a blue and green flowered housedress under a black bomber jacket. She had a purple scarf—a babushka—tied under her chin.

Anna and Nadia told her that we were interested in the Jewish history of the town, that my father was born and lived here until 1920, that Silvia's father was born in the town in 1922, that Silvia and I are cousins, my father and her grandfather, brothers. We were looking for where they might have lived. We told her that Silvia lived in Budapest, and I lived in New York.

The woman was now talking animatedly to Vilodin, Nadia, Zina, and Anna. Her name, also, was Zina, and she lived in the town all her life. She was 83, born in 1928. We were now standing in the street in the village, a crowd: Vilodin, Phil, Anna, Nadia, Silvia, myself, and the two Zina's, the older Zina and the younger Zina. Eight of us. Zina of Novokonstantinov told us that her father bought her house from a Jewish family, the Greenbergs, in 1936, and that she would like to show us the deed to her house.

All the while, Silvia had been looking for her Grandmother Dina's house: she knew that it was a two-story house with a balcony overlooking the street. There was an old house being renovated that she thought might be her grandmother's house. She said that her great grandfather had a library in the house. Her grandmother's parents had stayed behind and were killed by the Nazis.

Zina took us to her house, which was tucked away around the corner, and her daughter was there waiting for her. She was visiting her mother from Kiev, where she works. She apparently came often to see her mother, who does not want to leave her house in Novokonstantinov. We walked down a narrow path to the old house, passing through a long front garden that looked as if had been a fruit orchard.

There was a little chicken coop, with half a dozen baby chicks running about, cheeping. The coop was partially covered by a bright orange plastic sheet.

Zina's daughter asked if we wanted to see the cellar and went into the house for a flashlight—a torch—to light our way. The door was open to the cellar, and we stooped over, walked down a few steps, and entered a large dark hollow space. The earth was damp and cold under our feet, and smelled of animals. Here was where they used to keep the cows and other animals during the cold winters, Zina's daughter told us. The space felt familiar. This was like the dugout under the house that my father described to me, where the family could hide during a pogrom.

In the meantime, Zina had gone to find the deed to the house. She quickly returned and produced a hand-written sheet of lined paper, bearing an official stamp. The single page was yellowed and stained. It looked as if it has been handled repeatedly. This was the deed to the house that had been in her family for the past 75 years.

Zina invited us to come into the house, and we followed her up the steps. There were half a dozen cement steps leading up to an enclosed porch, with an oilcloth attached to the back wall. There was a little table covered with a plastic flowered tablecloth and two chairs. This could have been used as a *sukkah*, the shelter where the family eats during the holiday of Sukkot in the fall, after the High Holy Days. My father said there was one at the front of his house that also served as a sun porch. By Jewish law, the *sukkah* must have at least two and a half walls covered with a material that won't blow away—such as roll up blinds (at my father's house), canvas, or the oilcloth in the back of Zina's porch that I was looking at. Perhaps Zina's family had adapted the idea of the oilcloth that the Greenbergs had left on their house in 1936.

We followed Zina into the hallway and entered the front room on the right, which was the kitchen. It was a large spacious square room,

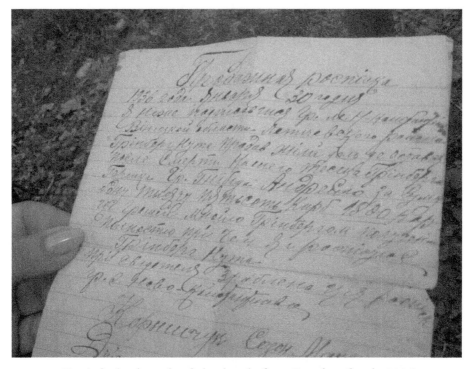

Zina's deed to house her father bought from Greenberg family, 1936

with high ceilings and a large front window looking out at the garden. There were flowered cottage curtains on the window. There was a long wooden table against the window, with freshly made bread and salads, a plate of potatoes and hard-boiled eggs. Some soup, it smelled like fresh vegetable soup, was in a pot. There were two chairs in front of the table. To our left, were four varying sized pans of water arranged on a counter next to a dry sink. There was a little pile of potato peels on the counter. There was no running water in the house. On the back wall was a wooden bench. There were a pillow and blanket neatly folded on it. Next to the bench was a wood-burning stove, which was apparently used for both cooking and heating. There was a kettle on the stove. There was a window behind, on this outer wall. But it had been boarded up to make room for the stove.

It was a big room, filled with light, even though there was only one big window, and a single light bulb hanging on a wire in the center of the ceiling. There was a floor lamp near the table. The room was large enough, I imagine, to do the cooking for a big family. The bench against the wall adjacent to the window could be used as a bed, as in my father's house. Someone else could sleep on two chairs put together. Several children could have slept in this room—the kitchen. And guests, too. It was large enough for a floor-to-ceiling stove that had a sleeping loft on top, as there had been in my father's house. Here was where Sofia slept. My father didn't sleep on the bench here in the kitchen. He slept on the wooden *couch* (what he called it) in front of the wall where there had been another stove, the *riba*, the inner-wall wood-burning stove that warmed both the kitchen and the room behind. In my father's house, this was the dining room, and the kitchen was behind it.

I asked if there had been a large floor-to-ceiling stove in the room, and Zina's daughter pointed out the plaster marks on the wall across from the window. Yes, her daughter said, there had been a stove against that wall, but it had been taken out.

The house was identical to the one my father described—it was not the house itself, we had seen where his house had been, I am sure of that, the last house in the row of houses that opened to the pasture, on the other side of the marketplace. That house had been destroyed. This house was closer to the marketplace. But the structure of the house was exactly the same. There were four rooms in Zina's house, we were told. We did not see the other rooms, only peeked into the room on our left, which was the living room. This house now included a hallway between the four rooms, so the rooms were smaller than they would have been in my father's house. The old stove had been replaced.

My father's house had the long garden at the front, with vegetables and fruit trees and lilacs. That house had a cellar—the dugout. My father's house also had a garden and stable in the back. We didn't see what was behind the house. There was the porch of Zina's house, the *sukkah*, leading into a center hallway, with two symmetrical halves on either side. The house was built of logs—Phil and Vilodin were examining the construction. The stucco was peeling off the corner of the house over the dugout, and the old logs were exposed. There was stucco on top of logs, dried mud holding them together, just as my father described it.

When was the house built, I wanted to know. Around 1880, Zina's daughter said. My grandfather's house was probably built around the same time. He moved to Novokonstantinov at that time. His first child was born in 1883. The house was new when he and Chana moved in. I have a sense now of where things were—and see, as if in a dream, my grandmother making tea on the samovar, a *glass tea*, as my father always said, as she sat at the table for a moment in the afternoon to take a break. My father, the youngest, sat with her, and Moishe, too. Sofia. Maybe, a neighbor walked in. In those twenty years, when the children were growing, and all seemed good in the world—before Meilach died, before Yeta, before the world changed.

Silvia wasn't sure that the front porch had been a *sukkah*, because it had an actual roof, but Zina's daughter said that they'd added it on themselves. Silvia also mentioned her grandmother's house, and Zina told us about the two-story house next to hers, and walked us through her garden and thicket of trees and brush to the foundation of a house, right next to her house. This was the house next door. Zina remembered it as a two-story house with a balcony. That house was gone. It was burned and razed by the Nazis. Zina's house was not.

We stood in front of the house talking. We talked about the Jews. The old woman knew what happened to the Jews. She knew what happened to the town. "*We watched them being marched out of town. Some handed their babies to their neighbors. They were good people*," she said, softly. "*They were our neighbors. One of them was my teacher.*" She was weeping now. Her daughter cried, too. We were all weeping. She did not want to leave the town, her daughter said, even though her children live in the cities. They tried to see her often, but they were worried about her, here alone. But it is her town, and she wants to stay. I wonder if the past is ever present: if she keeps seeing the absences, the neighbors who were taken away, her friends, her teacher.

Her surname translated, Anna tells us, means "of the borders." Zina of the Borders. She invited us into her home. How could she have known that I had been looking for this house? The way the house was built, the gardens, the shape of the rooms, the *sukkah*, and the dugout—my father had prepared me to find the house. Perhaps, she had been waiting for years to tell us, strangers from a land far away, that her house was spared because her father bought the house legitimately, legally, from people who left the town. The house next door was gone, all the houses around her were gone. But hers was saved.

It wasn't because her father had done something wrong. Her father had the deed to the house that he showed to the officials who determined which houses would be destroyed, and which would be saved. She had the deed in a safe place, in case she ever needed it again. Who knows? My father kept his papers handy, in case he ever needed them again. We thanked Zina of the Borders, and her daughter. Her daughter was still weeping. She hugged me, and we thanked her and her mother, again, and embraced them both.

We drove back to the school, to take Nadia back. She gave us her time—and her knowledge. She spent most of the morning with us. Without her, we would not have found the two rows of houses near the pasture. We wouldn't have known to look for the foundations of the houses. We wouldn't have been standing in the street when Zina came by. My understanding is that she was born and raised in the area—perhaps in Novokonstantinov. She was born twenty or more years after the Second World War, and I gather that she was leading the effort to create the town museum, to give the children a sense of their history. I would like to know more about what they are doing—and see the museum when it is finished. Perhaps they will record Zina and others who remember the past.

When we arrived back at the school, Nadia got out of the car. Ivan was there waiting for us, and with him was the mayor of the town. He greeted us warmly, and shook our hands. I think that Ivan had invited him to drive from another village to meet us. We were told that he serves as the mayor of a consortium of four neighboring villages, with the one school located in Novokonstantinov. I asked if they had met other Jewish visitors, and he said, no, we are the first they had met.

When we were in Ivan's office, he had shown us the hand-written text of a history of the town. He showed us the passage stating that the 1905 census lists 5000 residents of the town, 3000 of them were Jews. My father's entire family was probably listed on the 1905 census. My father would have been listed as a year or two years old, depending upon when his birth was registered. Ivan had prepared a copy of the hand-written history that was being written for the museum for the town—perhaps by Nadia, Vladimir, and others—to give to us.

Ivan, Nadia, and the mayor of the town all said goodbye to us, and asked us to come back, that we were welcome anytime. I told them again that my father loved this village, that it had been a good place for him to grow up, and that he always talked about Novokonstantinov and the people of the town. We thanked them all, Ivan, Nadia, and the mayor for all their help.

We thanked our guide from Letichev, too—the younger Zina, who had been with us now for two days. I hadn't realized that she was leaving now. She had been the local guide who knew this part of the world. She guided us to the mass grave in Letichev, and to the town, itself, and she made arrangements with Vladimir, the historian, to come with us in the morning, and also arranged for us to meet Ivan of the school.

And then we were ready to leave Novokonstantinov. We didn't see all there was to see, but I think that was all we were capable of seeing. It was as if all the pieces had fallen into place, that we had followed my father's map to the past, and while there may have been more to see of the present, the two shops in town, the café, the post office, a new section of town, down the road near the uranium mine, we had seen what we were prepared to see. We saw that in the old section of town, there is nothing left, and except for the school, there is nothing built in the spaces where the shtetl was, where the Jews lived. I kept wondering what had prevented them from building anything new on this land.

I wondered what those we met in the town thought about what we told them. In June 2011, we were talking with Nadia, Ivan, Zina of the Borders, and the mayor about events that happened long ago. My father left the town some ninety years ago. I must have appeared like a ghost speaking of a past impossibly long gone. The First World War began 100 years ago, the first of many disasters of the 20th Century that wrought havoc on the town. The history they are trying to recover is not this history, but they wanted to know about the Jews and how they had lived in the shtetl.

Vladimir, the historian, was writing about the *bloodlands*, where more blood was shed than in most parts of the world put together during the Second World War. Ukraine finally won its independence, just 20 years ago. This little town, by the time the Nazis invaded it, had already been lost through the pogroms of the First World War, the Russian Revolution, the Ukrainian Nationalist purges, the Soviet domination through the collectivization of the farms and the manufactured famine, Stalin's purges, and then the Second World War, and all that happened then and afterwards. This time from the past was a blip on the radar screen, a moment when my father slipped through the cracks of history. As did three of his brothers, including Silvia's grandfather, who all grew up in Novokonstantinov.

Khmelnitsky

For the last part of our journey, I hoped to find the site where my father's sister, Beila, and her family might be buried. Beila, the only one of my father's siblings who stayed in Ukraine, had married David Takser and moved to Dunaivtsi in 1918. Beila had taken my father in for half a year in 1920, before he left for America, and he never forgot her. Throughout the years before the Second World War, he wrote to her from America, regularly wired her money, and tried to convince her and her husband and three daughters to come to America, but they stayed on in western Ukraine, near the Polish border. My father never forgave himself for not finding a way for her to get out of Europe, and at the very end of his life, his mind wandering back to Novokonstantinov, he was calling her name.

Dunaivtsi is about about 70 miles west of Novokonstantinov. It was our good fortune that Anna, our guide, knew the area. She was born and raised in Dunaivtsi, and lived there with her husband and children. Her husband's sister was the Jewish Community Leader of Dunaivtsi. We planned to explore the area with Anna, then take her home, and then return to Kiev. We were staying in Khmelnitsky overnight, and Silvia wanted to arrive there early enough in the afternoon to get to the Jewish Museum and the public archives. Khmelnitsky, formerly Proskurov, is a large city, with a population now of 300,000. The city was renamed Khmelnitsky in 1954, despite the terrible Proskurov pogrom in the 17th century, that had been led by Bogdan Khmelnitsky.

Proskurov is where my father stopped on his way to Beila's house in Dunaivtsi. I was retracing his steps west toward Proskurov and Kamanetz-Podolsky. From Beila's, my father intended to slip over the border into Poland, and from there, find his way to America. In 1920, that was still possible, but the family prevailed upon him to stay. Beila probably wanted to keep her youngest brother close to her. All these turns of fate—who knows what might have happened had he tried to escape from Dunaivtsi? Meilach, who was Beila's twin, wanted to go to America in 1908, but Chana begged him not to go—stopped him from going, my father said, and Meilach took his own life. Meilach was about the same age as my father was in 1920. Perhaps my father reminded Beila of her twin brother. Who knows? But she and her husband begged him not to leave.

In the city of Khmelnitsky, Vilodin dropped us off at a large Soviet-era building, where Silvia had been directed to search for archives about her Grandmother Dina's family. Her grandmother had always told her that her family was descended from Bal Shem Tov, and she wanted to see what documents she could find. The grey building we entered was suddenly another world: it was an austere institutional construction, with wide steps leading to a bare lobby. There were no signs or directory or people around. Finally, someone appeared and sent us to the second floor.

Phil and I were directed to two wooden chairs off in a corridor, where we sat and waited and watched the men and women coming and going, in and out of the offices, carrying papers. They all seemed to be young and dressed in high-style Eastern European fashion. We could hear them speaking Ukrainian through the closed doors. Silvia's inquiry led her nowhere. It seems that the Department of Official Documents stored archives for Silvia's grandmother's family for the year 1894, none before, none afterwards.

Late afternoon, we found the Jewish Museum and Cultural Center in Khmelnitsky. The building, probably 19th century, looks as if it had been a baronial house, with dark oak doorways, window frames, floors, and staircase. On the first floor were several large rooms. One was used as a museum of daily furnishings and artifacts from Jews who lived in the area. There were displays of Sabbath candlesticks and linen tablecloths, phonographs, a sewing machine, and photographs on the walls. Two men were playing chess at a table. There was a room devoted to the history of Israel that was being used for a meeting. Another room was filled with historical documents of Jews of the area, and another was being used as a computer lab.

Upstairs was a pre-K and a Jewish cultural center with children's classes in session. In one, the children were making little beaded flowers. We were introduced to the boys and girls in the pre-K: they were intrigued that we were Americans. One little boy in the classroom was very excited to see us, and he gave us several little clay figures that he had made. Our young guide, Nadia, told us that the boy's father was an Israeli soldier, and that he had recently been killed. He was buried in Israel.

We could have met Nadia in any European city—or in New York. She was a fluent speaker of English, dressed in jeans and a tee shirt. She told us that she had studied Jewish Pedagogies in a university in Moscow, and she was very happy to have her job in the museum. Her cheerfulness was infectious. As we were leaving the second floor, the children in the arts and crafts room came out to the hallway with their teacher to say goodbye. They wanted to give us the little beaded flowers they had made. One little girl, whom I'd noticed before looking at us, gave me her artwork and a hug. I saved the little clay figures and the beaded flowers and placed them on a shelf in my study.

Today had been a long, full day. A lifetime in a day. We began in the morning in Novokonstantinov, and now we were here in what had been Proskurov in my father's day. I remember thinking that I'd probably not sleep that night—and I didn't. I kept thinking of my father, and how his story-map had taken us on this journey. What would he have made of the world that I'd entered? Knowing the historian/storyteller that he was, I feel certain that, if he were here today, he would still be in Novokonstantinov talking to the people we met there—to Ivan and Nadia, to the mayor and the younger Zina, to Anna and Vilodin and Vladmir, the military historian, and the older Zina, to all of them. He would have wanted to talk with Nadia in the Jewish Museum in Khmelnitsky this afternoon. He would have told them stories. And he would have realized that there is a history now being written, and it is in the hands of the teachers—Anna, Zina, Ivan, Nadia in Novokonstantinov, and this Nadia in Khmelnitsky—who want to know about the people who lived here a long time ago.

Dunaivtsi

In the morning, the five of us set off for Kamanetz-Podolsky, where Anna wanted to show us the old Polish castle and the former Jewish quarter. Kamanetz is a city of 100,000 that is listed as a National Historical–Archeological Sanctuary, one of the Seven Wonders of Ukraine and a UNESCO World Heritage Site. There is an impressive 14th century fortress set high on a limestone island, and connected by a bridge across the Smotrych River to the mainland. The Slavic word *kamin* means *stone*, and there are stone outcroppings everywhere, particularly around the old fortress. The castle, with its twelve towers, served various functions through the centuries, and the grounds surrounding it are extensive—as is the history of this city off in the border country of southwestern Ukraine.

Kamanetz[*] had been a strategic victory for the Nazis in their invasion east into Russia in 1941. It was one of the first cities conquered in Western Ukraine, and one of the first of the mass killings sites of the Jews. On August 27 and 29, 1941, an estimated 23,600 Jews were killed, 30% of the population. Many of them were Hungarian Jews seeking refuge here. We stood by the Holocaust Memorial, which was erected in 1998, and read:

> *Let the generations remember our fathers and mothers,*
> *brothers and sisters. The best sons and daughters of our*
> *people—who were murdered on the fifth day of Elul (August 28)*
> *in the year 1941 by the German fascists.*

The old Jewish sector, what once was a thriving Jewish world, one of the cultural triumphs of Eastern Europe, is crumbling. The old cobblestoned streets are largely empty—poor and neglected. The place feels haunted. Any money available for renewal evaporated in the late 1990's. There is a half-finished apartment house, left as is.

---

[*] Kamanetz-Podoloski www.yadvashem.org/untoldstories/database/index.asp?cid. . .

Anna and I walked along together, one of the first times we had to talk. I kept wondering what it is like to be a Jew here now. She told me that her mother lived close by, and that her uncle lived in a flat that we passed in the old city. He was her mother's brother, who had lived in Israel for ten years, and then returned to Ukraine. His children were in Israel, still. He was probably in his 80's. Wandering Jews. There had been a great influx of Russians to Israel in the 1990's—it was clear that some came back, even though they do not see themselves as Ukrainians. They are Jews first, and still Russians, perhaps. We got back in the van, and set out to find where Beila was buried. All I knew from my father was that she and her husband and three daughters had died together.

This was Anna's home territory, and she took us first to the house of her sister-in-law, Tatiana. As the Jewish community leader for Dunaivtsi, Tatiana had the key to the burial site. We had no idea what that meant. Tatiana got into the van with us, and we drove into a rural area and parked alongside the road. We got out of the car and walked along a narrow dirt path, overgrown by brush and trees, and hilly. It was a familiar site now. There were a few workmen sitting alongside the path, eating their lunch, a perfectly ordinary scene, I supposed. I realized that I'd lost sense of what I thought was ordinary or strange. Your perspective on the world changes when you see what we had seen: so, while it was curious that we were walking up a path somewhere and Anna's sister-in-law Tatiana was holding a large T-shaped vault key, I had come to expect anything now.

We came to a clearing at the top of the hill, and before us was a small white stone hut, with a Star of David near the top. Tatiana opened the vault door, and we walked into a small chamber that was filled on three sides with memorial—yahrzeit—candles. The space was no bigger than six feet deep and eight feet wide. Anna began to tell us what happened here at this site.

Holocaust memorial at potassium mine in Dunavitsi

On May 2, 1942, the Jews of the town of Dunaivtsi and the surrounding areas were marched to this place, and thrown, alive, into the
potassium mine, below. Bullets were getting to be expensive, and so a
local engineer suggested that to save money, the Jews be buried alive.
The Jewish men, women, and children were marched to the site and
thrown into the potassium shaft, and the door was sealed shut. The
Nazis then dynamited the entrance, leaving a few local sentries to guard

the door. The people who lived in the houses close by said they could hear the cries of the people trapped in the mine below for weeks on end.

The ways of killing were local. They were ingeniously executed, efficient, and expedient, tailored to fit the needs and economics of the place. Apparently, too, by 1942, there were adverse effects on those in charge of pulling the triggers. Here, the mine entrance was sealed in one swift blast, and the perpetrators, except for a few guards, could walk away.

We stood silently in the small memorial chapel, the four of us women, Silvia, Anna, Tatiana, and I. No one said a word after Anna told us what had happened here. The men, Vilodin and Phil, were standing outside, but they could hear Anna's story.

I left my father's gravesite stones on the ledge that holds the memorial candles. There were many stones here. The Jews from Dunaivtsi in America worked with the remaining Jews in the area to build the antechamber. Before the lock was installed, the site was frequently vandalized. There are about twenty Jews in Dunaivtsi now, Tatiana said, and she is the guardian of the key. Every year there is a memorial service for the Jews who were buried below in the potassium mine. Tatiana told us that they read the names of the dead every May 2. The Jews of the area are gathering names of those who died in the potassium mine seventy years ago. Tatiana and Anna said that they have some 200 names (out of nearly 3000). I asked if I could add Beila's name to the list.

We left the grave and returned to Tatiana's house to say goodbye. She had prepared a lunch for us. She brought out the handwritten list of names of those who were killed in the potassium mine in May 1942. There were exactly 200 names. I added these of my family to the list:

201: Beila Takser
201: David Takser
202: Daughter Takser
203: Daughter Takser
204: Daughter Takser

I don't know the names of Beila and David's daughters. They would have been in their twenties in 1942. Perhaps they were already married, so their husbands may have been with them too, and their babies. One of them, no doubt, was named Chana, after our grandmother. One may have been named Yeta after Beila's sister. I am sorry I don't know their names. I should have asked my father.

We left Anna at the door of her apartment house. She had been a judicious guide, taking us where we needed to go, making connections for us in Letichev and Novokonstantinov, and leaving us to find our own way, emotionally. We began the long trip back to Kiev, and then Budapest, and home. Vilodin drove us to the hotel in Kiev, and we said goodbye and thanked him. He was an expert driver and bodyguard, and while we couldn't speak with him in Ukrainian or English, we felt safe in his hands.

Twelve

Stories to Grow on

It was almost as though he were transported back through the ages on some mental, invisible breath.
    —*The Lost City*, Milton R. Peril[*]

Lost Places

My father's stories transported me back in time to the old world. He gave me a history that made it possible for me to link the present with the past. Ukraine's is a landscape of loss, of lost people, lost places, and lost history. Every place we went, there were mass killing sites among the green fields and river valleys if you knew where to look. Back home, the landscape was suddenly jarring. I kept seeing old gravesites and cemeteries in places I'd not seen before. Some I'd often passed but never noticed. Some were hidden away in parking lots in the town where I live. Another was on the grounds of the town high school, another on the old Revolutionary road near our house. Some I only imagined were there.

---

[*]   Peril, M.R. (May, 1934). 'The lost city," in *Amazing Stories*, Vol. 9, No.1.

I needed time to re-order my thoughts and wished that I could have told my father about where I'd been, but I knew that I wouldn't have told him everything. I took the small rocks that I'd pulled from the earth at the cemetery in Novokonstantinov and placed them on the headstone of my father's grave in New York.

That summer, my husband and I headed to the mountains in southwestern Pennsylvania. The timing was good. I had a reunion with three childhood friends from the town, and it felt right to be going back. Phil was going to explore nearby battlefields of the French and Indian War while we girls relaxed together at the old hotel and wandered about the mountains we all loved. I could talk freely with my friends about the trip to Ukraine and also share memories of growing up in the coal-mining town. We went to the falls at Ohiopyle and waded in the river under the iron bridge near the center of the little town, and climbed over the rocks. I remembered the times I was there with my father and Uncle Meyer, and I was now seeing the water and rocks through their eyes. I was here and at the river in Novokonstantinov at the same time.

Our last stop before heading back to New York was the Jewish cemetery in Hopwood where my father's brother Meyer is buried. Hopwood, known as the site of the opening battle of the French and Indian War, is spread out along Route 40 on the way south into the Alleghenies and on into West Virginia and the South. The town is a stretch of historic stone buildings, antique shops, and restaurants, and hardly a metropolis. But it is easy to get lost in the mountains.

At the first traffic light in the town center, we turned right off the main road, drove past a block of houses, and at the foot of the mountains, we found ourselves at an iron gate, with the sign for the Jewish cemetery. I'd been to Uncle Meyer's grave many times and knew exactly where the gravesite was, but this place looked different. I didn't think there were two Jewish cemeteries in Hopwood. So we began to look at the names on the graves, one by one, row by row.

Then Phil called out that he had found several graves with the name, *Peril*. Our spelling is *Pearl*. The family in Argentina is *Perel*. This was *Peril*. He had found a grouping of six graves, all belonging to my father's cousins: Mendel and Olta Peril and their children. I didn't know they were buried here. I had known the family primarily from my father's stories. They were the first of the family to come to the mountains in Pennsylvania from Ukraine. Mendel was my father's first cousin, and here in the Jewish cemetery in Hopwood were Mendel, his wife and their four children:

Mendel Peril, 1875—1930
Olta Peril, 1875—1958
Isadore Peril, 1909 - 1976
William Peril, 1900—1947
Milton Peril, 1908—1952
Anne Peril Stern, 1910—1987

We left without finding Uncle Meyer's grave. When I spoke to my cousin Karen, who is Uncle Meyer's granddaughter, she reminded me that in most small towns there were *always* two Jewish cemeteries. The Perils are buried in the Orthodox cemetery, and Uncle Meyer is buried in the Reform cemetery.

The Perils had provided a haven for my father when he returned from Buenos Aires in the 1930's. Their house in Uniontown was a place where young Jewish singles congregated. Anna—*Anna-la*, as my father called her—had been a favorite of my father, and she was on the lookout for a girl for him. They wanted to keep him in Pennsylvania for good. She did well when she found my mother, who had come to Uniontown during the depression to make a living. At that time, Izzy was married, as was Willy. And Milton, like Anna, was at home with their mother, Olta.

Milton was something of a legend, according to my father: As a young boy, he had polio and was confined to a wheel chair as an adult, but he found a way to live a full life. He played the piano—and drew a crowd of young people to socialize in the Peril living room. My father joined his cousins, Milton, Willy, Izzy, and Anna, in the Peril *salon* in their house in Uniontown.

Milton was also a science fiction writer. Several of his stories were published in the well-known pulp magazine of the time, *Amazing Stories.* His first story, "*The Dynasty of the Blue-Black Rays*" was published in 1930. A three-part series entitled "*The Lost City*" appeared in 1934. Part 1 was featured on the cover of the May 1934 issue. Another story, "*The Radium Dome,*" came out in 1937. My father had copies of all of Milton's stories.[*]

I wanted to know more about Milton, but there was no one in that branch of the family left to talk to. I wondered if he was known to science fiction writers. An Internet search on Milton R. Peril brought interesting results. In the standard reference, *The Early Years and Science Fiction,* the editors note that they could find no information about Milton R. Peril and, therefore, assumed that his name was a pseudonym for another writer. I was able to talk with one of the editors, who promised to make the correction. He said that he was pleased to rescue Milton from oblivion, at least in his publication.

Milton's story, "The Lost City" played on a popular theme in science fiction literature of the time, the discovery of lost worlds. In his story, a British archeologist uncovers a hidden passageway in the great Sphinx of Giza that takes him to the lost city of Atlantis. He finds a civilization under siege, a war between two races: the blonde, blue-eyed "Whites," who see themselves as a master race, are engaged in a war against the evil "Blacks." The archeologist escapes, but no one believes what he has seen. We assume that the city was destroyed. Milton, who

---

[*]   Bleiler. E.F. and Bleiler, R. (1991). *Science fiction, the early years: A full description of more than 3,000 science-fiction stories from earliest times to the appearance of the genre magazines in 1930.* Kent: OH: Kent State University Press.

died in 1952, at the age of 44, lived long enough to see his plot enacted in the horrors of the Second World War.

There were layers of history coming together for me, lost cities, lost family, getting lost in the mountains and finding a way out, going to the old country and coming back. In the "old" country, I am often aware that the ground I walk on is layered by civilizations that have come before. In Egypt, Italy, Greece, Turkey, Israel, the British Isles, the layers are, for the most part, a staple of tourism, although there are still, today, the inevitable new discoveries of the *old*, often of pre-history. But in the old country that we had just returned from, in the far reaches of western Ukraine, the lost civilization of the past century is still alive: the empty spaces that have not been rebuilt, the broken ground that you step on at every turn, you sense the dead under your feet. The mass killing sites have not yet been covered over or completely erased. The scarred earth has not been smoothed over by our shopping malls, parking lots, or new apartment buildings, as they are in the great urban centers.

Here in the new world, we have our layers of history, too. These are the same southwestern Pennsylvania hills that the young George Washington saw with its still thriving indigenous civilization. We've lost sight of the people who came before, except in the names of the rivers and towns: Monongahela, Youghiogheny, Ohio—and in several battlefields of the French and Indian War in these mountains. But the world of the American Indians here in the east is mostly gone.

There have also been profound changes to the world that my family and I knew in these parts of the country. McKeesport, a thriving city of the industrial age when my mother was growing up, and the river towns of southwestern Pennsylvania where I grew up, are broken, many of them derelict. The whole region has been stripped of the coalmines, the mills and factories of the industrial age. The steel mills are all but shut down. Many are rotting shells along the rivers, some turned into industrial museums.

McKeesport's Market Street is filled with empty stores—as are the other towns along the river. My grandparents' house was still standing the last time I was there, and the Jewish cemetery is still being cared for. My grandfather's synagogue, built in 1886, is still open, but the Jewish populations in the towns have all but vanished, and there are weeds growing between the cobblestones of the streets of McKeesport and the other towns nearby.

In our area, the coal mining villages are like ghost towns. Brownsville, where we went to synagogue, was bought up by a developer years ago to build a casino, but his plans have been snarled in litigation for decades, and most of the stores on Market Street are boarded up. Our synagogue was recently turned into a combination computer repair shop and gun store. There is a café in the basement where we held Sunday school classes. But the beautiful red brick building, O'Have Israel, is still standing. The ark and the stained glass windows are still there, as is the Star of David carved in the stone façade on the front of the building.

The whole area, though, is hurting. The population has declined dramatically. Conservationists are trying to hold off against *fracking*, shorthand for "hydraulic fracturing" or drilling for oil and gas that is done close to the surface of the earth.

Drive along the roads overlooking the green hills and valleys of southwestern Pennsylvania, and you'll see the hydraulic pumps and the pipelines throughout the area. We saw them last year when we went back to Fredericktown. The run-off from fracking poisons the rivers and streams, as well as the atmosphere.

Our town was showing a few signs of renewal. There is a river organization attempting to turn the area into a tourist destination. We found a restaurant—a boating club –on the Monongahela, and it was busy. There was a new meat market on Route 88, but Front Street in our town was pretty sad. The Methodist church is open once a month or so, on Sundays, and there is a traveling minister who officiates at weddings and funerals. There are a few stores open—a sporting goods store, a laundromat, a used furniture store, the old hotel, and the Italian restaurant along the river. The furniture store where my father worked, across the street from our house, burned down in the 1980's, and there's a big vacant lot with a bandstand in the middle of the space where the big store had been.

Our house is still there—the fence is gone, but the house looks neat and trim. It is freshly painted white, with a new porch. And now that the lot across the street is vacant, there is a river view from the front porch. The river and the hills around are still magical. We took what turned out to be a last ride across the river on our ferry, the *Frederick*. In 2014, the county governments closed the ferry, even though there was a steady ridership from Fredericktown to the new state penitentiary and the small town across the river. There was a newspaper article in the local paper about the 100 people who came down to the ferry to take a final ride. The closest bridge is eight miles east, near Brownsville, on Route 40. The road bypasses Brownsville. It used to go through the center of town.

Nothing stays the same. Those of us who come from these small towns of southwestern Pennsylvania have been watching the changes come over the past 50 years. Jennifer Haigh, a contemporary novelist, writes of the coal mining regions of central Pennsylvania in her stories. In the last part of the novel, *Baker Towers*,[*] she describes the decline: "The town wore away like a bar of soap. Each year, smaller and less distinct, the letters of its name fading. The thing it had been became harder to discern." The Mennonite or Amish farmers, whom she calls the *plain,* are driving their horses and carts into the emptying area and reclaiming the mining fields. "Each year the scarred places shrank a little. The green spread slowly, planted and harvested by the plain. The green covered, but did not fill the dark world that lay beneath" (334).

---

[*]　Haigh, J. (2005). *Baker Towers*. New York, NY: Harper Collins Publisher.

Going Meta: On Story, History, and Memory

"Whenever she had to warn us about life, my mother told stories like this one, a story to grow up on."
—*The Woman Warrior,* Maxine Hong Kingston[*]

The dark world that lay beneath the fields in southwestern Pennsylvania is nothing, though, like the dark world that lay beneath the earth in Ukraine or in Eastern Europe, where every place you go, the land is scarred and haunted by the dead who lie below in the mass killings fields of the last century. Those horrors cannot be erased or ignored.

My father's life and his stories are about his refusal to live in the dark world. His stories speak to the green that survives and to a past that illuminates and helps us make sense of our lives. In Jonathan Safran Foer's novel, *Everything is Illuminated,* a grandson journeys to Ukraine to find the lost world of his grandfather in the old country. He has little to go on, but through his adventures, the world of the past comes to life, primarily through those who know what happened to the Jews of his grandfather's village.[**] I am more fortunate. When I was a child, I had my father's stories to illuminate the past, and I had the opportunity to follow his stories to the world he had come from.

As I grew older, I began to wonder what he was doing when he was telling the stories *every day and every day* of his life. I began to listen to how he was telling the stories. In his later life, when he was retired and had more time to think about what had happened to him, he would occasionally "go meta," offering insights about what he was doing in the telling. "*I'm still living it through, living it over and over again . . . When you were living it, you couldn't stop and think about it. You can't do that.*"

His "stories" were a mélange of genres. He told stories of the family, where his people came from, how they got from here to there, how they lived and died, how they were connected to each other, always

---

[*]   Kingston, M.H. (1976). *The woman warrior: Memoirs of a girlhood among ghosts.* New York, NY: Knopf.

[**]   Foer, J. S. (2002). *Everything is illuminated.* New York, NY: Houghton Mifflin.

within the context of history and culture. There were re-presentations of actual events that had happened to him or others: his brother's suicide, his sister's death, his father's and brother's murders, his escape across the frozen river, the journey to America, his early years as an immigrant. He told a few fables or parables. He told of historical events: the Khmelnitsky massacres of the 17th century, the pogroms of 1905, the Bolshevik Revolution of 1917. In many ways, his story was a *Bildungsroman*—the story of a young man's coming of age—his education in a shtetl in Eastern Europe before the First World War, his journey that took him out into the wider world, and his transformation from Motye to Martin, from immigrant to American citizen.

It was always story in context. He was a storyteller-historian. He stayed close to the action, rarely embellished or exaggerated or talked about his feelings. He was committed to describing what happened, as he could bear witness or provide the facts, as he gleaned them from books, newspaper accounts, and others who had been there.

There were folkloric elements in what he told. As in many folk and fairy tales, he was the youngest son who left home on his own and took a dangerous journey. All he had with him were the clothes on his back and, in his case, a duck, rye bread, and his *tefillin*. There was danger on the road at every turn. "Fate" inexorably intervened: the stranger suddenly appearing with a message in a notebook, or telling him to run across the frozen river, or bringing him food when he lay dying of hunger fever. He described, in detail, the culture of the shtetl—what people did for a living, what they did to survive. He was focused on life, the games children played, the natural landscape, the roads, the river, the house, the garden, the wintery evenings, the Saturday night walks down the main street, the stores in the marketplace. He kept the world of the past alive– even though the place itself had been destroyed.

The metaphor of *green* was an essential part of his vocabulary. It was a land that was *green as green could be*. And the world was inescapably *beautiful.* Those were his tropes. He always turned to the light. His dog was caught and killed by the dogcatcher, but she left her pup behind. So it was with the family. Of the eleven children, four survived.

He was a lover of stories. He was the one who read me bedtime stories when I was a child: Mother Goose, the Golden Books, fairy tales. Why did *he* read me the stories, I asked, and not my mother? His answer was simply, *I loved those little stories.* There was something reassuring about reading stories where all worked out in the end. His own stories, I am convinced, were acts of resistance. They enacted the belief that stories could make a difference in how we see the world and how history is told. Such acts of resistance—*reading, walking, talking, stories*—are seen by the French historian, Michel de Certeau, as *tactics* that subvert those systems of power that limit where and how we can live and breathe. De Certeau dedicates *The Practice of Everyday Life* to the "ordinary man."* My father's story is a history through the eyes of an ordinary man.

Although nearly all was destroyed in the world my father came from, his stories secured the memories of the daily life. These cultural artifacts needed to be preserved in his memory as normative. Despite it all, he was saying, there was all this *life.* He told stories in order to live—in order so that he could live and so that the stories would live on. *So here's the story* was a refrain. *Words* enabled him to control the story, both the plot and the meaning.

He kept returning to the river—in the shtetl, in the southwestern Pennsylvania mountains he loved, in the town where he settled, in the place he chose to be buried. He was keenly aware of maps, of where places were and how you got from one place to another. Space, distance, place—they were all prominent in his memories. There was such appreciation of life: he was a connoisseur of simply opening the door and breathing the air. He loved to walk. He loved to stop and talk

---

*   de Certeau, M. (1984). *The practice of everyday life.* (Rendall, S., Trans.). Berkeley, CA: University of California Press.

with people. He loved to read and listen to music. His was an animating spirit. He took delight in the commonplace—he needed no trimmings on his food or his clothing or the house where he lived. There was beauty in the ordinary.

Perhaps all this was part of the tradition in which he was raised: I asked if the family was religious. Yes, it was the way things were. The letters to Meyer tell us that God was ever present: *God will help everything to pass, and we will be together, with God's help, and able to tell of everything, with great joy. May God help that we see each other very soon.* You lived your life by a Jewish calendar of holidays and festivals. You kept the Sabbath holy. You followed the traditions. The family wasn't part of a sect, as I understand it. But he grew up, I am certain, inheriting what Heschel talks of as a sense of *wonder,* a profound appreciation of being alive no matter where you were.

Of course, the modern world was calling, too. There were increasing summons to leave, for Palestine, for America, Brazil, Argentina. There were calls to join the rising socialist movements. I know that's where his sympathies lay, but he also knew what had happened to the promises of the revolution. He was no romantic about politics. He was a believer in the possibilities of democracy and emancipation.

We have glimpses of what he felt when he was living inside the event, as participant, in the letters he wrote to his brother during the year that he spent as a refugee in Romania. There we hear the despair in his voice. *Dear Brother, I beg you, do not change your mind about me. I don't know what to do or where I should go. I don't have any home, and I don't know now who to turn to, besides you.* But I never heard that despair in the stories he was telling.

Stories, as Freud says, are *belated;* they are constructed after events have occurred. The German term is *Nachtraaglichkeit,* meaning *afterwards.* He was using the term to discuss the ways one reported, retrospectively, on traumatic events in childhood. So it was with my father. Telling the stories throughout his life enabled him to create and hold onto a narrative that signified both the facts of his survival and the necessity of resilience. The French neurologist and psychiatrist, Boris Cyrulnik, in his work on narrative as anti-dote to trauma, describes narrative as a "way of working on meaning":

> The event is metamorphosed into a narrative by doing two things: we externalize events and situate them in time. . . .For those whose souls have been damaged, narration is an act that gives them the feeling that 'the events seem to be re-counting themselves'. Memories of images pass through their minds, and they are framed by words that comment on them, explain them, hesitate and then begin to describe the scene by using other expressions. Thanks to this work, the narrative can slowly extract the event from the self. The narrative exposition locates signifi-cant events that found their way into our minds in the past. [*]

Cyrulnik, himself the child of Holocaust victims, talks of "Resil-ience as Anti-Destiny." Narrative is represented as a "fog-lamp" that leads us through to the past, so that "the past, the absent and the dead can return to the present world of the living, to the stage of the text, and the image, to the stage of the representation. It is only then that they can become re-presentations."[**]

Cyrulnik talks of the storyteller as always needing a listener, even if it is an imaginary one. So it was with my father. I watched him time and time again capturing a listener. I'd bring friends to meet him in his later life, and he would ensnare them in his web. Three hours, four hours later, they would still be sitting there, listening. The stories were not rehearsed; each telling was different. He was telling some version for them at that moment. He was the master storyteller—performing the text, making it live.[***]

---

[*]   Cyrulnik, B. (2007). *Talking of love on the edge of a precipice.* (Macey, D., Trans.). New York, NY: Penguin.

[**]   Cyrulnik, 27.

[***]   Cyrulnik, B. (2009). Resilience. How damaged children can survive and recover. (Macey, D., Trans.) London, UK: Penguin.

He did it with his granddaughters (my children), when he got them after school to just sit and listen to him. My daughter, Lauren,* tells it like this:

> When I came to visit after school every week, my grandfather cooked dinner for me. Chicken soup. Chicken stew. Dessert. So much food that I could hardly move by the time I was finished. But he sat over me and urged me to eat—*essen.* And then he fed me stories.
>
> Every week after I ate, he would sit down in his armchair, settle in, and then say, 'Did you hear the story of the_____?' Mostly I hadn't heard the story of the day. Sometimes I had, but I knew that he was going to tell me a richer, more detailed version, usually adding something I hadn't heard before. His stories always had something cheerful about them, no matter how sad or desperate the landscape he painted. He often went back to the night he saw his father and brother get killed, but it wasn't scary to me. He made me feel that it was a place far, far away and that it was long gone. I knew that he felt safe here, that he was comfortable in his chair, grateful for having plenty of food every single day, and able to take a deep breath and bring what he called "the old country" back to life.
>
> He always talked about the *cheder*, where the boys learned Torah and had a community. He painted a world that had everything a child could want: family, a sense of wonder, a town with markets and horses and a river, with women preparing for Shabbat, keeping warm despite the cold winters.

Transgenerational trauma is the term used to describe the effects of trauma on the children and grandchildren of survivors. Some brain researchers are studying what they see as a genetic inheritance of extreme trauma on organisms.** I have no doubt that my father's stories shaped my own life and affected those of my children. Literary critic Frank Kermode echoes much of what the psychiatrists and neurologists say about the functions of narrative for those who had suffered trauma:

> Men, like poets, rush 'into the middest,' in medias res, when they are born; they also die in mediis rebus, and to make sense of their span they need fictive concords with origins and ends, such as give meaning to lives and to poems.***

---

*   Lauren Azuolay is a pediatric physical therapist, living in New York.

**   Kellerman, N. www.yadvashem.org/yv/en/education/. . . /kellermann.pdf

***   Kermode, F. (1967). *The sense of an ending: Studies in the theory of fiction*. London, UK: Oxford University Press, 7.

These "fictive concords" are narratives that we construct with beginnings and endings, so as to make sense of our lives—and our stories. My father said at times that some of the stories were *all mixed up. There were all kinds of mingled up stories.* Things happened that seemed incongruous. His job as the teller of the family's stories was to connect the parts, unite pieces of the family puzzle, construct coherent narratives to commemorate those who were lost and sustain those who survived. That he survived—that one could survive, against the odds—was the surprise, the gift. His life was testimony to that.

Our family story is one of loss and survival. More than a century has passed since my father's brother, Meyer, left Novokonstantinov for America. My father, Motye, followed him a decade later, and their brothers, Moishe and Duved, made their way to Argentina a few years after that. The four brothers all had children, and their children have had children. The next generations have only heard pieces of the stories that I'm telling. As fate had it, my father married in his middle years and had children late in life, so that my sister and I were born decades after the first in our generation were born. Of the nine grandchildren of my generation, there are only three of us left. So many of our contemporaries, our closest cousins, are great grandchildren of Chana and Joseph. From the nine grandchildren, there are 21 great grandchildren, and at last count 48 great-great grandchildren. There are a dozen or more great-great-great grandchildren. Eight new babies were born recently: Ana and Joaquín in Guadalajara; Olivia and Elisa in Buenos Aires; Klil, Ariel, and Yasmin in Tel Aviv; and Pearl in Maryland.

My cousin Rosa, Uncle Duved's granddaughter, says that *history is metabolized by story,* that constructing a story engages our whole being, psychologically, neurologically, to make the world make sense. She says that history doesn't come, just like that. It's built day by day. That's what my father was doing—telling stories to hold the world still, to construct his version of history, so that it made sense to him.

And, now, we have this story to keep on growing, this story of a family. It is a story about what we do with stories of the past.

Stories enable us to put together the pieces of our lives, to see the connections between the past and the present and to represent the past in ways that help us shape the future. "Each family has its own story and its particular way of telling and transmitting it from one generation to another," Rosa said. Each family has its own secrets and those things that you're not told. Those are things that no one talks about. That is also transmitted. "Each one of us has their own family in their own head. There isn't just one family history, or one that is the real one. There isn't a single truth. There is the truth of each of us." (Personal correspondence.)

My father left me these stories of the past as an inheritance, and they have become what some historians call a "usable" or "practical" past that sheds light on both the past and the future.* As curator of the stories of the family, my job now is to pass them on to the next generation. They can make the stories their own, add new ones to the old, and the stories will keep on growing, taking on new configurations, voices, and purposes.

My story here has been a long time in coming. It began years ago in conversation with my father, and it first took form as an imaginary dialogue with my grandmother, Chana the Long, who died long before I was born. I knew her only through my father's stories, but she was mostly in the background, much as mothers are. I have no photograph of her, nor can I hear her voice. But the story of her wedding captured my imagination. At 16, she stood under the chupah with her

---

*   Roskies, D. G. (1999). *The Jewish search for a usable past.* Bloomington, IN.: University of Indiana Press.
White, H. (2014). *The practical past.* Dimendberg, E. (Ed.). Evanston, IL: Northwestern University Press.
White, H. (1990). *The content of the form: Narrative discourse and historical representation.* Baltimore, MD: The Johns Hopkins University.
See also: Kirshenblatt-Gimblett, B. (1999). *Destination culture: Tourism, museums, and heritage.* Berkeley, CA: University of California Press.
Hardy, B. (1975). *Tellers and listeners: The narrative imagination.* London: The Athlone Press.
Zipperstein, S. J. (1999). *Imagining Russian Jewry: Memory, history, identity.* Seattle, WA: University of Washington Press.

groom, shoulder to shoulder. And after she married, she grew taller than he was, and everyone in the village called her Chana the Long. I identified with my Chana the Long, I'm sure, because I was named after her and, also, because she was tall, and so was I. My mother was short, my sister, too, and my other three grandparents were also short. So I had to come from somewhere.

For years, I imagined myself talking to her, telling her of my life, and wondering if she would approve. I wrote to her in my journal, in poems, and in letters. She figured into my teaching and scholarly work, and in an unpublished memoir. I wrote to her as a feminist expression about being a woman in the world and growing tall. Her story sustained me, and the metaphor of *being long* was shorthand for finding my way out of the small town and into the larger world. *Being long* translated into ontological questions about *belonging* that still persist here at the end. Where do any of us belong? How do we get from here to there?

In my imaginary conversations with my Chana the Long, I tell her about her children, the four sons who survived, married, had children and lived long lives. I tell her that my father, Motye, her youngest child, grew up to be a *mensch*—a good person—as did all her boys, and that, more than anything, my father held onto the memories of the life he lived in the house on the road past the marketplace in Novokonstantinov. He told the stories of the old world, the people, the places, and the way of life that he wanted us all to remember.

I tell Chana the Long about my own two daughters, who are taller than I am, and they have daughters who may grow even taller. The oldest is nearly as tall as her mother. I hope that they will all keep telling the story of their great-great grandmother Chana the Long and how she grew tall. I tell her that more than one-hundred years after the birth of her youngest child, the family keeps on growing, and that while we live in many parts of the world, many of us have connected to each other across time and space. The younger generation wants to know about the past. I will send them these pages, and we will all search through our drawers to bring out old photos and other artifacts. We connect to each other on the Internet, and some of us will meet next year where we live, in New York or Buenos Aires, Tel Aviv or even Hong Kong.

The family will tell stories of who we are and where we come from out of our particular needs and predilections. Many of the next generation are, in fact, in the business of stories. Some of us write stories. Some are poets, historians, archivists, filmmakers, and actors. Some are lawyers, therapists, and psychoanalysts. Others are musicians, singers, composers, and graphic artists. Some teach literature and languages. One is a linguist, another a cosmologist. Perhaps none of this is accidental. Perhaps this is the way we are genetically predisposed.

My version of the story is almost finished. I had promised to write down what I could of what my father told me, and now it is up to the others. There are more letters from the old country to be translated. There are still missing people in this version of the story. I don't know what happened to the family who stayed behind, to the cousin who was denied entry to the United States and went back to Podolia or the one who wanted my father to marry her. Did she ever get out? What about all those who couldn't leave? My father and his three brothers were the lucky ones.

A few weeks ago, my sister gave me my father's prayer shawl to give to my oldest granddaughter, and in the storage box we found an old worn brown velvet bag with an orange Star of David hand-stitched on the front. Inside is a pair of very old *tefillin*. Perhaps these are my father's that belonged to his father, Joseph of the Woods. Perhaps they are. There are still clues to the past all around us.

The tale is the teller, scholars of narrative tell us. Each time we tell a story, we make it our own. The story then becomes our responsibility. The next generations make them theirs, and the stories take on a life of their own, as they become part of our lives—the stories of our making.

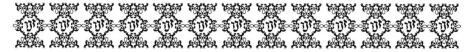

Afterword

A Storyteller Comes from Someplace

Who are we but the stories we tell ourselves, about ourselves, and believe?
—Scott Turow, *Ordinary Heroes*[*]

Each time we tell a story, we make it new.
—Barbara Hardy, *Tellers and Listeners: The Narrative Imagination*[**]

So, Here's the Story

There was a man who lived in a small town on the banks of a big river in a world long gone. Motye was the youngest of eleven children. He loved the little town. He loved being with his family, playing games with his brothers, riding his father's horse, and swimming in the river. He loved listening to stories, especially to those that his grandfather told when he came to visit. Then there were the terrible times, and Motye saw things he would never forget. Most of the family and the world he knew were suddenly gone.

One night in the dead of winter, with nothing but the clothes on his back, he set off on a long, dangerous journey to find his brother

---

[*]   Turow, S. (2005). *Ordinary heroes.* New York, NY: Farrar, Straus, and Giroux.

[**]   Hardy, B. (1975). *Tellers and listeners: The narrative imagination.* London: The Athlone Press.

in America. He wandered from place to place, carrying stories of the old world with him. After a time, Motye married, and he and his wife settled in a little town on the banks of a river in the new world, and had two children. Now, he had avid listeners – his two daughters – who grew up wanting to hear their father's stories. One of Motye's daughters became a teacher and a writer, who promised she would pass the stories on. What follows, here, in this new section of *A Man Comes from Someplace* is the story of how that daughter found her way to becoming the teller of her father's stories, and a storyteller, herself.

How the Book Evolved

Narrative is international, transhistorical, transcultural; it is simply there, like life itself.
—Roland Barthes, *"The Structural Analysis of Narrative"*

A Man Comes from Someplace was a long time in coming. It began early in my life with the sound of my father's voice in the Yiddish melodies he hummed when he walked me as a baby in our apartment above the American Legion Hall in the coal-mining town in southwestern Pennsylvania where we lived. And although I cannot remember when he began to tell me stories, I know that they grew with me as I grew, first, in versions that were fit for a child. These were sweet memories. He told of his privileged place as the youngest of the eleven children, the comfort of his home and family, and the vitality of the community in which he lived. I remember asking if the family was rich, and he said that, yes, for the times and the world they lived in, they were rich, but that everyone there was poor.

I became a reader and a want-to-be writer who always had a notebook at hand. I wrote and illustrated my first story in the third grade, and my teacher asked me to read it to the first and second graders

---

*   Barthes, R., & Heath, S. (1977). "Introduction to the structural analysis of narrative." In *Image, music, text*. New York, NY: Hill and Wang.

in the next classroom. (This was in our two-room schoolhouse, with first and second grades in one room, and third and fourth grades in the second room.) The story was about a girl who grew up in one place, knowing in her heart that she had come from a world far away. I have no doubt that the world my father described in his stories was that world. And I have no doubt that my father's stories shaped my own life.

I recently found a photograph of my father holding me in his arms in front of my grandparents' house (my mother's parents) in McKeesport, Pennsylvania.

My father and me, McKeesport, Pennsylvania, 1940's

In college, I took a double major in English and history, and it was as a sophomore in Robert Colodny's 20th century European history class at the University of Pittsburgh that I began to study the world my father had come from. I didn't write about him then. You didn't write about the "personal" in those days, particularly when having an immigrant father was not all that common in the worlds I inhabited then. I wrote the required 40-page paper on the American response to the Russian Revolution.

It was in Colodny's class, studying history and historiography, that I started to grapple with questions about how to represent events within the complex historical, political, and cultural worlds in which we live. I still have class notes from Colodny's course, which I recently included in a book that I edited on liberal education:

> To be is to be related.
> Since man makes his own history, however badly, but suffers it more than he controls it or understands it, nevertheless, he makes it.
> Men make their history in terms of beliefs and values; you cannot say "imperialism made war." Men make war, men may believe in war, in imperialism, nationalism.
> Do not reconstruct the narrative.
> Use the historical imagination.
> Historiography without philosophy is senseless chronicle, a blind conglomeration of facts.

I remember that in teaching the Russian Revolution, Colodny posited the question of how to represent the magnitude of the millions killed in Russia during those horrific times of the First World War, the Revolution and Civil War. Numbers would not do, he insisted: the human mind cannot grapple with such calamity – such "data." But to take us to the human experience itself, that was what he offered, as he read us a poem by Alexander Pushkin written from the perspective of a mother grieving the loss of her son. There were the facts, and there were also the voices of the witnesses, the survivors, the participants, those who were there at the time.

How and Why We Tell Stories

We tell stories in order to live…we interpret what we see….
—Joan Didion, *The White Album**

These questions of how and why we tell stories began to shape my studies and professional life. I eventually became a teacher/researcher/ scholar, and carried out a qualitative study for my dissertation at New York University on the oral stories of a group of multi-cultural students told in a freshman composition course. I continued the conversations with my father, asking questions, and eventually audiotaping our talks. By this time, now in his later years, my father wanted the stories to be told. He hoped that I would write a book to tell about the family and the world that was lost.

The book had actually begun earlier in hand-written notes I took as my father was telling me the stories. He was already seeing himself, I am sure, as an *informant*, giving me specific details of the place he had come from. I've just rediscovered this notebook of eleven single-spaced, hand-written, mostly back-to-back pages, and am surprised by what I read. I expected notes on the facts and a chronology of *events,* what happened, where, and when: 1911, his brother Meyer left for America; 1915, his mother Chana died; 1919, his father Joseph and oldest brother Paci were murdered; 1920, my father fled the shtetl.

But I find that I was taking notes in first person, in my father's "voice," beginning with the murders of his father and brother in 1919, and ending with the time he leaves Romania to sail to the United States in 1921. I am obviously writing quickly, trying to capture his language, phrasing. Now in re-reading, I see again how he moves between the family story and the historical and political contexts, the family struggling to survive within the unfolding events of the Bolshevik Revolution. Here are the first lines on the first notebook page, dated June 13, 1970. It is story in history:

---

*   Didion, J. (2006). "The white album." In *We tell stories in order to live: Collected nonfiction.* New York, NY: Knopf.

Author's notebook, June 1970.

It happened the day before Shavuot, 1919 – a nice spring day. Political situation – officially, Ukraine under Bol. Rule, but town itself was abandoned – no gov't. rule at that time. Officials had fled.... Chaos.... Moishe, Duved and his family, and I fled to next town. Nothing to eat. Learned that bandits had abandoned town. Father refused to go to next town. He stayed in NK. alone.

And on the last page, I hear yet another version of the journey to America in December 1921, as my father is finally packing to leave Romania:

I started to pack…went to see Bricks and Co. – agent for shipping co. – everything paid for by Meyer [his brother in the U.S.] – they reimbursed me $10. For visa …they told me to report Thurs. – there were 65 of us who were to be transported by train to Antwerp.

My notebook is dated early summer, 1970, and I had moved from southwestern Pennsylvania to New York. I imagine that I was visiting my parents back home, and in a quiet moment, I sat down with my father and asked him to tell me the stories, so that I could write them down. (*Why then?* I wonder.) I am struck again by his memory for detail, how many in the group of refugees, the route they took from Budapest by train and then boat, and another train to Liverpool. I am struck by the way he captures the strangeness of the journey in his discovery that he has eaten a ham sandwich on the train from London to Liverpool, and, when he found out what it was, he *opened the window and threw up*! A forbidden food for a boy who had eaten nothing but kosher food his entire life. He was a master-storyteller, and I became interested not only in what he was telling, but also in how and why he was telling the stories.

At this same time in my own life, I was finding my way professionally, in the midst of the immense cultural and political upheavals that were taking place all around me. I was teaching as an adjunct at The City University of New York (CUNY), the largest urban public university in the country. I taught, first, as an adjunct at Bronx Community College, and then at Queens College, where I was eventually hired full-time. There were stories all around me, with immigrant students arriving from across the world, and with the Civil Rights movement on the doorsteps of the colleges. At the same moment, CUNY was engaging in a controversial social experiment known as Open Admissions. On the campuses and around the country were colleagues coming together across disciplines to confront the big social questions of how we educate our students. It was a heady time for many of us, and we were learning from each other. I began to focus on how telling stories are ways of making meaning of our lives.

Connecting to the Past

We do not live in a void…we own the past and are, hence, not afraid of what is
to be.
          —Abraham Heschel, *The Earth is the Lord's*[*]

There was also my persistent longing to know what I would never
know, the people who were gone, the world of my father that had been
lost. These longings often came out in the journals/notebooks that I
began to keep. They came, too, in poems that needed to be written:
the poem to the grandmother I never knew, a poem about my father's
terrors that surfaced from time to time, another about how conversations with him would suddenly reveal parts of the stories he'd never
told. In an early poem, in May 1981, I invoke the story of my grandmother and grandfather at the *chupah* on their wedding day.

Chana the Long

I never knew my grandmother who died
Years back nursing the daughter, just died,
Of her daughter who died too of typhus
In one of those epidemics that wipe out.

The villagers in that Russian town tell
How she stood shoulder to shoulder
With my grandfather on their wedding day,
The same height.

Two years later, the story goes
They remember how she had inched
Above him. A young mother, now,
Still growing.

She bore my father and ten others,
Three to die in infancy, two as young
Adults, one in one war and one in
The next and the remaining four
To spend their lives continents apart.

After she died, for memory,
The family recorded their faces
Around the father, bearded;
My father, the youngest, straight
Against the painted roses.

I sit here, Grandmother, in my garden
The book on my lap, my daughters
Growing tall. I hear them laughing
In the kitchen and wonder about you.

---

[*]   Heschel, A. (1995). *The earth is the Lord's: The inner world of the Jew in Eastern Europe.* New York, NY:
      Jewish Lights Edition, published by arrangement with Farrar, Straus and Giroux.

For years after that, the "book" was taking form in several ways: at first, it was autobiographical, a first-person narrative about belonging, identity, and how the worlds we come from shape who we are, our beliefs, values, and ways of being in the world. In one version, I was writing letters to my grandmother, Chana the Long. Here is the brief opening to this project:

> My dearest Grandmother Chana,
>
> You don't know me. But I know about you through the stories my father told me throughout his life. My Hebrew name is yours, Chana Dina, and I am the older daughter of your youngest son – your eleventh child – Motye. Your baby was my beloved father, and despite the odds against it, he survived to live a long life in a land and a time far away from what you knew. He persisted and endured, and lived a life that I think you would have been proud of. Four of your sons in all survived the terrible times: the two older, Duved and Meir; and the youngest, Moishe and Motye. Your daughter and her daughters did not. But I will tell you all that I know from what my father told me. I will tell you what you could not have known.
>
> It is nearing sundown – Shabbos – and I find myself each Shabbos talking to you, imagining the details of your life, what you were doing as sundown neared every Friday, and wondering what you would think of my life, hoping that you would approve of who I have become, that you would know me, and that we would be able to talk to each other.

Another version, called "Chana the Long: A Family Memoir," was a chronicle of my father and the family within the history, politics, and culture of the times. Written in the third-person, it was a more objective rendering of my family story. Another draft followed, entitled *The Eleventh Child: A Father's Stories*, another move towards the objective. I recently found another title, *On Being Long: Stories My Father Told*. The question was the perspective: was he "a father" or "my father." There were other versions, one that I called *On Belonging*, and another called, *Chana's Children: Loss, Survival and Resilience*, which came back, autobiographically, to my own persistent questions of identity, how we know and define ourselves in the world.

My father's stories also found their way into my professional writing. In the opening pages of my 1986 dissertation, entitled, *Narrative*

Compositions: An Exploration of Narrative in The Teaching of College Composition, I begin with a postmodern flourish, representing three *roles* I bring together in the study: the daughter of a story-teller/survivor, the teacher, and the scholar-researcher:

> As she sat down to account for how she had come to this place, she began once and then again and then again.
>
> Beginning I
>   It is out of the stories of my own life that I come to narrative, particularly out of the stories of my father, who for me, is one of the great storytellers. And I offer here one of the stories he told me, one that has become part of my own life. The story is about his mother, who died in the Ukraine long before I was born. The story goes that when she married my grandfather, on the day that the bride and groom stood at the marriage altar, they were both exactly the same height, and then, after that, she grew, and came to tower over her husband. And the villagers renamed her: Chana, the Tall One or Chana the Long....
>
> Beginning II
>   It is out of the stories of my students' lives that I come to narrative....
>
> Beginning III
>   It is out of an abundant, eclectic, multi-disciplinary reading of and about narrative that I come to narrative....

The Narrator as Teller of the Tale

The use of the objective, "a father's stories," foregrounds this critical question of who is telling the story. Whose story is it? It was my story when I was writing the poetry and the draft about "belonging." These were letters to my grandmother as I imagined her being part of my life. What I was writing now was my father's story, but I was the teller of his tales. I couldn't name the struggle while in the middle of it – even though I had written, taught writing and literature for years. I could name the writer's "problems" in other texts for other writers, this common problem often referred to as "finding a voice." But my father's stories were too close, in a sense, they were like sacred texts, and I was trying to be the objective reporter, retelling his stories, *accurately*.

I could not find comfortable language to refer to my father. What to call him? He was – and continues to be – *my father.* I could not call him by his Anglicized name: *Martin.* I finally settled on the Yiddish, *Motye,* when I was telling of the life he led before I was born. And then, he slipped into *my father* in the rest of the book.

Belatedly, I find in the Jewish legal code and customs (*Halakha),* "The Laws of Honoring Father and Mother": *One may not call him by his first name either in life or in death, but rather should refer to him as my father, my teacher.**

Layers of Time

Looking back now, re-reading (and also teaching from) the published *A Man Comes from Someplace,* I see more clearly these writerly issues: these questions of time, of the here and now, the present as it connects to the past and the future, the not-so-simple question of verbs. I see the movements we often make through layers of time: the past merging with the present and the future. Virginia Woolf, in extracts from her 1939 notebooks, talks of these questions of time, and how to represent the past, in what she calls a relationship between an "I now, I then":

> 2nd May [1939]. I write the date, because I think that I have discovered a possible form for these notes. That is, to make them include the present – at least enough of the present to serve as platform to stand upon. It would be interesting to make the two people,

> 'I now, I then,' come out in contrast. And further, this past is much affected by the present moment. What I write today I should not write in a year's time.**

---

* *Shulchan Aruch Yoreh Deah* 240. See Goldberger, M. and Gevirtz, E. 1987). *A guide to Torah hashkofoh: questions and answers on Judaism.* New York, NY: Graphi Text Type Co. (in Handout from Westchester Jewish Center, Larchmont, New York.)

** Woolf, V. (1976). "A sketch of the past." In *Moments of being: Unpublished autobiographical writings.* In Jeanne Schulkind (Ed.). New York, NY: Harcourt Brace Jovanovich.

Learning from colleagues doing ethnography, I transcribed my father's stories into text, and then decided to re-present them as textual performances by setting them off in italics. Re-reading now, I see how his stories move through layers of time:

> *There was a mailman,* he said, *but there was a Jewish woman, for years and years and years, she'd go to the post office and get everybody's mail and bring it to you, and you'd give her a penny. She couldn't read or write, but she had somebody tell her who this was for, and she'd bend it this way or that, so she'd know who to take the mail to. It was an unofficial job. Her brother was in this country, and her daughter traveled on the same carriage as me when we left Novokonstantinov.* (11)

I see how my father moves back and forth, one moment giving way to another in the past, through layers of time: *a Jewish woman,* who *for years and years and years* delivered *your* mail. He moves across time, slipping in the brother in "this country," a daughter on the same carriage as he was on, and speaking to *you* in the here and now. You know the mail-delivery woman and the world she lived in, the community that took care of her so that she could make a living. He engages us as readers, she would "bring the mail to *you*." He is always aware of his listener – wanting to bring you into the conversation.

My father's stories were *oral performances*. The use of italics enabled me to set off his "voice" on the page. That was settled. But the questions of an 'I' as a first-person narrator, and where the "I" was in time and place were still unresolved. One question led to another about voice, role, point of view, stance, perspective. Who was I telling the story? What pronouns? Was the narrator a participant or spectator? And, still, what or who was the story for, its functions, purpose? Who was the audience?

Finding the Way In and Through

Leo Tolstoy said that the whole world of the novel comes out of the first line, as it does in his well-known opening of *Anna Karenina*: "All happy families are alike; each unhappy family is unhappy in its own way." The narrator asserts his worldview, distinguishing between happy and unhappy families. His vision of the world, in his third-person, all-knowing point of view, governs the following 800 pages.

Finding that perspective, the narrator's *voice* for *A Man Comes from Someplace* continued as a struggle for years. There was also a question of settling on genre: biography, historical nonfiction or cultural study. It wasn't memoir or autobiography, I insisted. It wasn't my story.

Several unexpected turns of event shifted my perspective: first, after my father died, my sister and I found our Uncle Meyer's boxes of letters, many of which we eventually had translated. Here, suddenly, were other voices from the past: my grandfather, my grandmother (through others writing for her), uncles, aunts, cousins. There were Uncle Meyer's many friends from Novokonstantinov writing to him in America. And here was my father's voice, at 17, on his year's journey to America, being urged by his brother Meyer to write to him every day. His 100+ letters enabled me to hear him as he was a participant in the unfolding events, and not as the storyteller looking back on the past. The stories were now in multiple voices from the past, in what I came to call "a chorus of voices."

Then, in 2011, I gained another view of my father's world as I traveled to Ukraine to experience, first hand, the place he had left nearly a century before. I also went back that same year to southwestern Pennsylvania, revisiting Fredericktown and the mountains I loved, and finding the graves of my father's cousins. My own relationship to the past was changing, growing more complicated. And I was still having difficulty situating an "I" within the text. These were my father's stories, but I was implicated in the stories, too.

I was fortunate to have trusted readers along the way among my family, friends, and colleagues, who read drafts, and urged me to keep writing: My sister, who corroborated details, and confirmed that I was not inflating my representation of our father, was my first reader. My friend from childhood, Carolyn Sacks, who grew up with me in Fredericktown, validated my depictions of the world we had come from in southwestern Pennsylvania.

My friend, Bette Moskowitz, was a critical reader, on the look-out for what she calls 'spinach,' that is, stuffing a 'moral' or 'message' down the reader's throat. The 'meanings' had to emerge from the details of the stories themselves, as they did in my father's oral telling.

There were others: my husband Philip, colleague, cultural critic, writer, who listened and read, throughout. My cousin Silvia Perel-Levin, who insisted that we take the journey to Ukraine, was an important reader, as were my daughters, who read parts of the manuscript. My friend and walking partner, Eleanor Dreyfus, walked through the pages. There were others along the way, particularly one, who played a critical role in the process.

Narrative Imagination

For who, after all, wants to think of oneself as traumatized, by one's very parentage, as having drunk victimhood, so to speak, with one's mother's milk?
—Eva Hoffman, *Memory, History, and the Legacy of the Holocaust**

You do not own the past, until you tell the story.
—Rabbi Jeffrey Segelman**

When I returned from Ukraine in 2011, my daughter Lauren introduced me to Jeffrey Segelman, the rabbi at Westchester Jewish Center (WJC) in my home town. She thought he might be interested in talking with me about the journey to Ukraine and the book I was writing. A conversation began and continues now, six years later in the fall of 2017.

I remember those early meetings in Rabbi Segelman's office at WJC, sitting at his table. He would clear a space, pushing aside papers and books, and ask me to read to him from the manuscript. He would

---

* Hoffman, E. (2003). *Memory, history, and the legacy of the Holocaust.* New York, NY: Public Affairs.

** In conversation with the author, October 17, 2017.

listen, often closing his eyes, and then we would talk. He'd comment on the manuscript, ask a question or two, offer interpretations, and challenges. I remember he was surprised at the details of ordinary life in my father's stories. He could see my grandparents standing at the *chupah*. He could see the town and the river and the house, smell my grandmother's challah baking on Friday mornings, and taste the fresh vegetables from the garden. He was struck by the way my father was telling stories of this lost world that we rarely hear about in this century: his escape from Ukraine, the details of the year that he was a refugee, the hazards on the road, the near-misses, the chances he took, his escape across the frozen river. It was a compelling story.

But he wanted to know where I was in the story. I was missing, he said. Where was I when my father was being urged to take a chance, to run for his life across the frozen river that early December morning in 1920? What might have happened had he hesitated? Even a moment?

"Aren't you standing there with him?" he asked. And what were the effects of my father's stories on my own life, the daughter of the man who dared to cross the frozen river, the daughter of a survivor?

I knew the dark side to the stories, the traumas that surfaced from time to time throughout my father's life. But Rabbi Segelman was asking how those traumas affect those of us in the next generations.

I find this entry in my December 2011 journal, as a possible ending for the book:

> I am always looking for escape hatches. What does a child do with the knowledge that your father's father and his brother were murdered in their own house and that your father, minutes before, had run out the back door into the back garden, to the house across the street, and up into the attic. My grandfather had been warned, and he said, 'This time will be no different from the other times.' And the family said, 'Let's eat, let's do the everyday things that we do.' And then my grandfather and his eldest son were murdered. What do you do with such knowledge? What is the moral of the story?

What was I, as the narrator of the story, to do with such knowledge? The rabbi said that the draft I read to him, while full of detail, seemed "dispassionate." He wanted to know what I was doing with my own "cauldron of feelings"? (These were his words that I jotted in my notebook in 2011.) There were other questions, too, about the larger history, about the ways that American Jews see the "old country" within the contexts of what happened in Europe a few years later. How was I going to tell my father's story within that history?

We mostly know the world of the *shtetl* from such iconic stories as *Fiddler on the Roof.* My father read Sholem Aleichem's Tevye's stories as he was growing up. But the world that my father knew was lost in what came later, in the Revolution and Civil War. The Soviet Union closed down its history to the west in the 1920's, and the Shoah in Ukraine is hardly known. I saw the scarred landscapes in Ukraine, the mass killing sites in Letichev, Chmelnick, and Dunaivitsi. For us in the West, this is a history that is not known. Rabbi Segelman asked the critical questions: Why are you telling this story? What does it matter, and to whom does it matter, what happened in the past, if it sheds no light on our lives now in the present, on who we are? And, more importantly, on what we do. It was a matter of bringing the lost histories of my father's stories into our own lives. It was Heschel's challenge to "own the past." But the Rabbi went further. "You don't own the past," he said, "until you tell the story."

I needed to tell my father's stories in history, but connected to the here and now, to the present. I needed to bring to the page what I had felt my whole life when he was telling the stories over and over again, and I was there with him, listening. These weren't fairy tales. All of what had happened to him, to the people and the world he had known, affected my life, too. He had acted, he had survived. He hadn't "drunk victimhood." He was a survivor. The stories were about coming to grips with the past, about his survival, resilience, and his gratitude and joy in being alive. I knew this was a pivotal moment in my understanding how I needed to tell the stories. I needed to bring the past into the present, to own it. I needed to step into the story, and to consider: *what if* my father had not dared to cross the frozen river?

We all engage with *what if's* as we tell and retell our own stories, and hear others' stories. We live a life of stories every day of our lives, immersing ourselves in stories on the big and little screens in our lives. Stories are in and around us in the air we breathe: we engage in a "narrative imagination," being able to step into and walk in another's shoes. I found a way into the book, creating a narrator who in the very first line stands at another river in Ukraine and moves the narrative between the *here and now* of her own present and the *then* of her father's past:

> It is June 2011, and I am standing near the rocky ford in the river at the place my father came from in southwestern Ukraine. There are stone outcroppings strewn about, on land and in the water –the erosional fragments indistinguishable from the remains of the gravestones...my father had described the site well....

I recall coming to this Prologue late in the project, realizing that I needed to establish the storytelling voice at the beginning. I realize, too, that I've taken another postmodern turn, in writing three beginnings:

> Prologue: "Ukraine, 2011"
> *It is June 2011, and I am standing....*
> The narrator's "I" introduces the story in the present.

> Introduction. "So, Here's the Story"
> *It was always that moment at the frozen river that made my stomach turn....*
> I use one of my father's favorite expressions, "so, here's the story" as the title of the introduction, and I begin, as narrator, with the story of the frozen river and its significance for me, as the listener of the story.

> Chapter 1, "Time and Place"
> *When you asked my father where he came from, he told you....*
> The *I*, as narrator, introduces my father's voice, inviting *you*, the reader into the conversation....

The number of voices in *A Man Comes from Someplace* was growing: there were my father's stories, his eyewitness accounts of history unfolding, in his own words. There were the voices in the letters from family and friends, and there were others' voices coming into the story from my own life, as I dived into the writing.

Italo Calvino chose the term, "multiplicity," as one of the distinctive qualities he was planning to discuss in the lecture series on literature that he was to give at Harvard in 1986. He died before completing the manuscript, but the lectures were published posthumously as *Six Memos for the Next Millennium*. Here is Calvino[*] near the end of what was to be the fifth memo, "Multiplicity":

> Who are we, who is each of us, if not a *combinatoria* of experiences, information, books we have read, things imagined? Each life is an encyclopedia, a library, an inventory of objects, a series of styles, and everything can be constantly shuffled and reordered in every way conceivable? (124)

That's what I was experiencing, a shuffling of voices that were entering *A Man Comes from Someplace*, from my "library" of experiences, from literature, history, poetry, philosophy, cultural studies, education. Isaac Babel, Joan Didion, Seamus Heaney, Nicole Krause, Abraham Heschel, William James, Maxine Hong Kingston, Barbara Hardy. These voices became part of the unfolding narrative, as associations, quotations, epigraphs that illuminated moments in the story, as I was coming to grips with the key questions: why did my father keep telling the stories, and what was I now doing in retelling them?

Calvino, in the last lines of "Multiplicity," enjoins us to step outside ourselves, and not be limited by our own "sensibilities or experiences," to imagine what it is like to be another, "to enter into selves other than our own...." In the narrator's voice that I was creating for *A Man Comes from Someplace*, I could stand with my father at the frozen

---

[*]   Calvino, I. (1993). *Six Memos for the Next Millennium*. (Geoffrey Brock, Trans.) New York, NY: Vintage Books.

river, engage a narrative imagination to travel with him on his journey, and take on the role as the teller of the tale.

Oral Performance to Written Text

When you listen to my father's voice on the tapes, you're in the presence of a master storyteller. Over the years, I collected a dozen hours of our ongoing conversation. Often, you'd hear my mother in the background, and others who were visiting, laughing, asking questions. Here is the beginning of my transcription of my father's telling the story of a traveler needing a ride to the next town (which I audiotaped in February1986):

> Judith: I brought you Jewish Week…and I know you said you were all "winded up," ready to go.
>
> Father: *I don't know if you want to tell some of the same stories again. How about that story of the man wanting a ride?*
>
> Judith: Oh, I love that story.

And so, my father begins the story of a man coming from someplace. What you hear in the voice is his delight in the telling. He's eager to get going again. And I am, too. I repeat to him one of his favorite locutions, of being "winded up." I am laughing when I say it.

He and my mother are living in my town, a few blocks away. The date tells me that I have just completed my dissertation, which draws from sociolinguistics and folklore studies, and I've been listening to *how* my father is telling the stories. His English is filled with Yiddish rhythms, inflections, and idioms, and what some would call "broken English," particularly in verb usage. He uses "winded up" for wound-up or tightly wound. Or excited. Later, when I begin to convert the oral into the written, I take what I've learned from anthropologists about "performance," particularly, as Victor Turner* puts it, about

---

*   Turner. V. (1986). *The anthropology of performance.* New York, NY: PAJ Publications.

"freeing" or "liberating" a text from cultural prejudices. I decide not to transcribe verbatim because I want to avoid the hesitations, repetitions, backtracking, and also the grammatical errors that distract us as readers from the fullness of the storytelling. My intent was to try to capture in text the richness of my father's oral storytelling.

After my father tells the story, our conversation continues:

Judith: Is that a true story?

Father: *I think, if I am not mistaken, it was one of Sholem Alecheim's stories…he was a humorist, but in a certain way he made fun of the way things were in real life …actually, he was born in the same part of the country that I was….and those stories were going around by mouth, his stories, like 'Fiddler on the Roof,' there was a story going around there…there was a song. According to that song, Tevye had seven daughters. In Russian, there was a song, everyone was singing it. (*He sings the beginning of the song in Russian.*)*

What it means is this: There was a man, a Jew, and he had seven daughters…just like flowers, each one of them was a beauty. He had to help them to get married… And each one of them wanted to get married…First one of them got engaged and then another and a third one and they all demanded a husband and he had to help them to get married.

Judith: That was a story that was circulating?

Father: *That was a real nice song. I remember how each one wanted what they wanted. This one wanted a tailor and this one wanted an engineer…and this one wanted this. And he had to work hard to try to get them married off.*

Listening to my father's stories influenced the research I was doing at Queens College at the same time: I was studying students' oral stories, particularly those students who spoke a non-standard English dialect in their local communities in Queens, which is still considered to be the most diverse county in the country. Their college work was often impeded by a preponderance of error in their writing, and the remedial courses they were placed in during that time at CUNY were seed-beds for changing the ways we were teaching writing in the country. What I was tapping into at CUNY was the richness of students' oral language, their rich indigenous knowledge across cultures, particularly of storytelling, as foundational to their learning to write standard English and to succeed as college students.

Audience

But what kind of book was *A Man Comes from Someplace*? And who was the book for? I sent the manuscript out into the world, to agents, academic journals, colleagues, and got similar responses: a 'compelling story,' but it doesn't *belong* here. What is it? Biography, memoir, cultural history, creative nonfiction? The book was a good read, some said, but it "fell between the cracks." The manuscript was called a "hybrid" by academics in specific fields and by commercial agents and publishers.

My editor, Shirley Steinberg, opened the door for me at Sense Publishers through her series, "Transgressions: Cultural Studies and Education," and I was suddenly home, able to offer the story to those of us readers who are part of these vital ongoing cultural and political conversations across disciplines and institutions. I found ways through, engaging multiple voices and roles, narrative structures and genres in what was becoming a cultural study of an oral storyteller. The story was both an ethnography that situates family story in historical, sociocultural, and political contexts, and an auto-ethnography, taking up questions of uprootedness, the loss of family, place, language, identity, and culture. It was a story of trauma, survival and resilience, the refusal to be silenced or erased. I could speak out of my own roles as the daughter of a storyteller, as well as my professional roles as a teacher, scholar, researcher, and writer.

The book was also a meta-narrative, a story about telling stories, as it is here in this new afterward. I could leave gaps in the narrative, as I realized them, without closing them. I could offer versions of the "same" story, recognizing that this is the way we tell stories. No oral story is ever the same, even if it is rehearsed to be so. A story shifts and changes, as the contexts for telling change. We don't tell the same story to the child, as we do to the adult. My father knew this well. David Schlitt,* historian at the Heinz History Center in Pittsburgh, who reviewed the book for *Western Pennsylvania History,* notes that this "study of family history and folklore, defies easy description," and that it "feels both innovative and familiar…It is not a conventional narrative." It is *a velt mit veltelekh,* he said, which is Yiddish for "a world within a world."

Story, History and Memory

As I was writing these pages, more than two years after publication of *A Man Comes from Someplace,* I was reading historian Saul Friedlander's new autobiography/historiography, *Where Memory Leads,* which is a sequel to *When Memory Comes,* published almost forty years earlier, in 1978.** Friedlander's own story of Jewish families trying to escape the Nazis is, sadly, not uncommon. Born in Prague in 1934, Friedlander was taken by his parents to Paris in 1934, where he was placed in a convent. As his parents were trying to cross the border to Switzerland, they were caught and sent to Auschwitz, where they died. Friedlander spent his life as a peripatetic student, teacher, scholar, lecturer, and researcher of the Holocaust.

An international ambassador for peace and social justice, he tells his story of where he came from, and how he spent a lifetime trying to find a place to belong in various cities in Europe, Israel, and the United States. He is best known for his award-winning history, *Nazi Germany and the Jews* (2007)*** in two volumes. Professor Emeritus of History at UCLA, his new book chronicles his own struggles as a historian to write about the Holocaust, particularly when many of his

---

* Schlitt, D. Review of *A Man comes from someplace: Stories, history, memory from a lost time* in *Western Pennsylvania History,* 99:2, Summer 2016.

** Friedlander, S. (1970). *When memory comes.* New York, NY: Farrar, Straus, Giroux.

*** Friedlander, S. (1997). *Nazi Germany and the Jews: The years of persecution, 1933-1939.* New York, NY: HarperCollins.

contemporaries in Germany were either denying events or attempting to "normalize" what had happened. He writes of his determination to find ways to represent *both* history *and* memory, so that the voices of "those who perished – and survived" could be heard.

In *Where Memory Leads,* Friedlander says that he wanted "to write as precise a historical rendition as possible, and at the same time re-create for the reader a momentary sense of disbelief that history has a tendency to eliminate in the case of extreme events. How could such contradictory aims be reconciled?" The answer, in the end, he says,

> …was the most obvious, and the simplest…to introduce into the historical narra-
> tive not only the Jewish dimension as such but the 'raw voices' of the victims….
> I would introduce extracts from diaries or letters that, mostly without the inter-
> mediary of postwar memory, carried the incomprehension or the fear, the despair
> or the hopes of the trapped victims. These cries and whispers would puncture,
> so to say, the normalizing pace of the historical narrative, and jolt, albeit briefly,
> the distanced intellectual understanding conveyed by historical narration as such.
> (264-265)*

I am stuck by Friedlander's perhaps unintentional allusion here to Samuel Taylor Coleridge's well-known treatise on a "willing suspension of disbelief."** Coleridge argues that that if a writer were to infuse a "human interest and a semblance of truth" into a "fantastic" tale, then the reader could experience that "willing suspension of disbelief for the moment, which constitutes poetic faith." I am wondering if Friedlander was implying that the German historians, who were try-ing to normalize the Holocaust, were seeing these horrors of their own times as a *fantastic* tale.

Friedlander's questions about historical narrative allow me to un-derstand more fully the choices I was making to tell my father's stories. It wasn't history that I was privileging. It was story. I wasn't reading eye-witness accounts from diaries. I was listening to an oral storyteller, who, himself, was an eye-witness to history, telling the stories out of

---

* Friedlander, S. (2016). *Where Memory Leads. My Life.* New York, NY: Other Press.

** Coleridge, S.T. (1817). *Biographia literaria.* Chapter XIV. (Ed.) Nigel Leask. London: J.M. Dent, 1997.

his prodigious memory. It was my father's stories as they were infused and shaped by memory and steeped in history that I needed to capture. I needed to represent the immediacy of his storytelling on the page, the stories in his own voice. And as I was coming to understand and own the past, I had to write the overall narrative in my voice. As I was nearing completion of the book, I arrived at a subtitle: *A Man Comes from Someplace: Story, History, Memory from a Lost Time.*

The Places We Come From, The Stories We Tell: A Writing Seminar

December 2016: The setting is the beautifully restored Larchmont Library, and this is the last session of the writing/reading/discussion seminar that I've been teaching for the past six weeks. The program is sponsored by the library and a grant from the New York State Council for the Humanities. There are twelve participants in the group, and *A Man Comes from Someplace* is our common reading, along with excerpts from such writers as Anton Chekov, Grace Paley, Seamus Heaney, Joyce Carol Oates, and Ta-Nehisi Coates. We're reading a mix of genres: poetry, fiction and nonfiction, including brief commentaries on writing, such as this adaptation from Virginia Woolf's dictum* on reading as a writer: *The best way to read a novel* [or any book] *is to write one.* We take our work from the program title's key words: *the places we come from, and the stories we tell.* We define *place* broadly as questions about our own identity, how we define ourselves. We have produced an in-house collection of our work, each of us writing a 500-word story to represent the places we come from. The cover painting, "Around the Bend," (here shown in B&W) is by Dorothy Rainier, a local artist, and a participant in our group.

We all write in the group. June Hesler, the librarian, who wrote the formal proposal to the Council for Humanities, is writing, as I am.

---

*   Woolf, V. (1932). "How should one read a book?" In *The second common reader.* New York, NY: Harcourt Brace &World, Inc.

Cover for collection of writers' stories, from Larchmont Library Seminar

We're experimenting, to use Virginia Woolf's phrase, with the "dangers and difficulties of words." We're reading as writers. In every session, we write impromptu, short pieces that we read aloud. We begin with these prompts in the first sessions:

List five places you come from.

Take one of the places and write for ten minutes, without crossing anything out,
just keep writing, writing, writing.
Recall a moment from the past from one of the places you come from.
Situate the moment in a larger context, a story in a time, as well as a place.

As each writer reads aloud, we pay attention to voice and to sound,
rhythm and cadence, to language, syntax, and form, the emergent
whole and parts – to beginnings and endings. We pay attention to
tense, to the past, present, and future, to how the verbs we choose
represent layers of time. We pay attention to nouns and pronouns,
who's telling the story, and from what perspectives. We pay attention
to qualifiers, to adjectives and adverbs. We need to learn how to become trusted listeners, making note of what strikes us as the strengths
of the piece, and only after we've all had the chance to read aloud, do
we offer observations, draw inferences, ask questions.

In that first session, we hear about the geographical places we come
from: New York (various boroughs: Brooklyn, Bronx, Manhattan,
and also here in the metropolitan area, our town and others nearby).
We come from other places, too: Pennsylvania. Alabama. New Jersey. Cuba. Austria, visitors from Buenos Aires (my cousins). We write
about our place in the family, the oldest of five, the youngest of seven.
Some explore questions of gender, race, religion, the era in which they
were born. Austria at the brink of the Second World War. Cuba, just
before Castro came to power.

We write about our roots, where our ancestors come from. Some
have stories passed down from generation to generation, from the
deep South before the Civil War, from Italy, Slovakia, Ireland, the
Pampas in the south of Argentina. We write about the present, describing the town or the house we're now living in. Some of us have
stories about the language or languages we speak and how translations
from one language to another evoke the various roles we play in our
lives.

We start a writer's notebook, a place to house our exercises, quick
writes that we do daily. A couple of pages or more a day of nonstop

writing, no worries about spelling or punctuation. We just write, all kinds of stuff related to this question of the worlds we come from. And we pull out artifacts, material objects, stuff we've inherited that we then provide contexts for – photographs, maps, letters, official documents, newspaper clippings, stories or bits of stories, recipes, jewelry, clothing. We draw from our experiences, memories, and the cultural, historical, political research that we do.

One participant found the exercises to be freeing, and came in after the first week with 113 pages written in her notebook. Another, whose family found their way out of Austria just as Hitler invaded the country in 1938, had never wanted to talk about the past, but wrote her way in through a passport she had rediscovered. Another began to sort through boxes of family archives and pulled out photographs, recipes, and letters that she had not read before.

Some of us, we came to know, are artists, poets, musicians, photographers. We decide that the piece we will write for our publication can be written in any genre, and that we will all include a photograph of an artifact to represent our story. We begin to work with these traces of the past, and discover that we understand more than we thought we did.

So, here in the library on this Tuesday afternoon in December, we have a full room of writers and our invited friends and family. All 50 seats are taken. Copies of our collection, *The Places We Come From, The Stories We Tell,* are distributed. And each of us (myself included) has the chance to read to the group, to make our work public. I review the syllabus and talk about how our workshop has grown out of my own experiences in writing *A Man Comes from Someplace*:

The Places We Come From, The Stories We Tell,

And how they speak to who we are, to our own lives and our own identity: these are the questions that will guide our work in the seminar. We'll explore the ways the stories we want to tell can take shape in various genres and forms: fiction, nonfiction, poetry. And we'll explore how, as writers, we can draw from memory, oral stories, history, genealogy, research, family artifacts (what anthropologists call "objects of ethnography"), and from our own imagination, to write our stories.

A Man Comes from Someplace: Stories, History, Memory from a Lost Time, a work of nonfiction literary narrative, will serve as the springboard for our work in the seminar. The narrative demonstrates the ways family stories can be collected, interpreted, and represented to situate story in history and to re-envision connections between the past, present, and future. Participants will keep a writer's notebook for their own experiments with reading and writing a variety of texts.

From NY State Council for the Humanities Grant Application for Larchmont Library, June Hesler and Judith Summerfield, June 2016

Syllabus: Six Sessions and a Reception/Readings from the Writers
October 18: The Places We Come From, The Stories We Tell

Getting Started: "Free Writing," Reading as Writers

Assignments for next session: A Writer's Notebook – writing daily, starting off from the first session about the 'places' you come from and the stories you tell or want to tell. (We're aiming for a whole piece(s) of writing by the end of the seminar.)

Virginia Woolf, "How Should One Read a Book?" (essay)

A Man Comes from Someplace: Prologue, Introduction, Chapter 1

(Who's 'speaking' in each chapter; What do epigraphs do?)

October 25: Tellers and Listeners: Who's Telling the Story, Who's the Audience? Narrator's

Stance, Voice, Perspective.

Discussing Woolf ("Moments of Being" and "The I now, and the I then") and A Man Comes from Someplace

Keep the notebook going. Do some 'focused' free writing, on a memory, an artifact (photo, etc.)

Read: Anton Chekov, "Misery: To Whom Shall I Tell My Sorrow?" (short story)

Grace Paley, "Wants" (short story)

Someplace, Chapters 2,3, and 4

November 1: So What's a Story?

Discussing Chekov, Paley, Someplace

Keep the notebook going. Write two or three 'place' memories, collecting artifacts.

Read: Marie Ponsot, "Among Women" (poem)

Seamus Heaney, "from Clearances" (poem)

Russell Banks, "Sarah Cole: A Type of Love Story" (short story)

Someplace, Chapters 5 and 6

November 15: The Narrative Imagination: Entering the Past
> Keeping the notebook going; finding a place to begin your own story.
> Discussing Ponsot, Heaney, Banks, Someplace
> Read: excerpt from Maxine Hong Kingston, "No Name Woman, from The Woman Warrior:
> Memoirs of a Girlhood Among Ghosts (memoir)Someplace, Chapters 7 and 8

November 22: Memory, Form, and Structure (Building a Building)
> Discussing week's readings – readings from your notebook
> Read: William Shakespeare Sonnet 30: "When to the sessions of sweet silent thought"
> Joan Didion, excerpt from Where I Came From (memoir)
> Patrick Modiano, excerpt from Pedigree: A Memoir
> Someplace, Chapters 9 and 10

November 29: Beginnings and Endings: Stories to Grow On, Stories to Make Sense of the World
> Discussing week's readings and reading from your own emerging stories.
> (This session might be a writers' workshop, reading and working on your own drafts.)
> Excerpt from Joyce Carole Oates, The Lost Landscape: The Making of a Writer
> Excerpt from Ta-Nehisi Coates, Between the World and Me (nonfiction/letters from the
> author to his son.)
> Someplace, Chapters 11-12

December 6: Reception/Readings from the Writers
> Reading (and publishing) your own stories.

Food for Thought
> We tell stories in order to live....
>> Joan Didion
> It is a labor in vain to try to recapture it: all the efforts of our intellect are useless. The past
> is hidden somewhere outside its own domain in some material object which we never
> suspected. And it depends on chance whether or not we come upon it before we die.
>> Marcel Proust
> Lacrimae rerum (the tears in things)
>> Lucretius

A Man Comes from Someplace is finding its way in the world, taking me on an unexpected journey, from Krakow, Poland, where I introduced *A Man Comes from Someplace* in the summer of 2015, back to the community where I live now, and to the world I came from in southwestern Pennsylvania. Just as my father tailored the stories to his listeners, so am I doing the same. This is a new kind of teaching. Each setting is different; I don't know many of these places or the audiences.

But the book is being defined by the listeners and readers, and I am having the chance to tell my father's stories to others, in places near and far.

I found myself in Krakow that summer of 2015, through a chance meeting with Jonathan Ornstein, Director of the Krakow Jewish Community Center, who invited me to talk about the book at the Krakow Festival.[*] This was the 25th anniversary of the Jewish Culture Festival, founded in 1988, the year before the fall of Communism in Poland. The project is committed to "building bridges between generations, traditions, cultures, and religions." Their maxim is *Mi Dor Le Dor* (Hebrew for 'from generation to generation'). The festival includes concerts, lectures, workshops, seminars, and exhibitions.

My cousin, Silvia, often our inspiration for taking such journeys, is with me and my husband, too. She has helped prepare the slide-show, with video from our trip to Novokonstantinov in 2011. Matias, a young cousin from Buenos Aires, a professional musician, teacher, and composer, has recorded an original piece for the occasion, "Recuerdos de un Tiempo Perdido." It is his aesthetic response to *A Man Comes from Someplace*. As the group enters the room, they hear Matias' music – a wistful blending of the classical with klezmer strains. They will also hear the recording of my father's voice, as he tells the story of "a man coming from someplace."

Standing in this small meeting room in the Jewish Community Center, I am aware that Novokonstantinov is due east, about 400 miles. My grandfather Joseph traveled to Krakow, I am certain, as part of his work as a manager of woodlands. I have a letter that he wrote to the family in Novokonstantinov from Warsaw, 70 miles north from where I am now. I am aware that he may have walked these streets.

As I write these lines today, at the end of September 2017, the Russian separatists have just destroyed another weapons factory in Ukraine, this one in Kalynivka, in the oblast of Vinnytsia, not far from

[*]   Krakow Jewish Festival web site: http://www.jewishfestival.pl/en/

Novokonstantinov. Google Maps notes that the road from Krakow east to Vinnytsia, M-12, the major east-west highway, is temporarily impassable.

"Your destination is on a road that is closed now."

Clearly, the road was damaged or destroyed by the attack, in which 30,000 residents were forced from their homes.

These layers of time, repetitions of history, in one guise or another, from generation to generation, are starkly apparent. Geography is present to me in ways I hadn't known before. Ukraine opened up the past as I had never expected; that part of the world is now part of my "combinatoria of experiences." And now, each telling of these stories from the past sheds light on the present in new ways.

At the talk to the philanthropic Woman's Club in my community, I spoke to women across generations, backgrounds, and interests, most of whom had never heard anything like these stories. At the Latin American Jewish Association conference at the City University of New York, my colleague, Nora Glickman scheduled me to speak about the book in a session on "literature and creative writing." Here were colleagues, who came from Central and South America, making films, writing poetry, fiction, "literary nonfiction" (as the book here was characterized). They were interested in my father's stories as they shed light on those in their families in Latin America who had come from the same worlds as my family in Russia at the turn of the last century.

At the University of Pittsburgh, my alma mater, I was invited to speak at their 2016 symposium on the humanities. I focused on the ways the stories took form, particularly as they related to our lives in Pittsburgh, McKeesport, and the neighboring cities and towns. These Eastern Europe immigrant stories of southwestern Pennsylvania are being collected by the Heinz History Center (an affiliate of the Smithsonian), where I am scheduled to give a book talk next year, and to create an exhibit of family artifacts, particularly those connected to both of my parents' lives in southwestern Pennsylvania.

In New York City, at the Holocaust Educators Network, a yearly seminar for teachers from around the United States and abroad, my colleague, Sondra Perl, suggested that I situate the stories within the contexts of a Ukrainian history that most of us do not know. I began this part of the talk with a brief history of Babi Yar in Kiev, and how the memorials of those murdered there in 1941, finally came to be built. It was the writers, the poets, who pressed for the site to be memorialized. It was only in 1961 that Yevgeny Yevtushenko's poem, "Babi Yar," became an international event, and the world suddenly became aware of another Holocaust: the Shoah in Ukraine.

That history, though, is not a dominant narrative. It was not known to the teachers in the room, who came from places near and far in this country, and even from parts of Eastern Europe. We spent time during the session talking about our own histories, and what parts of the stories are not known, have not become dominant narratives. These occasions for telling our stories, for crossing time and place, history, nationality, race, and class, are illuminating. I showed them the map of our journey, and where we found the burial sites of my family, from Babi Yar to Novokonstantinov to Letichev to Dunaivitsi. I read key passages from the book and presented images of photographs that we had taken in Ukraine, and other images that I have found to represent what I could only imagine.

There are no photographs of my grandparents at their wedding, but there are other ways to bring the past to life. I show them this image of Chagall's "Russian Wedding" (1909). And then I remember that when I had shown this same image to my father, he pointed out the water carrier on the far right of the painting. He said that there was always a water carrier in the wedding procession in the streets of the village. It was the tradition – to wish the newlyweds a long, happy, and blessed life.

Marc Chagall. Russian Wedding, 1909

And my cousin Claudia Perel, an archivist in Buenos Aires, found this painting of a wedding under a *chupah,* by the 19th century Polish Jewish artist, Mauricy Gottlieb. Here, the dancer, with his arm lifted high, represents the joyful spirit of the Jewish wedding celebration.

A story takes form in word and image, music and song, history and memory, and in material objects we take from our lives. These become objects of auto-ethnography for us to reflect upon, respond to – food, clothing, the weather, genetic predispositions that we only sense, perhaps, but may not as yet articulate. There are many ways of telling. And images, however we know them or find them, inform our stories. I recall John Berger's assertion: "There are no photographs which can be denied. All photographs have the status of fact. What

Mauricy Gottlieb, *Jewish "Huppa" Wedding,* 1876
https://commons.wikimedia.org/wiki/File:Maurycy_Gottlieb_Jewish_Wedding_sketch.jpg

is to be examined is in what way photography can and cannot give meaning to facts."*

I was having the chance to explore these other ways of telling, as the book took me to a next stop, back in my home town, with one of my trusted readers, Rabbi Segelman. We decided to talk about the conversations that we had when I was trying to find my way through to telling my father's stories.

Places We Come From, the Stories We Tell

A Conversation with Judith Summerfield and Rabbi Jeffrey Segelman

Tuesday, October 17th, 2017 8PM

How do you respond to the question: "Where do you come from?"

Join us for a lively discussion with Judith Summerfield, WJC member, author of *A Man Comes from Someplace: Stories, History, Memory From a Lost Time*, Professor Emerita in English, Queens College/CUNY. Judith introduced the book at the Krakow Festival in 2015, and since then, has been giving book talks and writing seminars, including a recent writing/reading workshop supported by the New York Council for the Humanities at the Larchmont Library.

---

* Berger, J. and Mohr. J. (1982). *Another way of telling.* New York, NY: Pantheon.

There are 20 people here in the synagogue library. The Rabbi and I are sitting in comfortable armchairs, surrounded by family, friends, neighbors in the community, some people I don't know. The conversation is the introduction to the writing seminar that I'll begin teaching in a couple of weeks. I'll follow the syllabus I wrote for the library workshop, but I am assuming that many in the group will want to focus on the question of Jewish identity. When we gather in any group such as this, new questions, ideas, topics, emerge. There are always surprises.

I talk about the Rabbi as an ideal listener, and how our conversations led to my finding the voice I needed to tell the story. I tell them how he urged me to imagine myself in my father's shoes on that early December morning long ago, when he stood on the bank of the frozen river, hoping to escape to the other side, and a stranger, who was standing nearby, said to my father, "Now's the time. Run, just run across." I showed an image of a frozen river, inviting the group to imagine what it might be like to stand there, alone, before a grey expanse of ice and sky, and dare to run across, not knowing what they would find on the other side.

Frozen river

https://blackboxblue.files.wordpress.com/2010/09/frozen-river-02.jpg

Rabbi Segelman then offers his thoughts about the stranger standing there at the frozen river with my father. He lingers a moment before going back with the rest of the crowd. He winks at my father and urges him to take the chance, to run across. Perhaps he is the prophet Elijah, the Rabbi suggests, who often appears as a stranger on the road to help travelers in distress. I mention these repetitions in my father's story, of a stranger appearing out of nowhere, urging my father on, telling him to take this road rather than that one. I also see now how quickly my father was to respond. He acts decisively, without hesitation. He takes the chance, runs this way and not that, follows this road and not the other.

I think about my own life, and think, sometimes, that I have a "shtetl mentality," that I am always on the look-out for escape routes.

I am becoming accustomed to marrying words and images of rivers, a map of Ukraine, family photos, epigraphs. I talk about the narrative imagination, entering into the text, imagining what we have no photograph of. I press a key on my lap-top, and here is my father's voice, the audio of his telling the story of a man coming from someplace.

My daughter Lauren is here tonight. She introduces and then reads her description from Chapter 12, "Stories to Grow On," of visiting her grandparents after school, where her grandfather cooks dinner for her and after dinner sits down in his armchair, waiting to tell her "some stories." "Did you hear the story of ____?" he asks her. And then Lauren begins.

> He often went back to the night he saw his father and brother get killed, but it wasn't scary to me. He made me feel that it was a place far, far away and that it was long gone. I knew that he felt safe here, that he was comfortable in his chair, grateful for having plenty of food every single day, and able to take a deep breath and bring what he called 'the old country' back to life. (215)

Lauren then reads a new text that she has written for the occasion about going to Israel at the age of 20, where she found:

…real living breathing Jewish communities, much like the landscape of the Old Country that he had painted with his stories. What was even more astonishing, was that this country was made up of so many new immigrants from different places, and everyone I met had a story to tell me about the miracle of their journey, their survival, their new beginning.

She says that her grandfather "would have fit right in," and she thanks Rabbi Segelman for helping her mother find her way into the book to "preserving [my grandfather's] spirit, faith, courage, struggles, and optimism."

We now look at an image on the screen that the rabbi has provided. It is a photograph of the rabbi, his sister, and their parents, just a few days before they both died, within days of each other. There is what we see before our eyes, as spectators, the rabbi reminds us, and then, there is the reality, of what the participant, who was there at the event, knows. The photograph may suggest one story, he says, but he knows what was actually happening that day. We interpret what we see before our eyes, but the rabbi was witness to the events. He knows the story.

Rabbi Segelman knows well how to engage us in conversation. He asks questions of me, the group, and he rephrases statements as questions. I had brought to the screen the Herschel quotation from Chapter 2:

> *We do not live in a void.*
> *We never suffer from a fear of roaming*
> *about in the emptiness of time.*
> *We own the past and are,*
> *hence, not afraid of what is to be.*

"To what extent do we own the past?" the rabbi asks us, and suggests that we cannot own the past until we tell the story.

The Places We Come From,
The Places We Wander

They have had no Jewish visitors, they tell us, who lived here before the First World War.
   —*A Man Comes from Someplace*, "Prologue."

In the spring of 2016, a pastor from a village in Ukraine not too far from Novo-kostantinov, was conducting research about Jewish life before WWI and the Russian Revolution. He asked the principal of the school if he had any information for him, any books, articles, archives, anything about Jewish life in Novokonstantinov, where his mother was born.

The principal suggested that I was the one to talk to, here in New York. I had written a book, he told him. So, the pastor wrote to our guide in Ukraine, who translated the pastor's letter to me, and then mine to him. After a number of letters back and forth, Sense Publishers sent copies of the book for students to read in their ESL classes – and for teachers to include in the local museum they are creating in the school in Novokonstantinov.

Here is a section from the letter that the pastor sent to me in January 2016:

Dear Judith Pearl Summerfield, peace to your home!

I want to share my impressions from the first 60 pages of the book "A Man Comes from Someplace," which I found in the internet. I read this extract with the help of a computer translation. However, in spite of the translation's imperfection, I felt I was in Novokonstantinov and in Podolya 100 years ago.

Now I can look at the past of my land from another side…. Such books are of great interest now, they enrich us and encourage to a deep rethinking of the present. I must confess, the book (at least its first part) impressed me greatly as a pastor of a church and researcher of the native land.

This is not only the biography of one separate family, but also a big source of information about local history. I am looking forward to reading the whole book and learning more about the life of those who were in the first part. I thank G-d that he helped you make your dream true and bring closer our past. I am sure it was also His Holy will. The words from the 1 chapter of "Time and Place" are true. 'We do not live in a void…We own the past and are, hence, not afraid of what is to be

We send prayers for you,
Alexander Kozubovsky

Novokonstantinov, Ukraine, 2016, Presentation of
A Man Comes from Someplace *to area school.*

The pastor also sent photographs of the book being presented to the students, teachers, and administrators in the area school in Novokonstantinov.*

One day, perhaps, I'll return to meet the students and teachers in Novokonstantinov, and read my father's stories to them and listen to the stories they want to tell me about the world that they live in now in this moment in time. We will talk, I hope, about how they can "own their past."

---

* Permission from Pastor Alexandr Kozubovsky for school photograph and letter. Letter translated by Anna Royzner.

Sabbath

The meaning of the Sabbath is to celebrate time rather than space.
—Abraham Heschel, *The Sabbath*[*]

It is Yom Kippur, 2017, the Day of Atonement, and I am doing what I need to do, what I typically do on the day. I am reflecting upon the past year, promising to do better in the next. As American Jews, we are fortunate to have two new-year commemorations every year: we have the Days of Awe, this chance for repentance and renewal in the fall, and then in exactly three months to the day this year, we celebrate another New Year. Two chances in one year to begin again.

We are a traveling lot. My father's brother Meyer was a peddler up until the moment he died. My father always lived in two places at the same time, here and there. The past was ever present to him. But he found a home place here in New York in his later years, in Fredericktown for much of his life, in Buenos Aires for a short while, and, of course, in the world he left behind in Novokonstantinov. He found his final resting place by the riverbank in Valhalla, New York, within earshot of a running stream that perhaps reminded him of the cemetery that overlooks the Southern Buh, where his parents and four siblings are buried.

Ukraine is now a familiar place that I revisit frequently in my mind. It is for my husband Philip, as well. He is the primary map-reader, geographer, and geologist in the family, who routinely searches various devices for his writing and research, and for mine, as well. This week, he was the one who heard through his newsfeed about the attacks on weapons factories in Ukraine – the last a short distance from Novokonstantinov. These days, the news is so overwhelming, that this story has not been reported in the mainstream press, and it may not reach the front page, for the world that my family came from is not newsworthy. It wasn't in the past, and it isn't now.

---

[*]   Heschel, A. (1951). *The Sabbath*. New York, NY: Farrar Straus and Giroux.

But we wandered there, miraculously, in 2011, and we revisit the places we traveled, Novokonstantinov, Letichev, Dunaivtsi, Khmelnitsky, Letichev, Chmelnick, Medzhibozh, Kiev, Kamanetz-Podolsky, in our daily lives in conversations, correspondence, and in the talks and seminars that I've been giving, and the writing that I continue to do. Our old house in New York, built in 1906 on the old colonial road, feels like home. We've been here a long time, longer than either of us has ever lived in a house. I like to think of it as a home place for my family, particularly, for the Sabbath dinners we have Friday nights with my daughter Lauren, her husband, Avi, and the three children, Danielle, Naomi, and Gabriella. Lauren and her family live around the corner, in this still-new century, nearly 100 years since her grandfather left Ukraine.

We were talking a few weeks ago about several of Avi's family taking a pilgrimage from Israel to the gravesite of Ba'Al Shem Tov in Medzhibozh, a few miles from Novokonstantinov. I wondered how they had traveled. He said that they flew and then took a bus to the site. I asked if they had flown into Kiev. He said, no, someplace else. And my husband and I said, simultaneously, 'Oh, then, maybe, they flew into Kamanetz-Podolsky."

Danielle, my oldest granddaughter, looked at me for a moment, and then said, wryly, "Oh, but, of course, who *wouldn't* fly right into Kamanetz-Podolsky?" A brief pause around the table – and we all laughed. That part of Ukraine is now commonplace for me: I figured that Kamanetz was the closest airport to Medzhibozh.

The little group of us on Friday night is part of a large, connected family who live in many places across the world. Thanks to my father, who insisted on taking my sister and me to meet the family in Argentina, thanks to the internet, and now to *A Man Comes from Someplace*, we are more than ever connected, this transnational family that we are. We've had family from near and far this past year – and the stories grow on.

For my sister, Janet, at her house in Maryland, and me, here in New York, Friday night is a time to take a breath, have a meal, and tell stories to "stop time," as I tend to think of it. We rush about the whole week, and the Sabbath matters. Janet and Allan host their son and daughter-in-law and their little girl, whose name is Pearl. Janet lights Sabbath candles in our mother's candlesticks. And I light candles in the three brass candlesticks that belonged to my Grandmother Lena, my mother's mother, who died when I was five.

A few years back, in her first-grade class, in November 2011, our granddaughter Naomi's assignment was to draw a "picture of my family and our tradition." Here is our Sabbath table, with my husband and me, and her parents and the three sisters.

She is in the seventh grade now, and she says that in her art class, she is creating our Sabbath table again, this time out of clay. She has just finished it. She apologized that she didn't have enough space on the board for all of us, but it still signifies our Sabbath gatherings, given that at times we're all coming and going.

Gabriella, at 10, is the youngest of Lauren's girls. She is now in the fifth grade. Her class assignment was to respond to questions on a worksheet entitled, "Where I Am From." Students were asked to write descriptions of family traditions, ancestry, where they live, the places they come from, and to turn their responses into a poem.

I am struck by the creative ventures in these classrooms, where children are being encouraged to see the worlds they live in as part of cultural traditions, of a world within worlds. The classrooms are a mix of religions and races, and places the families come from. Naomi's best friend was born in Ireland. Gabriella's new classmate is from Kenya, and speaks with a "British accent," which Gabriella delights in imitating. In her first year at college, Danielle is taking courses that introduce her to diverse cultural practices and multiple languages and literacies. Their great-grandfather's stories in *A Man Comes from Someplace* would fit right in.

Here is Gabriella's poem:

I Am From[*]

I am from my bedroom, from the house
I live in

I am from the messy, but cozy and
noisy family where you can smell
delicious food scent drifting from the
kitchen to the living room

I am from the grass, leaves, and trees
in my backyard, the gravel of my
neighbors' driveway rough and hot
under the bright sun

I am from Friday night Shabbat at
Grandma's house and mostly brown
haired people, from my dad and sisters

I am from the always late, hilarious family
from 'get up' and 'make your bed' or 'love
you' and 'see you after school.'

I am from Connecticut, Israel, and New
York, salmon and seltzer from the
kitchen counter.

I am from the photograph box in the
closet, old, but almost full to the top.

I am from loving and gigantic hearts

September 15, 2017

---

[*]   Poem by Gabriella Azuolay.

Home Places

> None of us has one definite
> Home Place
> We haunt the shadowy woods,
>   bed down on riverbanks,
> On meadowland in earshot of
>   running streams.
> —Seamus Heaney, *Aeneid, VI*

One of my "home places" is the house in Fredericktown, Pennsylvania, the two-story 1910 house, a block away from the great Monongahela River. The river runs parallel to the one street in the town, and is a place I often return to in my memories. We lived on the first floor and rented out the second. I had seen the top floor only a few times when I was growing up.

My sister doesn't remember the second floor at all. This spring, in wandering through the internet, I found the house posted for sale, with photos of all the rooms in the house, the back porch, the yard, and a view of the river. My sister and several cousins suggested that we might buy it as a summer house, and now that some of the stores across the street have vanished, we'll have a clear view of the river from our front porch. The house was sold quickly, almost at asking price. Here is the river across the street, a few steps away from the house, captured by my friend from childhood, Carolyn, who was in the town a short while ago.

I keep thinking of rivers: The frozen Dniester at Yaruha that my father ran across early that December morning long ago. The river in Novokonstantinov that he loved, and the world that he left behind. And our river, the great Monongahela in the hills of southwestern Pennsylvania, at the place he and my mother came to, and where my sister and I grew up.

---

*   Heaney. S. (2016). *Aeneid* VI. New York, NY: Farrar, Straus and Giroux. (69)

Photograph of Monongahela River, Carolyn Sacks

For me, the daughter of a survivor, I know that for my father, our little town along the river became a "home place." And he was ever grateful.

Index